Study Guide

Amy Pearce
Arkansas State University

Understanding Psychology

SEVENTH EDITION

CHARLES G. MORRIS

University of Michigan

ALBERT A. MAISTO

University of North Carolina at Charlotte

PEARSON

Prentice
Hall

Upper Saddle River, New Jersey 07458

© 2006 by PEARSON EDUCATION, INC.
Upper Saddle River, New Jersey 07458

ISBN 0-13-193746-4

Printed in the United States of America

TABLE OF CONTENTS

How to Use
This Study Guide

Preface

Your Time Is Valuable

Invest your study time so you get the greatest benefit!

The following techniques have been shown to increase a student's mastery of new information:

- Use as many of your senses and abilities as possible—writing, reading, hearing, speaking, drawing, etc.

- Organize information so it is meaningful to you.

- Study with other people whenever possible.

- Have FUN. We remember what we enjoy.

This study guide has been designed to provide you with ideas and resources in all of these areas. This preface explains how to effectively use the sections in each chapter.

Chapter Focus

This section provides you with a summary of the key topics covered in the chapter. You should read this section after reading the entire chapter in your text.Practice exams are an important way to check your progress.

Learning Objectives and Questions

After you have read and studied each chapter, you should be able to complete the learning objectives and short essay questions. Your exams are written based on the learning objectives so it is important to practice writing them.

Chapter Outline

Making an outline is a good way to organize your notes taken from the lecture and the text. This section should help you determine which concepts will be emphasized on an exam.

Multiple Choice Posttest

The questions in your textbook after each section measure your starting point and the questions in the Posttest in the study guide measure how far you have progressed toward your goal of mastering the material.

Short Essay Questions

Many college courses are designed to help you develop your writing skills so completing short essay questions can be useful. This is especially true if your psychology course will include essay exams. You will find these questions on the Learning Objectives page.

Language Support

The *Language Support* section contains words students have identified from the text as needing more explanation. This section is for anyone who can benefit from extra support in English.

This page can be cut out, folded in half, and used as a bookmark in the appropriate chapter.

Most students have trouble finding enough time to study. Try carrying these flash cards with you so if you ever have to wait you can pull out a couple of cards and make good use of your time. Flash cards can also serve a very useful function during times of stress. Stress is much worse when we feel overwhelmed; in fact, we tend to shut down and do nothing. At those times divide up what you have to do and do a small portion every day. Studying 10 flash cards today is less overwhelming than thinking about the 100 pages on your next exam.

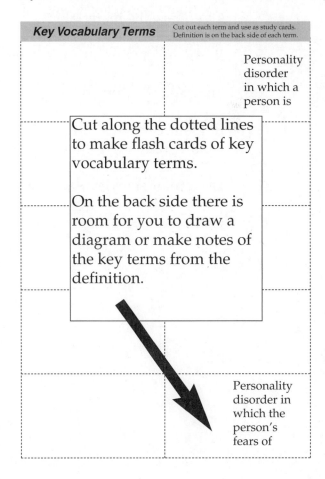

Key Vocabulary Terms Cut out each term and use as study cards. Definition is on the back side of each term.

Personality disorder in which a person is

Cut along the dotted lines to make flash cards of key vocabulary terms.

On the back side there is room for you to draw a diagram or make notes of the key terms from the definition.

Personality disorder in which the person's fears of

STUDY TIPS

Improving Your Memory

1. Learn general information first and then specific.

2. Make material meaningful to you.

3. Create associations with what you already know.

4. Learn it actively.

5. Imagine vivid pictures.

6. Recite out loud.

7. Reduce noise and interruptions.

8. Overlearn the material.

9. Be aware of your attitude toward information.

10. Space out learning over several days.

11. Remember related information when you are having trouble recalling something.

12. Use mnemonic devices (rhymes or words created from material).

13. Combine several of these techniques at once.

Memorizing Complex Information

There are memory techniques that make learning easier and faster. One technique, known as the "loci memory system," involves picturing yourself in a familiar setting and associating it with something you need to learn. Let's assume that you needed to memorize the function and structure of a neuron. Begin by picturing yourself walking into the entry hall of your home. At the same time pretend that you are walking through a dendrite. As you walk down the hall toward the living room, imagine that you are traveling in the dendrite to the cell body. As you exit the living room and walk down the hall toward the bedrooms, think of traveling down an axon toward the terminal button that contains the neurotransmitter. In this example you are connecting new information with something very familiar. We recall information much better when we involve our imagination. An even better way to perform this exercise would be to actually walk through your home while you visualize the parts of a neuron. In this situation you would not only be using your imagination but at the same time doing something physically. It is important to realize that we have strong memories for what we do physically. Just think how long you have remembered how to ride a bike even though you may not have ridden a bike for years.

When and How to Study

1. Plan two hours of study time for every hour you spend in class.
2. Study difficult or boring subjects first.
3. Avoid long study sessions.
4. Be aware of your best time of day.
5. Use waiting time by studying flash cards.
6. Use a regular study area.
7. Don't get too comfortable.
8. Use a library.
9. Take frequent breaks.
10. Avoid noise distractions.

Study in Groups

Research has shown that one of the most effective ways to learn is to study with other students. Your grades on exams will be better and you will have a lot more fun doing it!

How to Form a Group

1. Look for dedicated students who share some of your academic goals and challenges.
2. You could write a note on the blackboard asking interested students to contact you, or pass around a sign-up sheet before class.
3. Limit groups to five or six people.
4. Test the group by planning a one-time-only session. If that session works, plan another.

Some Activities for a Study Group

1. Compare notes.
2. Have discussions and debates about the material.
3. Test each other with questions brought to the group meeting by each member.
4. Practice teaching each other.
5. Brainstorm possible test questions.
6. Share suggestions for problems in the areas of finances, transportation, child care, time scheduling, or other barriers.
7. Develop a plan at the beginning of each meeting from the list above or any ideas you have.

Better Test Taking

1. Predict the test questions. Ask your instructor to describe the test format—how long it will be, and what kind of questions to expect (essay, multiple choice, problems, etc.).

2. Have a section in your notebook labeled "Test Questions" and add several questions to this section after every lecture and after reading the text. Record topics that the instructor repeats several times or goes back to in subsequent lectures. Write down questions the instructor poses to students.

3. Arrive early so you can do a relaxation exercise.

4. Ask about procedure for asking questions during the test.

5. Know the rules for taking the test so you do not create the impression of cheating.

6. Scan the whole test immediately. Budget your time based on how many points each section is worth.

7. Read the directions slowly. Then reread them.

8. Answer easiest, shortest questions first. This gives you the experience of success and stimulates associations. This prepares your mind for more difficult questions.

9. Next answer multiple-choice, true-false, and fill-in-the-blank questions.

10. Use memory techniques when you're stuck.
    - If your recall on something is blocked, remember something else that's related.
    - Start from the general and go to specific.

11. Look for answers in other test questions. A term, name, date, or other fact that you can't remember might appear in the test itself.

12. Don't change an answer unless you are sure because your first instinct is usually best.

Tips on Test Taking

Multiple-choice questions

1. Check the directions to see if the questions call for more than one answer.

2. Answer each question in your head before you look at the possible answers, otherwise you may be confused by the choices.

3. Mark questions you can't answer immediately and come back to them if you have time.

4. If incorrect answers are not deducted from your score, use the following guidelines to guess:
   - If two answers are similar, except for one or two words, choose one of these answers.
   - If two answers have similar sounding or looking words, choose one of these answers.
   - If the answer calls for a sentence completion, eliminate the answers that would not form grammatically correct sentences.
   - If answers cover a numerical range, choose one in the middle.
   - If all else fails, close your eyes and pick one.

True-False Questions

1. Answer these questions quickly.

2. Don't invest a lot of time unless they are worth many points.

3. If any part of the true-false statement is false, the whole statement is false.

4. Absolute qualifiers such as "always" or "never" generally indicate a false statement.

Machine-Graded Tests

1. Check the test against the answer sheet often.

2. Watch for stray marks that look like answers.

Open-Book and Notes Tests

1. Write down key points on a separate sheet.

2. Tape flags onto important pages of the book.

3. Number your notes, write a table of contents.

4. Prepare thoroughly because they are usually the most difficult tests.

Essay Questions

1. Find out precisely what the question is asking. Don't explain when asked to compare.

2. Make an outline before writing. (Mindmaps work well.)

3. Be brief, write clearly, use a pen, get to the point, and use examples.

Reading for Remembering

1. **Skim**
   Skim the entire chapter.

2. **Outline**
   Read the outline at the front of the chapter in the text.

3. **Questions**
   Write out several questions that come to your mind that you think will be answered in the chapter.

4. **Read**
   Read material with the purpose of answering your questions, critical evaluation, comprehension, and practical application.

5. **Highlight**
   While reading highlight the most important information (no more than 10 percent).

6. **Answers**
   As you read, get the answers to your questions.

7. **Recite**
   When you finish reading an assignment, make a speech about it. Recite the key points.

8. **Review**
   Plan your first review within 24 hours.

9. **Review again**
   Weekly reviews are important—perhaps only four or five minutes per assignment. Go over your notes. Read the highlighted parts of your text. Recite the more complicated points.

More about review

You can do short reviews anytime, anywhere, if you are prepared. Take your text to the dentist's office, and if you don't have time to read a whole assignment, review last week's assignment. Conduct five-minute reviews when you are waiting for water to boil. Three-by-five cards work well for review. Write ideas and facts on cards and carry them with you. These short review periods can be effortless and fun.

Anxiety Interferes with Performance

Do you freeze up on exams, worry that you won't do well? We can turn one exam into a "do or die" catastrophic situation. Yes, we should try our best but we are not doomed for life if we fail at something. Perhaps the following examples will help you see a failure for what it is, just one more step in the process of life.

- Einstein was four years old before he could speak and seven before he could read.
- Isaac Newton did poorly in grade school.
- Beethoven's music teacher once said of him, "As a composer he is hopeless."
- When Thomas Edison was a boy, his teachers told him he was too stupid to learn anything.
- Woolworth got a job in a dry goods store when he was 21, but his employers would not let him wait on a customer because he "didn't have enough sense."
- A newspaper editor fired Walt Disney because he had "no good ideas."
- Leo Tolstoy flunked out of college.
- Louis Pasteur was rated as "mediocre" in chemistry when he attended college.
- Abraham Lincoln entered the Black Hawk War as a captain and came out as a private.
- Winston Churchill failed the sixth grade.

Failures mean very little in the big picture of our life. It is just important that we keep trying.

Effective Note-Taking During Class

1. **Review the textbook chapter before class.**
   Instructors often design a lecture based on the assumption that you have read the chapter before class. You can take notes more easily if you already have some idea of the material.

2. **Bring your favorite note-taking tools to class.**
   Make sure you have pencils, pens, highlighter, markers, paper, note cards, or whatever materials you find useful.

3. **Sit as close to the instructor as possible.**
   You will have fewer distractions while taking your notes.

4. **Arrive to class early.**
   Relax and get your brain "tuned-up" to the subject by reviewing your notes from the previous class.

5. **Picture yourself up front with the instructor.**
   The more connected you feel to the material and the instructor, the more you will understand and remember the topic.

6. **Let go of judgments and debates.**
   Focus on understanding what the instructor is saying because that is what you will find on the test. Do not get distracted by evaluating the instructor's lecture style, appearance, or strange habits. When you hear something you disagree with, make a quick note of it and then let it go.

7. **Be active in class.**
   It is the best way to stay awake in class! Volunteer for demonstrations. Join in class discussions.

8. **Relate the topic to an interest of yours.**
   We remember things we are most interested in.

9. **Watch for clues of what is important.**
   - repetition
   - summary statements
   - information written on the board
   - information the instructor takes directly from his or her notes
   - notice what interests the instructor

When Instructors Talk Too Fast

1. Read the material before class.

2. Review notes with classmates.

3. Leave large empty spaces in your notes.

4. Have a symbol that indicates to you that you have missed something.

5. Write down key points only and revise your notes right after class to add details.

6. Choose to focus on what you believe to be key information.

7. See the instructor after class and fill in what you missed.

8. Ask the instructor to slow down if you think that is appropriate.

1 The Science of Psychology

Chapter Focus

The authors begin this chapter with a personal story that highlights the many realms of query engaged in by psychologists. Psychology is then defined as the scientific study of behavior and mental processes. The reader should grasp that psychology is a multi-faceted science consisting of many separate but sometimes overlapping fields; these include developmental, physiological, experimental, personality, clinical and counseling, and social psychology and the newer fields of industrial organizational, evolutionary, humanistic, positive, and cognitive psychology. Psychology is defined as a science because its tenets are based on the scientific method, a process that involves collecting data, systematic observation, generating explanatory theories and testable hypotheses, empirically testing the hypotheses, and then using the results of studies to describe, understand, and predict. Along with the scientific method, psychologists employ critical thinking skills to further examine information before making judgments and decisions.

A historical overview of the science of psychology is presented in this chapter so that the reader may gain additional insight into psychology's brief but dynamic past. Wilhelm Wundt is credited with founding psychology in 1879 and described his views of the field through the term voluntarism. Wundt was followed by many others, each committed to their own ideas of the focus of psychology. Among the major contributors and their respective schools of thought were James (Functionalism), Freud (Psychodynamic Psychology), Watson (Behaviorism), and Skinner (Behaviorism).

Although early studies in psychology were conducted on and by white males, psychologists now appreciate that understanding human diversity is essential. Topics integral to human diversity include studies on gender and gender stereotypes, feminist theory, race, ethnicity, and culture.

Certain research methods are used by psychologists to ask and answer their questions. All scientific studies must obtain evidence, or data. The primary research methods are naturalistic observation, case studies, surveys, correlational research, and experimental research. Each method has its strengths and weaknesses and the most appropriate method to employ is determined based on the types of questions asked; many researchers may use a combination of these methods to approach a problem, but only experimental research can establish cause and effect. When conducting research, psychologists must adhere to ethical guidelines regarding the use of human and animal subjects. These guidelines are regulated by the facility hosting the research, and are often based on the American Psychological Association's ethical standards for psychologists and the U.S. government's Code of Federal Regulations.

Finally, for students considering further explorations into psychology, careers in this field are varied and numerous. The career options available depend on the type of degree held, such as a bachelor's, master's, or doctorate in psychology. Many doctoral psychologists become clinicians or counselors. For people who desire to become therapists the main career paths are psychiatrist, psychoanalyst, clinical psychologist, counseling psychologist, and social worker.

Learning Objectives and Questions

After you have read and studied this chapter, you should be able to complete the following statements.

LEARNING OBJECTIVES

1. Describe the major subdivisions of psychology including developmental, physiological, experimental, personality, clinical and counseling, social, and industrial/organizational psychology.

2. Define psychology and explain the role played by the scientific method in psychological research, including the four goals of psychologists.

3. Summarize the five enduring issues of psychology.

4. Describe the early schools of psychology (Structuralism, Functionalism, Psychoanalysis, Behaviorism) and their founders.

5. Distinguish among the five basic research methods used by psychologists to gather information about behavior and give an example of a situation in which each method would be used appropriately.

6. Discuss cognitive psychology, how it differs from behaviorism, and its impact on the field of modern psychology.

7. Explain the importance of human diversity for researchers and how a lack of understanding of diversity, lack of diversity, and cultural bias can affect research results.

8. Discuss the ethical concerns in psychology and how they affect both humans and animals in research and treatment.

9. List the differences in training and activities of psychiatrists, counseling and clinical psychologists, psychoanalysts, and social workers.

10. Discuss the benefits of taking a course in psychology.

SHORT ESSAY QUESTIONS

1. Describe the importance of sampling related to issues of gender, race, and culture in research.

2. Explain Milgram's study, why it was so controversial, how it affected the APA's ethical guidelines, and the issue of deception and punishment in psychological research.

3. Discuss the differences between structuralism and functionalism; behaviorism and cognitive psychology, and how Freud's psychoanalytic differed from these schools.

4. Discuss the design of an experiment studying the effects of alcohol on aggressive behavior. Label the hypothesis, independent variable, dependent variable, control and experimental group, and the measures taken to avoid experimental bias.

5. Define the terms: sample, population, random sample, and representative sample. Explain how researchers can overcome obstacles to obtaining a good sample.

6. Explain the goals and interests of evolutionary psychologists and give two examples of the types of findings they have uncovered.

7. Describe the role played by women in the history of psychology, some obstacles that have prevented women from achieving equal status with men, and the current status of women in psychology.

8. Define and discuss the emerging field of positive psychology and its unique perspective on mental wellness as opposed to mental illness.

Chapter Outline

The following is an outline conveying the main concepts of this chapter.

1.   What Is Psychology?   page 3
   A.   The Fields of Psychology   page 4
      • Developmental Psychology
      • Physiological Psychology
      • Experimental Psychology
      • Personality Psychology
      • Clinical and Counseling Psychology
      • Social Psychology
      • Industrial and Organization (I/O) Psychology
   B.   Enduring Issues   page 7
      • Person–Situation
      • Nature–Nuture
      • Stability–Change
      • Diversity–Universality
      • Mind–Body
   C.   Psychology As Science   page 8
      • Scientific Method
         – Collecting Data
         – Systematic Observation
         – Generating Theory to Explain Data
         – Producing Testable Hypotheses Based on the Theory
         – Testing the Hyptheses Empirically
         – Used to describe, understand, and predict

UNDERSTANDING OURSELVES: The Benefits of Studying Psychology   page 10
   • Self-understanding
   • Critical thinking skills
   • Study skills
   • Job skills

2.   The Growth of Psychology   page 12

Indicate A, B, C, D, or E and write the correct name of each psychologist below his picture

1. _____   2. _____   3. _____   4. _____   5. _____

Multiple Choice Posttest

After studying the text and completing the Study Guide activities, answer these questions to determine if you need to review any areas before the course exam.

1. Psychology is the science of _____.
   a. behavior and mental processes
   b. objective introspection
   c. inductive reasoning
   d. emotions

2. Psychologists use the scientific method to do each of the following except ____ what they study.
   a. describe
   b. circumvent
   c. predict
   d. control

3. The scientific method has been applied to psychological issues for about the last ____ years.
   a. 100
   b. 200
   c. 300
   d. 400

4. A specific, testable prediction about a phenomenon, usually derived from a theory, is a _____.
   a. thesis
   b. hypothesis
   c. principle
   d. prognosis

5. The basic atoms or units of experience and their combinations were the foundation of _____.
   a. functionalism
   b. structuralism
   c. behaviorism
   d. psychoanalysis

6. Consciousness as a continuous flow is an important concept to ____.
   a. structuralism
   b. functionalism
   c. objective introspection
   d. behaviorism

7. Freud's theories differed radically from the views of American psychologists of the time because of _____.
   a. its extensive use of laboratory research to support its claims
   b. the emphasis it placed on Eastern philosophies and culture
   c. the emphasis it placed on unconscious processes
   d. its emphasis on environmental learning as the source for most personality characteristics

8. The idea that psychology should be based only on observable, measurable behaviors is central to _____.
   a. behaviorism
   b. cognitive theory
   c. structuralism
   d. psychodynamic theory

9. Gestalt theory emphasizes _____.
   a. flow of consciousness
   b. the atoms of thought
   c. environmental stimuli
   d. our tendency to see patterns

10. The scientific study of the ways in which people perceive, interpret, store, and retrieve information is central to _____ psychology.
    a. humanistic
    b. behavioral
    c. existential
    d. cognitive

11. Research that observes behavior in its actual setting without controlling anything is called _____.
    a. correlational method
    b. naturalistic observation
    c. survey research
    d. case study method

12. The _____ is a detailed description and analysis of a single individual or a few individuals and may include a variety of information gathering methods.
    a. correlational method
    b. naturalistic observation
    c. survey research
    d. case study method

13. The degree of relationship between two or more variables is _____.
    a. correlation
    b. naturalistic observation
    c. reliability
    d. synchronicity

14. The only research method that can demonstrate a cause-and-effect relationship between variables is the _____ method.
    a. correlational
    b. naturalistic observation
    c. survey research
    d. experimental

15. A researcher manipulates the _____ variable to see how it affects a second variable.
    a. placebo
    b. independent
    c. dependent
    d. correlational

16. A sample carefully chosen so that the characteristics of the subjects correspond closely to the characteristics of the general population is known as a _____ sample.
    a. random
    b. controlled
    c. biased
    d. representative

17. Subjects in Milgram's studies were told they were taking part in studies on ___ but were really being tested on ____.
    a. learning, biofeedback
    b. pain thresholds, biofeedback
    c. learning, obedience
    d. obedience, learning

18. Milgram's studies on obedience raised significant controversy regarding _____.
    a. the quality of laboratory equipment used in psychological research
    b. laboratory research on human sexuality
    c. the use of placebo techniques to treat severe psychological disorders
    d. ethics and the use of deception in research

19. Which of the following mental health professionals is the only one who can prescribe medicine?
    a. a psychologist
    b. a social worker
    c. a counselor
    d. a psychiatrist

20. Critical thinking involves all of the following EXCEPT _____.
    a. examining evidence
    b. considering alternatives
    c. accepting common knowledge
    d. analyzing assumptions

21. Wundt used the term _____ to convey the concept of attention as a selective process actively controlled by intentions and motives.
    a. experimentation
    b. voluntarism
    c. stream of consciousness
    d. introspection

22. Genetic or evolutionary influences were largely unexplored in the psychology of the 1960s. Rather, behaviors were explained as a result of learning and experience. This tendency is conveyed by the term _____.
    a. environmental bias
    b. deception
    c. observer bias
    d. experimenter bias

23. Susan gives students a word list to memorize, then she tests the number of words remembered from the list and how long the students retain certain words in memory. Susan is most likely a _____ psychologist.
    a. behavioral
    b. developmental
    c. evolutionary
    d. cognitive

24. Which of the following statements concerning women in psychology is NOT true?
    a. The number of women enrolled in psychology graduate programs has increased steadily over the last 50 years.
    b. Women receive approximately 75 percent of the bachelor's degrees awarded in psychology.
    c. In the early years of psychology, females were openly invited to participate in the field, but few accepted, opting instead for more traditional occupational roles.
    d. The absence of females in the early years of psychology may reflect a larger problem—the inattention to human diversity.

25. Which of the following statements supports the case for including studies on human diversity in the field of psychology?
    a. It is important to recognize and understand the similarities and differences found in people of diverse backgrounds.
    b. Interpersonal tensions such as prejudice and conflict may be better understood.
    c. Comprehension of human diversity may lead to appreciation of different values, behaviors, and approaches to situations used by others.
    d. All of the above.

26. _____ is based on genetic similarity while _____ is based on cultural characteristics.
    a. Race; ethnicity
    b. Ethnicity; race
    c. Gender; sex
    d. Diversity; feminism

Answers and Explanations to Multiple Choice Posttest

1. a. Psychology is the science of behavior and mental processes. p. 3

2. b. The second goal of psychology is to explain behavior. p. 8

3. a. It was in the late 1800s that the scientific method was applied to questions about human behavior and mental processes. p. 12

4. b. A hypothesis is a testable prediction about the phenomenon in question. p. 9

5. b. Structuralism focuses on basic units or atoms of experiences and their combinations. p. 12

6. b. Consciousness as a continuous flow is important to functionalism. pp. 12–13

7. c. Freud believed that people are motivated by unconscious instincts and urges. p. 13

8. a. Behaviorists believed that psychology was the study of observable, measurable behavior—and nothing more. p. 14–15

9. d. Gestalt theory emphasizes our tendency to see patterns. p. 16

10. d. Cognitive psychology is the study of mental processes in the broadest sense. p. 16–17

11. b. Naturalistic observation involves watching a research subject in the natural setting. p. 24

12. d. A case study is a detailed description of one person or a few individuals and may include real life observation, interviews, psychological test scores, and interviews with others. p. 25

13. a. Correlational research is based on a naturally occurring relationship between two variables. pp. 26–27

14. d. Only the experimental method can prove cause and effect. pp. 27–28

15. b. A researcher manipulates the independent variable. p. 28

16. d. A representative sample is carefully chosen to correspond closely to the characteristics of the larger population. p. 30

17. c. Milgram's subjects were told the research was about learning but it was really about obedience. p. 33

18. d. Milgram's study sparked such a public uproar that the APA was forced to reassess its ethical guidelines. p. 33

19. d. Psychiatrists are medical doctors and the only mental health professionals licensed to prescribe medication. p. 35

20. c. Critical thinkers question common knowledge. pp. 9–11

21. b. Wundt's primary interest was selective attention and he used the term voluntarism to describe his view of psychology. p. 12

22. a. The tendency to explain virtually all behaviors as aspects of learning and experience is referred to as an environmental bias. p.15

23. d. Cognitive psychologists study mental processes including, but not limited to, learning and remembering. pp. 16–17

24. c. In the late 1800s and early 1900s academic careers in psychology remained closed to women. Still, women were attracted to the field and many pursued careers in related nonacademic settings such as child development and education. pp. 18–20

25. d. Understanding human diversity is essential in today's world. Psychologists no longer accept that what is true of white, Western males is true of others as well. p. 20

26. a. Race is a biological term used to refer to a genetically similar subpopulation. Ethnicity is based on cultural characteristics shared by a category of people. pp. 20–22

Language Support

Students identified the following words from the text as needing more explanation. This page can be cut out, folded in half, and used as a bookmark for this chapter.

A

Adherents of	those who believe in, devoted followers of
Advocate	speak, plead, or argue in favor of
Affiliate with	accept as a member, associate, or branch of
Against all odds	surprisingly winning over major difficulties
Anonymity	unknown or unacknowledged name, authorship, or agency
Ascribe	attribute to a specific cause, source, or origin
Assimilate	include, absorb, accept, make similar to

B

Blank slate	unmarked surface, 'tabula rasa'
Blunder	make a mistake, to flounder
Breadth	wide range or scope

C

Colleague	people who work together, associates, companions
Commingle	mix together
Competent	well qualified, adequate or properly trained for the purpose
Conjecture	inference based on incomplete evidence, guess
Constraints	restrictions, limitations, restraints
Contradict	to deny, discrepancy, to say something that doesn't agree
Controversial	dispute between sides, holding opposing views
Criteria	standard or basis for making a judgment

D

Decorum	behavior within social conventions
Derive	obtain from a source; originate, deduce, or infer
Devote	dedicate, give oneself totally to
Differentiate	perceive a distinction or difference between
Discrete	individually distinct, keep separate
Dissimilar	different or distinct, not alike
Distinct	of marked difference, clear, well defined
Distinguish	observe the difference between, keep apart, discern
Dominate	influence strongly

E

Elicit	to bring or draw out, call for, evoke
Embedded	insert, enclose, locate, or fix in surrounding area
Emergence	to come forth into view, come into existence or notice
Empower	to invest with power or authority
Encompass	include or contain
Encounter	meet face to face, confront
Enduring issues	topics that sustain interest, continue or last over time
Establish	set up, settle, make stable, prove, institute, or verify
Evolve	develop gradually, unfold naturally
Expel	drive or force out
Explicit	fully and clearly expressed, defined, or formulated
Extent	degree, scope, or range to which something extends

F

Fascinate	intense interest or attraction
Faulty generalization	deciding without gathering all the facts or prematurely
Flair for	talent or aptitude, instinctive discernment
Formulate	to express, state, or prepare in systematic terms
Fundamental	essential, basic, involving all aspects, of central importance

G

Ghetto	inner city neighborhood occupied by minority groups, slum
Grasp	understanding, comprehension

H

Holistic	interdependence and importance of all the parts of a whole
Heresy	controversial opinion in opposition to tradition

I

Impartial	unbiased, unprejudiced, neutral
Improvise	make up, invent, or recite without preparation
Inaccessible	unapproachable, not having entry point or opening
Infamous	having a bad reputation, notorious
Inference	conclude from evidence or premises
Influential	exerting influence or power, important
Inhumane	cruel, without compassion or feeling
Initiative	ability to begin or follow through with a plan or task
Intercede	mediate, act as a go-between
Intervene	come between, alter or hinder an event or action
Investigate	examine thoroughly, inquire into
Irrelevant	unrelated to the matter at hand
Ivy league	prestigious, traditional colleges, mostly on East Coast

L

Liaison	communication between groups, rendezvous or meeting
Loopholes	opening in premise or law allowing another interpretation

M

Magna cum laude	graduating with high honors
Mean streets	dangerous neighborhood
Miracle cure	medical discovery considered very helpful, wonder drug
Monopolize	dominate by excluding others
Morale	state of mind of person or group, spirit of the group
Mutual	shared, have in common

O

Obsolete	no longer in use or needed, outmoded
Opponent	against another or others, opposite viewpoint or stance
Orthodox	adhering to traditional, accepted ways
Overrequest	asking for too much
Override	to prevail over, set aside, consider more important than
Overwhelmingly	overpowering, irresistible, to decisively, strongly

P

Penchant	preference, strong inclination, definite liking
Phenomena	unusual fact or occurrence
Pioneer	innovator especially in research and development
Precursor	one that comes before, indicates or announces something
Predisposed	inclined to something in advance, susceptible or likely
Prohibitions	forbidding by law, taboo, not allowed
Prestigious	prominent, distinguished, respected
Prevalent	widely occurring, common

Prominence	widely known, eminent
Proximity	closeness, nearness
Puzzled	confused or baffled by, bewildered by
R	
Realm	area, field, or location
Reassign	transfer from one location or task to another
Repertoire	range of skills, aptitudes, or accomplishments
Resurface	come out at another time
S	
Scrutiny	very close look, examine carefully
Shed light on	help to understand more clearly
Sentient	conscious, perceptive, and alert beings
Skeptical	doubt, question, or disagree
Stringent	vigorous or severe standards
Superstition	irrational belief or practice in magical or chance happening
Supplant	supercede, take place instead of
T	
Transform	change markedly in form, nature, appearance, or condition
U	
Underlying	basic, fundamental, implicit, present but not obvious
V	
Voodoo	using fetishes, spells, curses, magical power, or deception
Vulnerable	susceptible to attack, easily affected, not protected
W	
Wooed	seeking to gain or achieve, seeking romantic affection
Y	
Yield	give way to pressure, force, or persuasion; give in return
Z	
Zapped	exposure to electric current or radiation

Key Vocabulary Terms

Cut out each term and use as study cards.
Definition is on the back side of each term.

Psychology	Structuralism
Scientific method	Functionalist theory
Theory	Psychodynamic theories
Hypotheses	Behaviorism
Representative sample	Gestalt psychology

School of psychology that stresses the basic units of experience and the combinations in which they occur.

The scientific study of behavior and mental processes.

Theory of mental life and behavior that is concerned with how an organism uses its perceptual abilities to function in its environment.

An approach to knowledge that relies on collecting data, generating a theory to explain the data, producing testable hypotheses based on the theory, and testing those hypotheses empirically.

Personality theories contending that behavior results from psychological factors that interact within the individual, often outside conscious awareness.

Systematic explanation of a phenomenon; it organizes known facts, allows us to predict new facts, and permits us to exercise a degree of control over the phenomenon.

School of psychology that studies only observable and measurable behavior.

Specific, testable predictions derived from a theory.

School of psychology that studies how people perceive and experience objects as whole patterns.

Sample carefully chosen so that the characteristics of the subjects correspond closely to the characteristics of the larger population.

Feminist theory	Culture
Humanistic psychology	Race
Cognitive psychology	Ethnicity
Evolutionary psychology	Positive psychology
Gender	Naturalistic observation

The tangible goods produced in a society, and the values, attitudes, behaviors, and beliefs that are passed from one generation to another.

Theories offering a wide variety of views on the social roles of women and men, the problems and rewards of those roles, and prescriptions for changing those roles.

A subpopulation of a species, defined according to an identifiable characteristic (i.e., geographic location, skin color, hair texture, genes, facial features).

School of psychology that emphasizes nonverbal experience and altered states of consciousness as a means of realizing one's full human potential.

A common cultural heritage, including religion, language, ancestry, that is shared by a group of individuals.

School of psychology devoted to the study of mental processes in the broadest sense.

The view that psychology should devote more attention to the "good life" and the origins and nurturance of mental wellness rather than mental illness.

An approach and subfield of psychology concerned with the evolutionary origins of behaviors and mental process, their adaptive value, and the purposes they continue to serve.

Research method involving the systematic study of animal or human behavior in natural settings rather than in the laboratory.

The psychological and social meanings attached to being biologically male or female.

Observer bias	Participants
Case study	Independent variable
Survey research	Dependent variable
Correlational research	Experimental group
Experimental method	Control group

Individuals whose reactions or responses are observed in an experiment.

Expectations or biases of the observer that might distort or influence his or her interpretation of what was actually observed.

In an experiment, the variable that is manipulated to test its effects on the other, dependent variables.

Intensive description and analysis of single individual or just a few individuals.

In an experiment, the variable that is measured to see how it is changed by manipulations in the independent variable.

Research technique in which questionnaires or interviews are administered to a select group of people.

In a controlled experiment, the group subjected to a change in the independent variable.

Research technique based on the naturally occurring relationship between two or more variables.

In a controlled experiment, the group not subjected to a change in the independent variable; used for comparison with the experimental group.

Research technique in which an investigator deliberately manipulates selected events or circumstances and then measures the effects of those manipulations on subsequent behavior.

Experimenter
bias

Random
sample

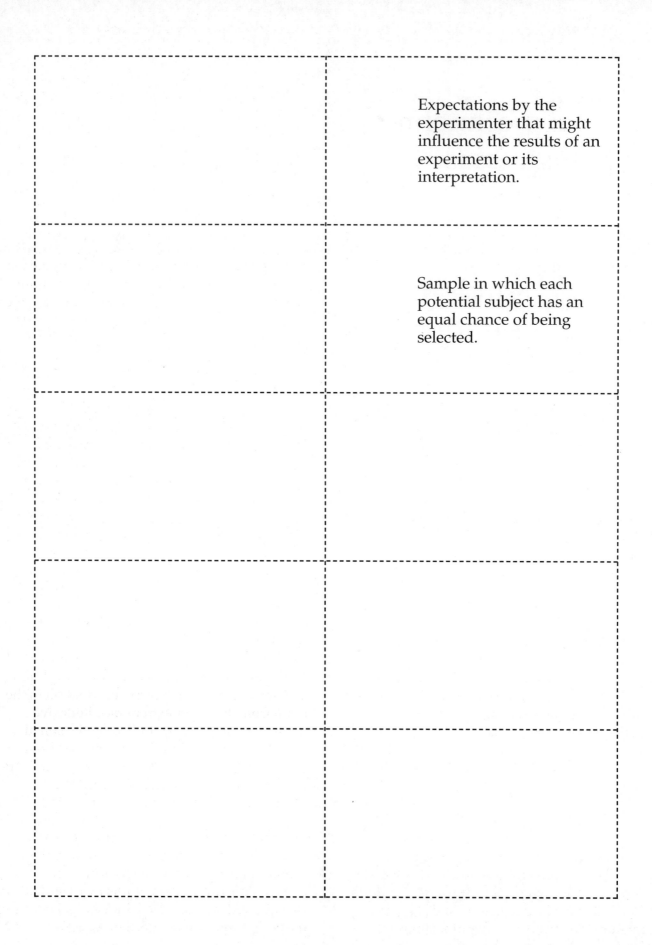

Expectations by the experimenter that might influence the results of an experiment or its interpretation.

Sample in which each potential subject has an equal chance of being selected.

2

The Biological Basis of Behavior

Chapter Focus

This chapter introduces the field of psychobiology. The authors begin by exploring the basic components of the brain and nervous system. Neurons are nerve cells that allow communication throughout the brain and spinal cord. The typical neuron has dendrites, a nucleus located within the soma, an axon, which may or may not be myelinated, and terminal branches. Neural cells called glia serve as support cells. Neurons communicate by sending impulses that run on electrochemical gradients and by forming synapses with other neurons. Neural impulses do not vary in strength, either a neuron fires an impulse or it does not. This is known as the all-or-none law. Neural impulses travel in one direction down the axon to the terminal button. Terminal buttons contain synaptic vesicles filled with neurotransmitters. Neurotransmitters are released into the synaptic cleft; many of them will bind to receptors located on the opposing neuronal membrane. The primary neurotransmitters are acetylcholine, dopamine, serotonin, and endorphins. Neural plasticity, the ability of the brain to change in response to experience has been observed in both humans and nonhumans. New evidence has shed light on neurogenesis, the production of new nerve cells.

The central nervous system consists of the brain and spinal cord. The three basic divisions of the brain are the primitive central core, the limbic system, and the cerebral hemispheres. Within these divisions lie structures that have specialized functions; many interact with each other. Structures within the central core include the medulla, pons, cerebellum, and reticular formation. The thalamus, hypothalamus,

olfactory bulb, hippocampus, and amygdala are structures within the limbic system. The outer cerebral cortex regulates complex behavior and is comprised of different lobes known as the frontal, parietal, occipital, and temporal lobes. Split-brain operations performed on patients with severe epilepsy have revealed specialized functions of the left and right hemispheres. The left hemisphere appears to be dominant in language tasks as well as analytic, logic, and rationalizing. The right hemisphere appears dominant at visual and spatial tasks including face recognition, perception of emotions, and solving problems that require creative solutions.

Neuroscientists use four basic techniques for studying the brain—microelectrodes, macroelectrodes, structural imaging, and functional imaging. Often researchers will use a combination of these techniques to observe anatomy (CT), energy use (PET), blood movement (fMRI), and electrical activity (EEG).

The brain and spinal cord join at the brain stem. Two major pathways exist in the spinal cord; motor pathways descend from the brain, and sensory pathways carry information to the brain from the lower extremities. Reflexive movements are also controlled by the spinal cord, but do not require input from the brain.

Another division of the nervous system is the peripheral nervous system (PNS). Afferent neurons carry sensory information from the periphery to the CNS and efferent neurons carry information from the CNS to muscles and glands. The PNS is further divided into the somatic and autonomic nervous systems.

The endocrine system works together with the nervous system and exerts widespread effects on the body by producing hormones. Like neurotransmitters, hormones carry messages, but at a slower pace through the bloodstream. Hormones play a role in development and activate behaviors. Hormones affect moods and play a role in psychological disorders. Endocrine glands are located throughout the body and include the thyroid, parathyroid, pineal, pancreas, adrenal, and pituitary glands, as well as the gonads.

Researchers are deeply interested in the influences and determinants of human behavior. It is now known that many traits are passed from one generation to another through genes. Genes are carried via chromosomes; humans have 46 chromosomes, arranged as 23 pairs. Chromosomes contain DNA. The Human Genome Project was launched to map the entire human genome. Human traits may be determined by the expression of one dominant gene or two recessive genes. However, most genes are polygenic. Behavior geneticists aim to determine the genes that contribute to characteristics like intelligence, temperament, and even predispositions to psychological and neurological disorders. Human behavior geneticists use family, twin, and adoption studies to examine how genes may influence a trait.

Evolutionary psychology examines origins of behaviors and mental processes and attempts to explain them by the process of natural selection. Natural selection states that organisms best adapted to their environment tend to survive. Hence, if the traits that provide a survival advantage are genetically based, then those genes will get passed on to offspring.

Finally, as society gains more control over genetics ethical issues arise. Science has widespread effects on society, and these effects must be critically examined. Questions to be considered include: Should genetic replacement be allowed in an abnormally developing fetus? How will genetic tampering affect our gene pool? How will results from new genetic studies be applied and interpreted? Although opinions may be divided on these issues, recent evidence has revealed that the environment heavily influences which genetic predispositions are expressed and which are not. Therefore, it is important to keep in mind that both heredity and environment contribute to behaviors and traits.

Learning Objectives and Questions

After you have read and studied this chapter, you should be able to complete the following statements.

LEARNING OBJECTIVES

1. Describe the structure of the neuron. Trace the path of a neural impulse and explain how it transmits messages from one neuron to another.

2. Describe the process by which a neuron moves from a resting state to firing and then back to a resting state.

3. Describe the effects of the neurotransmitters acetylcholine, dopamine, serotonin, norepinephrine, and endorphins.

4. Describe the location and function of the medulla, cerebellum, thalamus, hypothalamus, and cerebral cortex.

5. Describe the functions of the frontal lobe, temporal lobe, occipital lobe, and parietal lobe of the brain.

6. Compare and contrast the functions of the left and right hemispheres of the cerebral cortex. What role does the corpus callosum play in this functioning?

7. Compare and contrast the functions of the sympathetic and parasympathetic nervous system.

8. Describe the basic functions of the endocrine system, including the specific functions of the thyroid gland, pancreas, pituitary gland, gonads, and adrenal glands.

9. Define genes, chromosomes, and DNA and describe their role in the genetic transmission of traits.

10. Define and describe the uses for and limitations of family studies, twin studies, and adoption studies. What has been learned about the role of heredity in shaping human personality?

11. Discuss the field of evolutionary psychology and identify the types of human behaviors that interest evolutionary psychologists. Briefly discuss the criticisms of this field and how evolutionary psychologists respond to these criticisms.

12. Discuss the Human Genome Project and its contribution to understanding genetics and mapping the chromosomes. Give at least two examples of traits or diseases that have been identified and marked on the human chromosomes.

SHORT ESSAY QUESTIONS

1. Discuss how cocaine, curare, caffeine, opiates, and LSD block or disrupt neural communication. Which receptor sites do these drugs specifically affect?

2. What are the reasons for, and the results of, split-brain operations? What is the difference between split-brain surgery and hemispherectomies?

3. Briefly describe the functions of the reticular formation, the limbic system, and the spinal cord. What kind of problems can result from damage or destruction of these areas?

4. Briefly discuss the purposes of and procedures for studying the brain within each of the following general areas: microelectrode techniques; macro electrode techniques; structural imaging, functional imaging.

5. Compare and contrast strain studies and selection studies. What are they used for and what has been learned from them. Discuss any limitations of these techniques.

6. Identify and briefly explain the four major principles of Darwin's theory of natural selection. What scientific fields have been impacted by his ideas and how large has that impact been?

7. Discuss some social implications of behavior genetics.

8. Identify several approaches to studying heritability of a trait.

9. Explain the concepts of dominant and recessive genes and discuss how a child's eye color may be influenced if the father has blue eyes and the mother has brown eyes.

10. Briefly summarize the research regarding stem cells and the possibility of growing new neurons in the human brain. Define neuronal plasticity and neurogenesis. Which specific disorders or diseases may be helped by this method?

11. What are some of the ethical concerns regarding stem cell research and development?

Chapter Outline

The following is an outline conveying the main concepts of this chapter.

1. Neurons: The Messengers   page 41
   A. Dendrites
   B. Axon
   C. Nerve or tract
   D. Myelin sheath
   E. Support cells—Glial cells
2. The Neural Impulse   page 43
   A. Resting Potential
   B. Polarization
   C. Neural Impulse or Action Potential
   D. Graded Potential
   E. Threshold of Excitation
   F. All-or-None Law
3. The Synapse   page 44
   A. Synaptic Space or Synaptic Cleft
   B. Synapse
   C. Terminal Button or Synaptic Knob
   D. Synaptic Vesicles
   E. Receptor Sites
   F. Neurotransmitters
      – Acetylcholine (ACH)
      – Dopamine
      – Serotonin
      – Norepinephrine
      – Endorphins

UNDERSTANDING OURSELVES   page 47

4. Neural Plasticity and Neurogenesis   page 47
   A. Neural Plasticity
   B. Neurogenesis
5. The Central Nervous System   page 50
   A. Spinal Cord
   B. The Brain
      • Brain Stem
      • Medulla
      • Pons
      • Cerebellum
      • Midbrain
      • Thalamus
      • Hypothalamus
      • Reticular formation
      • Limbic system
      • Cerebral Cortex
         – Association areas
         – Occipital Lobe
         – Temporal Lobe
         – Parietal Lobe
         – Frontal Lobe
   C. Hemisphereic Specialization page 55
      • Corpus Callosum
      • Left Hemisphere Dominance
      • Right Hemisphere Dominance
      • Split-brain patients
   D. Tools for Studying the Brain page 57
      • Microelectrode Techniques
      • Macroelectrode Techniques
      • Structural Imaging
         – Computerized Axial Tomography (CAT or CT scan)
         – Magnetic Resonance Imaging (MRI)
      • Functional Imaging
         – EEG imaging
         – Magnetoencephalography (MEG)
         – Positron emission tomography scanning (PET)
         – Functional magnetic resonance imaging (fMRI)
6. The Spinal Cord page 60
7. The Peripheral Nervous System page 62
   A. Afferent neurons
   B. Efferent neurons
   C. The Somatic Nervous System
   D. The Autonomic Nervous System
      • Parasympathetic Nervous System
      • Sympathetic Nervous System
8. The Endocrine System   page 64
   A. Hormones
   B. Endocrine Glands
   C. The Thyroid Gland
   D. The Parathyroid Glands
   E. The Pineal Gland
   F. The Pancreas
   F. The Pituitary Gland
   G. The Gonads
   H. The Adrenal Glands
9. Genes, Evolution, and Behavior page 67
      • Behavior Genetics
      • Evolutionary Psychology

A. Genetics
- Genes
- Chromosomes
- Deoxyribonucleic acid (DNA)
- Human Genome
- Dominant gene
- Recessive gene
- Polygenic Inheritance

UNDERSTANDING THE WORLD AROUND
US: In Search of the Human Genome   page 68

B. Behavior Genetics
- Animal behavior genetics
  - Heritability
  - Strain studies
  - Selection studies
- Human behavior genetics
  - Family studies
  - Twin studies
  - Identical twins
  - Fraternal twins
  - Adoption studies
- Molecular Genetics
- Evolutionary Psychology
  - Natural selection
- Social Implications

Multiple Choice Posttest

After studying the text and completing the Study Guide activities, answer these questions to determine if you need to review any areas before the course exam.

1. The term "plasticity" as it regards the brain, refers to _____.
   a. brittleness or rigidity
   b. levels of complexity
   c. softness or crevices
   d. ability to adapt to new conditions

2. The field of psychobiology explores the ways in which ____.
   a. biological processes affect our behavior
   b. our mental state affects our physical health
   c. behavioral patterns affect biological development
   d. evolution has shaped our instincts, drives, urges, and needs

3. The smallest unit of the nervous system and the cell that underlies the activity of the entire nervous system is the _____.
   a. glial cell
   b. epidermal cell
   c. neuron
   d. T-cell

4. Neurons that receive information from sensory organs and relay that information to the spinal cord and the brain are called _____.
   a. association neurons
   b. efferent neurons
   c. afferent neurons
   d eons

5. When a neuron is polarized, _____.
   a. potassium ions pass freely through the cell membrane
   b. the electrical charge inside is positive relative to the outside
   c. it cannot fire
   d. the electrical charge inside is negative relative to the outside

6. The entire area composed of the axon terminal of one neuron, the synaptic cleft, and the dendrite or cell body of the next neuron is called the _____.
   a. synaptic vesicle
   b. synaptic knob
   c. synaptic space
   d. synapse

7. The "all or none" law refers to _____.
   a. a group of neurons firing together
   b. a neuron fires at full strength or not at all
   c. all the dendrites must be receiving messages telling the neuron to fire or it will not fire at all
   d. all the neurons in a single nerve fire simultaneously

8. People with Parkinson's disease and schizophenia probably have a deficiency of the neurotransmitter _____.
   a. norepinephrine
   b. serotonin
   c. dopamine
   d. acetylcholine

9. Morphine and other opiates are able to bind to the receptor sites for _____.
   a. acetylcholine
   b. hypothalamus
   c. dopamine
   d. endorphins

10. Eating, drinking, sexual behavior, sleeping, and temperature control are regulated by the _____.
    a. thalamus
    b. hypothalamus
    c. cerebral cortex
    d. corpus callosum

11. The outer covering of the brain and the part most people think of when they consider the brain is the _____.
    a. cerebral cortex
    b. pons
    c. medulla
    d. cerebellum

12. What structure connects the two hemispheres of the brain and coordinates their activities?
    a. reticular formation
    b. amygadala
    c. hippocampus
    d. corpus callosum

13. The part of the brain that helps regulate hearing, balance and equilibrium, certain emotions and motivation, and recognizing faces is the _____.
    a. occipital lobe
    b. temporal lobe
    c. parietal lobe
    d. frontal lobe

14. A part of the brain that sends the signal "Alert" to higher centers of the brain in response to incoming messages is _____.
    a. limbic system
    b. reticular formation
    c. amygdala
    d. hippocampus

15. The thyroid gland controls _____.
    a. glucose absorption
    b. emotions
    c. metabolism
    d. sexuality

16. The _____ hemisphere of the cerebral cortex is usually dominant in spatial tasks while the _____ hemisphere usually dominant in language tasks.
    a. frontal, lateral
    b. left, right
    c. right, left
    d. lateral, frontal

17. The limbic system is responsible for _____.
    a. controlling learning and emotional behavior
    b. providing a bridge for numerous brain areas
    c. analyzing problematic situations
    d. fighting pathogens

18. The system that coordinates and integrates behavior by secreting chemicals into the bloodstream is called the _____.
    a. somatic system
    b. autonomic system
    c. limbic system
    d. endocrine system

19. The endocrine glands located just above the kidneys that release hormones important for dealing with stress are the _____.
    a. gonads
    b. adrenal glands
    c. parathyroid glands
    d. pituitary glands

20. The complex molecule that forms the code for all genetic information is the _____.
    a. DNA
    b. messenger RNA
    c. RNA
    d. monoamine oxidase

21. _____ is a test on a fetus to determine if there are any genetic abnormalities.
    a. Amniocentesis
    b. Positron emission tomography
    c. Magnetic resonance
    d. CT-scans

22. Which of the following would provide the best map of physical structures in the brains of living human beings?
    a. magnetic resonance imaging (MRI)
    b. magnetoencephalography (MEG)
    c. positron emission tomography (PET) scan
    d. electroencephalography (EEG) imaging

23. The goal of the Human Genome Project is to:
    a. clone humans
    b. slow the aging process by identifying genes that play a role in development
    c. find cures for people afflicted by Alzheimer's disease and schizophrenia
    d. identify chromosomes and determine which genes influence human characteristics

24. Studies of heritability in humans that assume that if genes influence a certain trait, close relatives should be more similar with that trait than distant relatives are called _____.
    a. family studies
    b. twin studies
    c. strain studies
    d. selection studies

25. Research on human brain tissue has found that human adult brains ____ have stem cells and neurogenesis ____ occur in human adult brains.
    a. do not, does not
    b. do, does not
    c. do not, does
    d. do, does

26. Messages transmitted and received by neurons may be either _____ or ____ telling a neuron to fire or not to fire an action potential.
    a. all; none
    b. excitatory; inhibitory
    c. synaptic; nonsynaptic
    d. dendritic; axonic

27. Which of the following statements is true regarding research findings on the role of experience in neural development?
    a. Rats raised in impoverished conditions showed no difference in the number of synaptic connections later in life when compared to rats raised in enriched environments.
    b. Rats raised in stimulating environments performed worse on problem-solving tasks than rats raised in impoverished conditions.
    c. Rats raised in stimulating environments may form more synapses as a result of performing complex cognitive tasks.
    d. Rats raised in impoverished environments may form more synapses as a result of barren conditions.

28. Damage to the cerebellum is most likely to result in which of the following?
    a. severe problems in movement
    b. loss of language
    c. reduced ability to think abstractly
    d. vision impairment

29. Which of the following is true regarding split-brain operations?
    a. It has been performed on patients with severe epilepsy.
    b. The two hemispheres of the brain are disconnected by severing the corpus callosum.
    c. Normal functioning is possible since sensory information is sent to both hemispheres.
    d. all of the above

30. Distinctions between Broca's and Wernicke's areas came from studying ____.
    a. people with schizophrenia
    b. victims of stroke
    c. Parkinson's patients
    d. none of the above

31. Which of the following is most likely to describe a person with an overactive thyroid?
    a. feeling tired and wanting to sleep
    b. depressed and low excitability
    c. difficulty focusing on tasks and reduced concentration
    d. increased attention span

32. The gland connected to the hypothalamus that influences blood pressure, thirst, sexual behavior, body growth, and other functions is the ____ gland.
    a. pituitary
    b. pancreas
    c. thalamus
    d. pineal

33. Which statement regarding sex hormones is true?
    a. Wwomen perform better on cognitive tasks during the ovulatory phase of their menstrual cycles.
    b. Elderly men with lower testosterone levels perform better on cognitive tasks.
    c. <arried men with children have higher testosterone levels than unmarried men.
    d. all of the above

Label Drawings

A. Label the parts of a neuron.

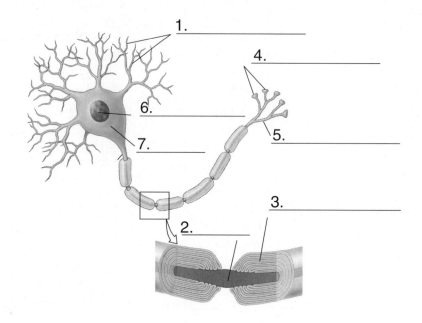

1. _____

4. _____

6. _____

7. _____

5. _____

3. _____

2. _____

B. Label the parts of the neuron at the synapse.

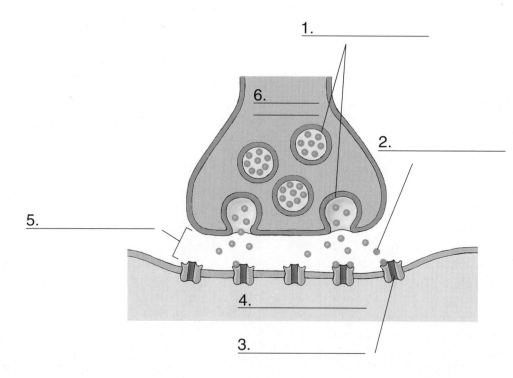

1. _____

6. _____

2. _____

5. _____

4. _____

3. _____

C. Name each lobe of the brain and identify the parts of the brain.

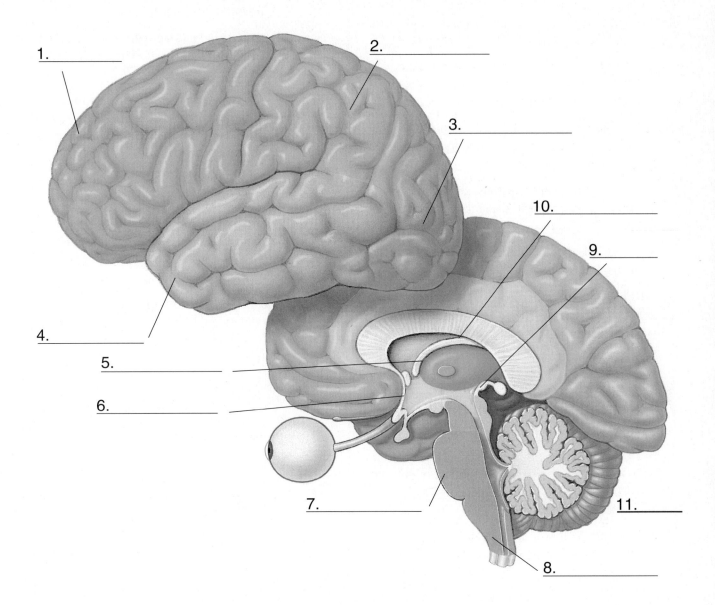

1. _____

2. _____

3. _____

10. _____

9. _____

4. _____

5. _____

6. _____

7. _____

11. _____

8. _____

Answers and Explanations to Multiple Choice Posttest

1. d. Plasticity in the human brain is the ability to adapt to new environmental conditions. p. 47

2. a. Psychobiology is the branch of psychology that deals with the biological basis of behavior and mental processes. p. 41

3. c. A neuron is the smallest unit of the nervous system and underlies the activity of the entire nervous system. p. 41

4. c. Afferent (sensory) neurons carry messages from sense organs to the spinal cord or brain. p. 62

5. d. When the electrical charge inside the neuron is negative relative to the outside, it is called polarized or polarization. p. 43

6. d. A synapse is composed of the axon terminal of one neuron, the synaptic space, and the dendrite or cell body of the next neuron. pp. 44–45

7. b. The all-or-none law operates on the principle that the action potential in a neuron either fires at full strength or not at all. p. 44

8. c. The neurotransmitter dopamine is involved in a wide variety of behaviors and emotions and is implicated in schizophrenia and Parkinson's disease. p. 46

9. d. Opiates such as morphine and heroin bind to the receptor sites for endorphins and shed information on addictive behavior. p. 46

10. b. Portions of the hypothalamus govern hunger, thirst, sexual drive, body temperature, rage, terror, and pleasure. p. 52

11. a. Most people think of or refer to the cerebral cortex when talking about 'the brain.' p. 53

12. d. The corpus callosum is a thick, ribbonlike band of nerve fibers that is the primary connection between the left and right hemispheres. p. 55

13. b. The temporal lobe of the brain regulates hearing, balance, equilibrium, some emotions and motivation, and facial recognition. p. 54

14. b. The reticular formation's main job is to send "alert!" signals to the higher brain in response to incoming messages. p. 52

15. c. The thyroid gland regulates the body's rate of metabolism and how alert and energetic people are. p. 64

16. c. The right hemisphere tends to dominate in spatial and holistic tasks; the left hemisphere tends to dominate in language and sequential activities. pp. 55–56

17. a. The limbic system plays a role in learning and emotional behavior and forming new memories. pp. 54–55

18. d. The endocrine system secretes hormones into the bloodstream that coordinate and integrate behavior. p. 64

19. b. The adrenal glands (adrenal cortex and adrenal medulla) affect the body's reaction to stress by releasing hormones into the bloodstream. pp. 64–65

20. a. Deoxyribonucleic acid (DNA) is a complex, double helix shaped molecule that is the main ingredient of chromosomes and genes and forms the code for all genetic information. p. 67

21. a. Amniocentesis is a prenatal screening procedure that harvests cells taken from the amniotic fluid to determine defects. p. 73

22. a. (MRI) Magnetic resonance imaging observes computerized colored brain images to detect abnormal brain activity and map structures in the brain. p. 59

23. d. The Human Genome Project was launched in 1990 with the goal to map all 23 pairs of human chromosomes and to determine which genes influence which characteristics. p. 67

24. a. Family studies assume that close relatives should have more heritability than distant relatives on certain traits. p. 70

25. d. Major breakthrough research in 1998 has proven that adult brains do have stem cells and that neurogenesis does occur in human adult brains. p. 48

26. b.   Excitatory signals tell neurons to "fire," while inhibitory signals tell them to "rest." p. 43

27. c.   Studies have shown that rats raised in enriched conditions have larger neurons with more synapses compared to rats raised in impoverished conditions. p. 47

28. a.   Also known as the "little brain," the cerebellum is known primarily for control of balance and coordinating action; jerky movements and stumbling may result if the cerebellum is damaged. New evidence shows it may be involved in psychological processes. p. 52

29. d.   In severe cases of epilepsy, the corpus callosum may be cut separating the two brain hemispheres. Normal functioning is possible, but certain experiments have revealed the specialized roles of the left and right hemispheres. pp. 55-57

30. b.   Strokes often produce language problems called aphasias. Expressive aphasias are seen in damage to Broca's area and receptive aphasias are seen in patients with damage to Wernicke's area. p. 57

31. c.   The thyroid gland affects alertness and energy. Among other things, hyperthyroidism results in overexcitability, insomnia, reduced attention span, agitation, as well as reduced concentration and difficulty focusing on a task. p. 64

32. a.   Often called the "master gland," the pituitary produces many different hormones and has a wide range of effects on the body functions. p. 64

33. a.   Sex hormones such as estrogen and testosterone influence performance on cognitive tasks. Also, testosterone levels vary in males, they are lower in married men and married men with children. p. 66

Answers to Label Drawings

A.   Parts of a neuron. Refer to Figure 2-1, p. 42
   1. dendrites
   2. axon
   3. myelin
   4. terminal buttons
   5. axon terminals
   6. cell nucleus
   7. cell body

B.   Parts of the neuron at the synapse. Refer to Figure 2-3, p. 45
   1. synaptic vesicles
   2. neurotransmitters
   3. receptor
   4. dendrite or cell body
   5. synaptic space
   6. terminal button

C.   Lobes and parts of the brain. Refer to Figure 2-6, p. 51
   1. Frontal lobe
   2. Parietal lobe
   3. Temporal lobe
   4. Occipital lobe
   5. Thalamus
   6. Hypothalamus
   7. Pons
   8. Medulla
   9. Pineal gland
   10. Corpus callosum
   11. Cerebellum

Language Support

Students identified the following words from the text as needing more explanation. This page can be cut out, folded in half, and used as a bookmark for this chapter.

A

Aftereffects	delayed or prolonged response to a stimulus
Astonished	fill with or cause wonder, amazement, or surprise
Artificial	made to imitate something in nature, not genuine
Assumption	accept as true without proof
Attention deficit	unable to concentrate due to impulsiveness and inattention
Attraction	arouse the interest, admiration, or attention of

B

Bizarre	strikingly unconventional, odd or weird
Boost	increase, lift, raise up

C

Cadaver	dead body, often used for dissection (autopsy)
Cite	quote as authority; use as support, proof, or to illustrate
Clone	replica or copy of a DNA sequence, closely resemble
Concentrate	focus, direct thoughts or attention to something
Continuous	uninterrupted in time, sequence, substance, or extent
Coordinate	to harmonize in a common action or effort

D

Delayed onset	to postpone or begin at a later time
Deleterious	harmful, dangerous, injurious
Deliberately	action done with full awareness of the effect, intentional
Destiny	predetermine course of events, inevitable fate
Dexterity	skill in the use of one's body, hands, or mind
Dilemma	a situation that requires a choice between options
Disrupt	break apart, throw into confusion, stop or interrupt
Docile	easily managed or taught
Double helix	2 coiled strands of DNA forming a spiral shape

E

Ebullient	enthusiastic, lively, bubbly
Enable	supply with means or knowledge, make possible
Environment	surroundings, circumstances, or conditions around one
Equilibrium	balance between opposing forces, influences, or actions
Equivalent	equal, similar or identical in form or effect
Exceed	go beyond the limits, surpass
Exhibit	to show or display
Exterminate	destroy completely, wipe out

F

Facet	an aspect, part or one side of
Facilitate	to assist or make easier

H

Hastily	rapid, speedy action made too quickly to be accurate
Harvest	result or consequence of an activity
Heighten	intensify, increase, or strengthen in quality or degree

I

Impaired	diminished or weakened functioning
Implied	express or indicate indirectly, suggest
Impoverished	deprive of strength or nourishment, poverty
Inaugurate	begin or introduce formally
Inbred	mating of closely related individuals
Indirectly	not straight to the point, diverging from plan or course
Induce	persuade or move to action, influence
Ingenious	imaginative, resourceful, clever
Insulate	protective covering to prevent loss of heat, sound, etc.
Integrate	join together, unify, unite without restriction
Interplay	reciprocal action and reaction, interaction
Interpret	explain or clarify meaning based upon one's understanding
Intricate	having complex elements, requiring effort to understand
Intriguing	arousing interest or curiosity
Irreverent	disrespectful act or remark

K

Keen	intellectually sharp or sensitive, enthusiastic

L

Landmark	historically significant event or location

M

Merge	blend together or be absorbed, often gradually
Migraine	severe, recurring headache often affecting one side of head
Misguided	led in the wrong direction or astray
Minute (my-nute)	exceptionally small, beneath notice, insignificant, tiny
Mysterious	something that is unexplainable or not fully understood

N

Notion	idea, whim, or impulse; belief or opinion

O

Obstinate	difficult to manage, control or subdue, stubborn
Opposite effect	sharply contrasting results or outcomes
Origin	ancestry, point at which something comes into existence

P

Paradigm	example that serves as a pattern or model
Patent	invention protected by a grant
Perpetuate	prolong the existence or duration of
Pinpoint	to locate, target, or identify with precision
Pioneer	innovator in research and development
Plausible	believable, apparently true or likely, credible
Predominate	controlling power or influence, greater importance
Primitive vertebrates	animals with simple body structure
Profane	irreverent, contempt for what is sacred, vulgar language
Prognosis	prediction of possible or probable outcome
Promising	likely to develop favorably
Provocative	inciting anger or resentment, stirring up action or feelings

R

Replicate	duplicate, copy, repeat, or reproduce itself (DNA)
Reveal	to show, bring to view or light

S

Sequentially	following one after another in time or continuous series
Shallow	lacking depth of intellect, emotion, or knowledge
Spark	to set in motion or spur

Strenuous	requiring great effort, energy, or exertion
Specialized	to choose or adapt to a specific function or field of study
Spontaneously	arising without apparent external cause or thought
Subdue	to quiet or bring under control, make less intense
Subtle	difficult to detect, not obvious, requiring fine distinction
Susceptibility	likelihood of being influenced, allowing or permitting
Sustain	maintain, provide with necessities to survive, support

T

Tamper	interfere with harmfully or meddle
Temperament	one's nature or character
Tendency	inclination to think, act, or behave a certain way
Three-dimensional	extending in depth, width, and height in space and time

U

Urgency	requiring immediate action

V

Voluntary	using free will or volition, intentionally, deliberately

W

Wander	lose clarity of thought, go astray, to move aimlessly

Key Vocabulary Terms

Cut out each term and use as study cards.
Definition is on the back side of each term.

Neurons	Glial cells/ glia
Dendrites	Ions
Axon	Resting potential
Nerve or tract	Polarization
Myelin sheath	Neural impulse or action potential

Cells that insulate and support neurons by holding them together, providing nourishment, removing waste products, preventing harmful substances from passing into the brain, and forming the myelin sheath.

Individual cells that are the smallest unit of the nervous system.

Electrically charged particles found both inside and outside of the neuron.

Short fibers that branch out from the cell body and pick up incoming messages.

Electrical charge across a neuron membrane resulting from more positive ions concentrated on the outside and more negative ions on the inside.

Single long fiber extending from the cell body; it carries outgoing messages.

The condition of a neuron when the inside is negatively charged relative to the outside; when the neuron is at rest.

Groups of axons bundled together.

The firing of a nerve cell.

White, fatty covering found on some axons.

Graded potential	Terminal button or synaptic knob
Threshold of excitation	Synaptic space or synaptic cleft
Absolute refractory period	Synapse
Relative refractory period	Synaptic vesicles
All-or-none law	Neurotransmitters

Structure at the end of an axon terminal branch.

A shift in the electrical charge in a tiny area of a neuron.

Tiny gap between the axon terminal of one neuron and the dendrites or cell body of the next neuron.

The level an impulse must exceed to cause a neuron to fire.

Area composed of the axon terminal of one neuron, the synaptic space, and the dendrite or cell body of the next neuron.

A period after firing when a neuron will not fire again no matter how strong the incoming messages may be.

Tiny sacs in a terminal button or synaptic knob that release chemicals into the synapse.

A period after firing when a neuron is returning to its normal polarized state and will fire again only if the incoming message is much stronger than usual.

Chemicals released by the synaptic vesicles that travel across the synaptic space and affect adjacent neurons.

Principle that the action potential in a neuron does not vary in strength; either the neuron fires at full strength or it does not fire at all.

Receptor sites	Neuropsychology
Central nervous system	Cerebellum
Peripheral nervous system	Brain stem
Spinal cord	Midbrain
Medulla	Thalamus

Branch of psychology that focuses on the brain and nervous system	Locations on a receptor neuron into which a specific neurotransmitter fits like a key into a lock.
Structure in the hindbrain that control certain reflexes and coordinates the body's movements.	Division of the nervous system that consists or the brain and spinal cord.
The top of the spinal column; it widens out to form the hindbrain and midbrain.	Division of the nervous system that connects the central nervous system to the rest of the body.
Region between the hindbrain and the forebrain; it is important for hearing and sight, and it is one of several places in the brain where pain is registered.	Complex cable of neurons that runs down the spine, connecting the brain to most of the rest of the body.
Forebrain region that relays and translates incoming messages from the sense receptors, except those for smell.	Part of the hindbrain that controls such functions as breathing, heart rate, and blood pressure.

Hypothalamus	Temporal lobe
Neuroscience	Parietal lobes
Cerebral cortex	Frontal lobe
Association areas	Corpus callosum
Occipital lobe	Reticular formation

Part of the cerebral hemisphere that helps regulate hearing, balance and equilibrium, and certain emotions and motivations.	Forebrain region that governs motivation and emotional responses.
Part of the cerebral cortex that receives sensory information from throughout the body.	The study of the brain and the nervous system.
Part of the cerebral cortex that is responsible for voluntary movement; it is also important for attention, goal-directed behavior, and appropriate emotional experiences.	The outer surface of the two cerebral hemispheres that regulate most complex behavior.
A thick band of nerve fibers connecting the left and right cerebral cortex.	Areas of the cerebral cortex where incoming messages form the separate senses are combined into meaningful impressions and outgoing messages from the motor areas are integrated.
Network of neurons in the hindbrain, midbrain, and part of the forebrain whose primary function is to alert and arouse the higher parts of the brain.	Part of the cerebral hemisphere that receives and interprets visual information.

Limbic system	Sympathetic division
Somatic nervous system	Parasympathetic division
Afferent neurons	Hormones
Efferent neurons	Endocrine glands
Autonomic nervous system	Thyroid gland

Branch of the autonomic nervous system; it prepares the body for quick action in an emergency.	Ring of structures that plays a role in learning and emotional behavior.
Branch of the autonomic nervous system; it calms and relaxes the body.	The part of the peripheral nervous system that carries messages from the senses to the central nervous system and between the central nervous system and the skeletal muscles.
Chemical substances released by the endocrine glands; they help regulate bodily activities.	Sensory neurons that carry messages from sense organs to the spinal cord or brain.
Glands of the endocrine system that release hormones into the bloodstream.	Motor neurons that carry messages from the spinal cord or brain to the muscles and glands.
Endocrine gland located below the voice box; it produces the hormone thyroxin.	The part of the peripheral nervous system that carries messages between the central nervous system and the internal organs.

Parathyroids	Adrenal glands
Pineal gland	Genes
Pancreas	Neural plasticity
Pituitary gland	Genetics
Gonads	Primary motor cortex

Two endocrine glands located just above the kidneys.

Four tiny glands embedded in the thyroid; they secrete parathormone.

Elements that control the transmission of traits; they are found on the chromosomes.

A gland located roughly in the center of the brain that appears to regulate activity levels over the course of a day.

The ability of the brain to change in response to experience.

Organ lying between the stomach and small intestine; it secretes insulin and glucagon, to regulate blood sugar levels.

Study of how traits are transmitted from one generation to the next.

Gland located on the underside of the brain; it produces the largest number of the body's hormones.

The section of the frontal lobe responsible for voluntary movement.

The reproductive glands–testes in males and ovaries in females.

Chromosomes	Polygenic inheritance
Deoxyribonucleic acid (DNA)	Behavior genetics
Primary somatosensory cortex	Evolutionary psychology
Dominant gene	Family studies
Recessive gene	Hindbrain

Process by which several genes interact to produce a certain trait; responsible for our most important traits.

Pairs of threadlike bodies within the cell nucleus that contain the genes.

Study of the relationship between genetics and behavior.

Complex molecule in a double-helix configuration that is the main ingredient of chromosomes and genes and forms the code for all genetic information.

A subfield of psychology concerned with the origins of behaviors and mental processes, their adaptive value, and the purposes they continue to serve.

Area of the parietal lobe where messages from the sense receptors are registered.

Studies of heritability in humans based on the assumption that if genes influence a certain trait, close relatives should be more similar on that trait than distant relatives.

Member of a gene pair that controls the appearance of a certain trait.

Area containing the medulla, pons, and cerebellum.

Member of a gene pair that can control the appearance of a certain trait only if it is paired with another recessive gene.

Twin studies	Psychobiology
Identical twins	Interneurons (association) neurons
Fraternal twins	Primary motor cortex
Adoption studies	Human genome
Natural selection	

The area of psychology that focuses on the biological foundations of behavior and mental processes.	Studies of identical and fraternal twins to determine the relative influence of heredity and environment on human behavior.
Neurons that carry messages from one neuron to another.	Twins developed from a single fertilized ovum and therefore identical in genetic makeup at the time of conception.
The section of the frontal lobe responsible for voluntary movement.	Twins developed from two separate fertilized ova and therefore different in genetic makeup.
The full complement of genes within a human cell.	Research carried out on children adopted at birth by parents not related to them, to determine the relative influence of heredity and environment on human behavior.
	The mechanism proposed by Darwin in his theory of evolution, which states that organisms best adapted to their environment tend to survive, transmitting their genetic characteristics to offspring.

3

Sensation and Perception

Chapter Focus

This chapter begins by describing the nature of sensation, the basic experience of stimulating the body's senses. Receptor cells that respond to energy are located in each of the sense organs, such as the eye, ear, tongue, and skin. To be detected, a stimulus must reach an absolute threshold else neural impulses will not be fired and no sensory experience will result. Sensory thresholds are not static; they adapt to the levels of stimulation in the environment. Weber's law states that the difference threshold, or just noticeable difference, is a constant proportion of the original stimulus. Methods used to examine subliminal messages and ESP have been heavily criticized; even well-designed studies have produced inconsistent results.

Of all the senses, vision has received the most attention by researchers. Light is the stimulus that creates visual experience, but only visible light is converted into neural impulses by the visual system. Structures within the eye include the cornea, pupil, iris, lens, retina, fovea, and receptor cells. Two kinds of receptor cells are located in the retina: the rods which are responsible for night vision; and the cones that allow color vision. Rods and cones adapt according to the amount of light available. Sometimes removal of a stimulus results in an afterimage.

Rods and cones form synapses with retinal bipolar cells, which transmit information to ganglion cells. Axons of the ganglion cells bundle together in the retina at the blind spot forming the optic nerve. Optic nerves extend from the back of each eye to the brain. Some of the fibers comprising the optic nerves separate and cross to the opposite sides of the brain at a point called the optic chiasm. The main destinations of these projections are the visual processing areas within the cerebral cortex, primarily located within the occipital lobe. The brain is finally able to register and interpret the signals translating them into meaningful visual images. Specialized neurons, known as feature detectors, play an important role in this process.

The ability to see colors is an adaptation present in most animals. Color properties are referred to by hue, saturation, and brightness. All 150 basic hues can be made by combining red, green, or blue lights. The process of mixing lights of different wavelengths to create new hues is known as additive color mixing; whereas the process of mixing paints in known as subtractive color mixing. Some people have color blindness, the partial or total inability to perceive hues. Dichromats are blind to either red-green or yellow-blue, while monochromats are totally color-blind and respond only to shades of light and dark.

Hearing is another important sense. Sound is a psychological experience created by air molecules that collide with one another creating soundwaves; these soundwaves then hit the eardrums. The frequency of soundwaves is measured in hertz and changes in frequencies produce the pitches of different sounds. The amplitude of the soundwave helps determine the loudness of a sound and is measured in decibels. The ear's main structures are the outer ear, the middle ear consisting of the hammer, anvil, and stirrup, and the inner ear. The stirrup is connected to the inner ear by the oval window. On the inner basilar membrane lies the organ of Corti; it is embedded with tiny hair cells whose fibers send signals to the auditory areas of the brain via the auditory nerve. Three theories of hearing have been proposed: the place theory, frequency theory, and the volley principle. Hearing disorders vary in their level of impairment type and origins. Most hearing loss is caused by exposure to noise. Some types of hearing loss are irreversible while other types may be treatable using implants or electrical stimulation.

Other senses include smell, taste, kinesthetic and vestibular senses, skin senses, and pain. Smell is activated by proteins produced in the nasal glands. Receptor cells in the nasal cavity send axons to the olfactory bulb, which then sends impulses to the temporal lobes where they are interpreted as smell. The sense of taste is detected by receptor cells housed within the taste buds located on the tongue. Kinesthetic and vestibular senses help our bodies to determine the speed and direction of movement and the orientation in space. Disruption to the vestibular sense results in motion sickness in some people. Sensitive nerve fibers in the skin convey information about the sensations of pressure, temperature, and pain to the brain. Pain is a complex sense not easily understood as scientists have great difficulty identifying pain receptors. Individuals vary widely in their thresholds for pain and for pain tolerance. Approaches to managing pain vary by culture and alternative treatments for pain are increasing.

The final sections of this chapter are devoted to perception. Gestalt psychologists believed that perceptual experience is created in the brain in predictable ways. In optical illusions, however, things are perceived that could not exist in reality. An important concept is perceptual constancy. Familiar objects are perceived to be the same size (size constancy), the same shape (shape constancy), the same color (color constancy), and of the same brightness (brightness constancy) despite changes in distance, position, or the amount of available light. The perception of distance and depth are largely accounted for by the use of monocular and binocular cues. The location of sounds is determined by monaural and binaural cues.

Movement perception is a complicated process requiring visual information from the retina and information from muscles around the eyes as they track objects. It is believed that real movement is determined by the changes in the positions of objects as they move across a stationary background. Apparent movement is the perception of movement in stationary objects. Forms of apparent movement include autokinetic illusion, stroboscopic motion, and the phi phenomenon. Visual illusions can create perceptual experiences that may (or may not) correspond to real-world situations. Distinctions are generally made between physical and perceptual illusions. Finally, personal factors play a large role in perception. Perception is strongly influenced by personal motivations, values, expectations, cognitive style, experience, culture, and personality.

Learning Objectives and Questions

After you have read and studied this chapter, you should be able to complete the following statements.

LEARNING OBJECTIVES

1. Compare and contrast sensation and perception and describe the events that produce each of them.

2. Describe the difference between the absolute threshold and difference threshold and how consistent these thresholds are across people, place and time.

3. Describe the process of adaptation. Discuss light and dark adaptation and the phenomenon of afterimages.

4. Explain how messages entering the eye are processed in the brain.

5. Describe the two main theories of color vision.

6. Identify the characteristics of sound.

7. Describe the structure of the ear and explain the functions of the various parts.

8. State the two theories of pitch discrimination.

9. Summarize the theories that explain how the sense of smell is activated by chemical substances and describe the role smell plays in our daily lives.

10. Explain the processes involved in the sense of taste and name the four primary qualities of taste.

11. Explain how the sensations of pressure, warmth, and cold originate and how people respond to them.

12. Discuss three theories of pain: gate control theory, biopsychosocial theory, and placebo effect. Describe the role played by endorphins and people's subjective experience of pain.

13. Define perceptual constancy and identify four kinds.

14. Describe four observer characteristics that can affect perception.

15. Identify the contributions of both monocular and binocular cues of depth.

SHORT ESSAY QUESTIONS

1. Define pitch, amplitude, decibels, overtones, and timbre.

2. Differentiate among hue, brightness, and saturation. Explain the difference between additive and subtractive color mixing.

3. Distinguish between rods and cones and list their characteristics and functions with respect to light, color, and how they connect to other cells.

4. Describe hearing disorders and explain the causes of deafness and tinnitus.

5. Describe autokinetic illusion, stroboscopic movement, the phi phenomenon, and the illusion of induced movement.

6. Explain subliminal perception and discuss research findings on the effectiveness of subliminal messages on people's behavior.

7. Explain extrasensory perception, telepathy, and clairvoyance. Define parapsychology and discuss research findings in this field.

8. Describe how we use monaural and binaural cues to locate the source of sounds.

9. Discuss the principles of perceptual organization identified by the Gestaltists.

10. Compare and contrast real and apparent movement and provide three examples of apparent movement.

Chapter Outline

The following is an outline conveying the main concepts of this chapter.

1. The Nature of Sensation   page 79
   A. The Character of Sensation
      - Receptor Cell
      - Doctrine of Specific Nerve Energies
   B. Sensory Thresholds
      - Absolute threshold
      - Adaptation
      - Difference threshold or just noticeable difference (jnd)
      - Weber's law
   C. Subliminal and Extrasensory Perception
      - Advertisements
      - Self-Help tapes
2. Vision   page 83
   A. The Visual System
      - Cornea
      - Pupil
      - Iris
      - Lens
      - Retina
      - Fovea
      - The Receptor Cells
        – Wavelengths
        – Rods
        – Cones
        – Bipolar cells
        – Visual acuity
      - Adaptation
        – Dark adaptation
        – Light adaptation
        – Afterimage
      - From Eye to Brain
        – Ganglion cells
        – Optic nerve
        – Blind spot
        – Optic chaism
        – Feature detectors
   B. Color Vision
      - Properties of color
        – Hue
        – Saturation
        – Brightness
      - Theories of color vision
        – Additive Color Mixing
        – Subtractive Color Mixing
        – Trichromatic (3 Color) theory
        – Colorblindness
          1. Trichromats
          2. Dicromats
          3. Monochromats
3. Hearing   page 92
   A. Sound
      - Sound waves
      - Frequency
      - Hertz (Hz)
      - Pitch
      - Amplitude
      - Decibels
      - Overtones
      - Timbre
   B. The Ear
      - Outer ear
      - Middle Ear
        – Hammer
        – Anvil
        – Stirrup
      - Inner Ear
      - Oval window
      - Cochlea
      - Basilar membrane
      - Organ of Corti
      - Auditory Nerve
      - Neural Connections
   C. Theories of Hearing
      - Place Theory
      - Frequency Theory
      - Volley principle
      - Hearing disorders
        – Deafness
        – Tinnitus
        – Remedies
4. The Other Senses   page 97
   A. Smell
      - Detecting common odors
      - Olfactory bulb
      - Pheromones

UNDERSTANDING THE WORLD AROUND US: Pheromones   page 98

   B. Taste
      - Taste buds
   C. Kinesthetic and Vestibular Senses
      - Kinesthetic Senses
      - Stretch receptors
      - Golgi tendon organs
      - Vestibular senses

- Semicircular canals
- Vestibular sacs
- Motion Sickness
D. The Skin Senses
- Paradoxical heat

UNDERSTANDING OURSELVES   page 101
E. Massage: Rubbing People the Right Way
- Phantom limb phenomenon
- Individual differences
- Pain threshold
- Pain tolerance
- Individual Differences
  - Gate Control Theory
  - Biopsychosocial Theory
- Alternative Approaches
  - Placebo effect
5. Perception   page 103
A. Perceptual Organization
- Gestalt
- Figure/Ground relationships
- Optical illusion
  - Proximity
  - Similarity
  - Closure
  - Continuity
B. Perceptual Constancies
- Size constancy
- Shape constancy
- Color constancy
- Brightness constancy
C. Perceptions of Distance and Depth
Monocular cues
- Interposition
- Linear perspective
- Aerial perspective
- Elevation
- Texture gradient
- Shadowing
- Motion parallex
Binocular cues
- Stereoscopic vision
- Retinal disparity
- Convergence
D. Location of Sounds
- Monaural cues
- Binaural cues
E. Perception of Movement
- Real movement
- Apparent movement

- Autokinetic illusion
- Stroboscopic motion
- Psi phenomenon
F. Visual Illusions
- Real-world illusions
- Physical illusion
- Perceptual illusion
- Induced movement
G. Observer Characteristics
- Motivation
- Values
- Expectations
- Cognitive Style
- Experience and Culture
- Personality

Multiple Choice Posttest

After studying the text and completing the Study Guide activities, answer these questions to determine if you need to review any areas before the course exam.

1. Sensation is to _____ as perception is to _____.
   a. stimulation; interpretation
   b. interpretation; stimulation
   c. sensory ability; sensory acuity
   d. sensory acuity; sensory ability

2. The _____ is reached when a person can detect a stimulus 50 percent of the time.
   a. difference threshold
   b. just noticeable difference threshold
   c. absolute threshold
   d. separation threshold

3. Which of the following is NOT true of subliminal perception?
   a. The effects attributed to subliminal perception may be the results of conscious expectations.
   b. Subliminal messages may be able to change attitudes.
   c. People can perceive stimuli they cannot consciously describe.
   d. It works equally as well in all people.

4. _____ are receptor cells in the retina responsible for night vision and perceiving brightness, and _____ are receptor cells in the retina responsible for color vision.
   a. Rods; cones
   b. Rods; reels
   c. Cones; rods
   d. Cornea; iris

5. The ability of the eye to distinguish fine details is called _____.
   a. visual dilation
   b. visual acuity
   c. visual sensitivity
   d. adaptation

6. On the chart below, label the energies in the electromagnetic spectrum in order: FM radio waves, AC circuits, X-rays, radar, TV radio waves, infrared rays, gamma rays, AM radio waves, ultra violet rays.

7. Motion sickness arises in the _____.
   a. kinesthetic organs
   b. cutaneous organs
   c. cerebral cortex
   d. vestibular organs

8. The process of mixing various pigments together to create different colors is called _____.
   a. blending
   b. trichromatic color mixing
   c. subtractive color mixing
   d. additive color mixing

9. The psychological experience created by the brain in response to changes in air pressure that are perceived in the auditory system is known as _____.
   a. vibration
   b. harmonics
   c. sound
   d. amplitude

10. On the chart below, label the amount of decibels of the following common sounds: patter of rain; revolver firing at close range; subway train; normal conversation; whisper; average office interior; sonic boom; power lawnmower; food blender; air raid siren; live rock music; heavy truck; leaves rustling; window air conditioner, jet plane; personal stereo; pain threshold; potential ear damage; heavy traffic; vacuum; dishwasher.

11. Hertz is a unit of measurement of _____.
    a. the timbre of a sound
    b. how high or low a sound is
    c. the frequency of a sound
    d. the amplitude of a sound

12. A chemical that communicates information to other organisms through the sense of smell is called _____.
    a. a saccule
    b. a pheromone
    c. odorant protein binding
    d. a scent

13. Flavor is _____.
    a. a combination of texture and taste
    b. a combination of taste and smell
    c. a combination of texture and smell
    d. taste

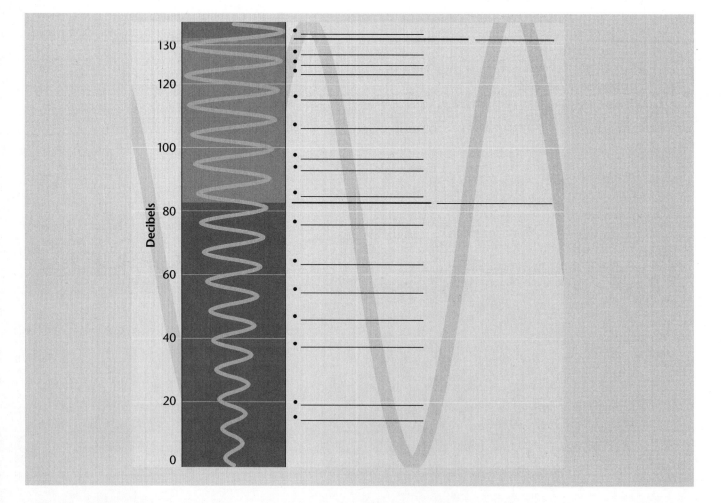

14. The _____ has the most numerous receptors.
    a. eye
    b. ear
    c. nose
    d. skin

15. Optical illusions result from distortion in _____.
    a. transduction
    b. sensation
    c. perception
    d. adaptation

16. You know a house is the same size whether you are standing right next to it or a mile away from it because of _____.
    a. phi phenomenon
    b. the figure-ground distinction
    c. retinal disparity
    d. perceptual constancy

17. Our general method for dealing with the environment is known as _____.
    a. intelligence
    b. perceptual style
    c. personality
    d. cognitive style

18. Visual distance and depth cues that require the use of both eyes are called _____.
    a. monocular cues
    b. diocular cues
    c. binocular cues
    d. dichromatic cues

19. Placebo pills and acupuncture have been effective in reducing pain. The common element in these methods may be their ability to stimulate the ____.
    a. production of adrenal hormones
    b. opening of neurological gates in the spine
    c. arousal of the peripheral nervous system
    d. production of endorphins

20. The phenomenon whereby items that continue a pattern or direction tend to be grouped together as part of a pattern is _____.
    a. proximity
    b. similarity
    c. closure
    d. continuity

21. The phenomenon in which we perceive movement in objects that are actually standing still is known as _____.
    a. apparent movement
    b. real movement
    c. biological movement
    d. induced movement

22. On the chart below, match the Gestalt principles of perceptual organization with the appropriate pattern.
    a. continuity
    b. closure
    c. proximity
    d. similarity

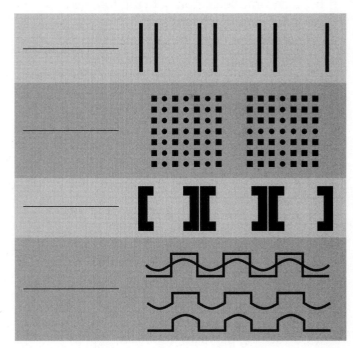

23. Which of the following best describes the process of adaptation in a dimly lit environment?
    a. Rods and cones have equal sensitivity to light in low levels of illumination.
    b. The best vision will occur once the rods have adapted.
    c. Cones will become increasingly sensitive to the dim light.
    d. Once the rods and cones have adapted, seeing in color is possible.

24. The term blind spot refers to _____.
    a. the place on the retina that does not have any receptor cells
    b. the place on the retina that does not have cones
    c. the place on the retina that does not have rods
    d. the complete inability to process vision

25. A person who has tinnitus suffers from _____.
    a. the perception of a constant visual image, as if seeing stars
    b. a chronic sensation of being touched
    c. hearing a persistent sound, like screeching or ringing, from inside the head
    d. an inflammation of the sensory receptors

26. Which of the following statements is true regarding anosmia?
    a. It is most commonly reported in the elderly.
    b. Taste buds detect salty, bitter, sour, or sweet flavors.
    c. It is the complete loss of smell.
    d. all of the above

27. Which of the following is NOT true regarding the sensation of touch?
    a. No medical benefits have been reported from the act of touching.
    b. Touching plays an important role in human interaction.
    c. Receptors for touch are found in our skin.
    d. Touch may be influenced by expectations.

28. Which of the following is NOT true regarding the experience of pain?
    a. Individuals vary widely in their thresholds for pain.
    b. Genetics may play a role in the perception of pain.
    c. Culture and belief systems play a role in coping with pain.
    d. Pain receptors are easy to locate in the body.

Answers and Explanations to Multiple Choice Posttest

1. a. Sensation is the stimulation of a receptor cell (p. 79) and perception is our interpretation of that stimulation (p. 103).

2. c. Absolute threshold is a sensation detected 50 percent of the time. p. 80

3. d. Subliminal perception has not been shown to affect everyone in the same way. p. 82

4. a. Rods are receptors for night vision and brightness, and cones are receptors for color vision. p. 84

5. b. Visual acuity refers to our ability to see fine details. p. 84

6. Fig. 3–4, p. 84. From left to right: gamma rays; x rays; ultraviolet rays (visible light); infrared rays; radar; radio waves: FM – TV – AM; AC circuits.

7. d. Motion sickness originates in the vestibular organs. p. 100

8. c. Mixing of pigments is called subtractive color mixing. p. 90

9. c. Sound is our brain's interpretation of the changes in air pressure in our eardrums. p. 92

10. Fig. 3–16, p. 93 From top to bottom: revolver; *130 decibels:* pain threshold; *sonic boom;* air raid siren; jackhammer; *120 decibels:* jet plane; personal stereo; live rock music; *100 decibels:* subway train; heavy truck; power lawn mower; food blender; *80 decibels: potential ear damage;* heavy traffic/vacuum/dishwasher; normal conversation; *60 decibels:* window air conditioner; patter of rain; *40 decibels:* average office interior; *20 decibels:* leaves rustling; whisper.

11. c. Hertz refers to the frequency of the sound wave. p. 92

12. b. Pheromones are chemicals hat communicate information to other organisms through smell. p. 98

13. b. Flavor is a combination of taste and smell. p. 98

14. a. The skin is the largest sense organ and contains the most receptors. p. 100

15. c. Optical illusions are the result of distortions in perception. p. 104

16. d. Perceptual constancy enables us to see distant objects as the same size as when viewed close by. p. 106

17. d. Our cognitive style determines how we deal with our environment. p. 113

18. c. Binocular cues require both eyes. p. 109

19. d. Placebos and acupuncture both work through the release of endorphins. p. 103

20. d. Continuity is perceived as a pattern or direction of items grouped together. p. 106

21. a. Apparent motion is when we perceive movement in objects that are actually standing still. p. 110

22. Fig. 3–28, p. 105. c. proximity; d. similarity; b. closure; a. continuity

23. b. Rods continue adapting until they reach maximum sensitivity about 30 minutes after entering the environment. This is when the best vision occurs. p. 86

24. a. The place on the retina where the axons of all ganglion cells join to form the optic nerve is called the blind spot and has no receptor cells. p. 87

25. c. Tinnitus is a persistent sound that seems to come from inside the head. p. 96

26. d. Although taste buds may still work, anosmia is a devastating disorder resulting in the loss of smell. It is reported in greater prevalence in people over 65 years old. p. 99

27. a. Research has shown that some kinds of touch may be medically beneficial. pp. 100-101

28. d. There is no simple relationship between pain receptors and the experience of pain. In fact, finding pain receptors has proven difficult. p. 102

Language Support

Students identified the following words from the text as needing more explanation. This page can be cut out, folded in half, and used as a bookmark for this chapter.

A

Adage	traditional saying about a common experience or observation
Adept	very skillful, proficient, expert
Ad campaign	media plan to promote, make known, or sell
Ambiguous	having several possible meanings or interpretations
Ancestry	one's lineage or the origin of an idea, object, or phenomenon
Apparent	obvious, easily understood
Assess	estimate the value of, determine, judge the value or character of
Assume	take for granted without proof, suppose
Attune	bring into harmony or relationship with, adjust

B

Bland	not highly flavored, mild, lacking in interest
Blip	brief interruption, short erratic movements, spot of light on screen
Blotches	large irregular spot or stain
Blurred	make indistinct, smudge, smear
Bombard	to attack vigorously
Bypass	to avoid or circumvent by going around, neglect or ignore opinion

C

Characteristic	typical of, distinctive quality or feature
Coherent	logically connected, consistent, harmonious
Collision	clash, conflict, forceful impact
Consequent	following as the result or logical conclusion
Contend	hold or maintain a position; struggle or oppose
Contour	outline of a figure, edge, or defining line
Contradictory	inability of opposing view or evidence to be true or false
Conversely	opposite or contrary in direction, action or sequence
Convey	communicate, move
Correspond	agree or conform with, match
Cue	guiding suggestion, stimulate to action, sensory signal
Customary	long continued practice according to custom or habit

D

Decipher	make meaning of something difficult to understand
Defect	shortcoming, imperfection, weakness
Displace	remove, replace, or move out of usual place or position
Discrepancy	difference, inconsistency, disagreement
Dramatically	vivid, highly compelling or effective

E

Ebb	decline, decay, fade, flow backward or away
Enhance	magnify the intensity, increase in quality, degree or value, improve
En route	on or along the way
Evidence	support for a belief, that which proves or disproves something
Exclusively	excluding or limiting; singularly, reserved for something alone
Excruciating	causing intense suffering, torment, or torturous action
Exert	put forth into vigorous action or effort

F

Fateful	of great significance, controlled by fate or destiny
Feat	noteworthy or extraordinary act or achievement
Flexible	easily modified, adaptable
Fooled	tricked, deceived, or imposed on
Foreknowledge	knowing something before it happens, foresee
Fraction	small portion or segment of a whole

H

Hazy	vague, misty, indefinite
Hidden	concealed from sight, obstructed, covered up, kept secret
Hypersensitive	excessively affected by external influences or emotions

I

Implant	insert, plant, or establish firmly
In sync	in agreement with, at the same time and rate, together
Interpretation	assigning meaning or understanding of something
Interrelated	reciprocal, in mutual association or connection between or among
Irresistible	tempting, unable to oppose
Irreversible	incapable of being changed

L

Limbo	intermediate, transitional, or midway state or place

M

Manipulate	influence or change something to suit one's purpose or advantage
Mimic	to imitate or copy

O

Optimally	most favorable condition for obtaining desired results
Overall	covering or including everything

P

Particular	specific, exceptional, separately, distinct
Pedestrian	person traveling on foot; lacking in distinction or imagination
Perplexing	puzzling or bewildering, uncertainty, confused
Pool	to join together in common interest, combine
Precisely	specifically, exactly, fixed
Predatory	preying upon others, greedy, selfish
Pretend	to make believe, false appearance, deceive
Prompt	quick to act or respond, on time, assist by suggestion
Protracted	drawn out, lengthen, prolong
Pygmy	of small size or stature, African tribe of tiny people

Q

Quiver	to shake, slight but rapid motion, tremble

R

Radical	drastic, extreme, having strong convictions
Rarely	exceptional, unusual, infrequent
Realistic	based on what is practical or actual, representing what 'is'
Relevant	having practical value, applicable, pertinent to the matter at hand
Remarkable	worthy of note, unusual
Remedy	counteract; something that cures, corrects, or relieves
Resonate	echo or ring with sound, amplify or sustain sound

S

Sophisticated	worldly wise, intricate, complex
Sparse	thinly scattered or distributed, scanty, meager
Speculate	think curiously about, reflect, to wonder
Stationary	not moving, standing still, fixed position
Sufficient	adequate, enough

T

Tactile	having to do with the sense of touch
Transpose	change or reverse position, order, or sequence; interchange
Transmute	change from one substance, condition, or form into another

U

Uncanny	extraordinary, mysterious, having an unexplainable basis
Unique	unusual, not typical, no equal, sole example

V

Vice versa	reverse order from the preceding statement, conversely
Vintage	high quality of past time, classic

Key Vocabulary Terms

Cut out each term and use as study cards.
Definition is on the back side of each term.

Sensation	Weber's Law
Perception	Cornea
Absolute threshold	Pupil
Adaptation	Iris
Difference threshold or just noticeable difference (jnd)	Lens

The principle that the just noticeable difference (jnd) for any given sense is a constant fraction or proportion of the stimulation being judged.

Basic experience of stimulating the body's senses.

The transparent protective coating over the front part of the eye.

Process of creating meaningful patterns from raw sensory information.

Small opening in the iris through which light enters the eye.

The least amount of energy that can be detected as a stimulation 50 percent of the time.

Colored part of the eye that regulates the size of the pupil.

Adjustment of the senses to the level of stimulation they are receiving.

Transparent part of the eye behind the pupil that focuses light onto the retina.

The smallest change in stimulation that can be detected 50 percent of the time.

Retina	Bipolar Cells
Fovea	Dark adaptation
Wavelengths	Light adaptation
Rods	Afterimage
Cones	Ganglion cells

Neurons that have only one axon and one dendrite; in the eye, these neurons connect the receptors on the retina to the ganglion cells.	Lining of the eye containing receptor cells that are sensitive to light.
Increased sensitivity of rods and cones in darkness.	Area of the retina that is the center of the visual field.
Decreased sensitivity of rods and cones in bright light.	The different energies represented in the electromagnetic spectrum.
Sense experience that occurs after a visual stimulus has been removed.	Receptor cells in the retina responsible for night vision and perception of brightness.
Neurons that connect the bipolar cells in the eyes to the brain.	Receptor cells in the retina responsible for color vision.

Optic nerve	Brightness
Blind spot	Additive color mixing
Optic chiasm	Subtractive color mixing
Hue	Trichromatic theory
Saturation	Colorblindness

The nearness of a color to white as opposed to black.

The bundle of axons of ganglion cells that carries neural messages from each eye to the brain.

The process of mixing lights of different wavelengths to create new hues.

Place on the retina where the axons of all the ganglion cells leave the eye and where there are no receptors.

The process of mixing pigments, each of which absorbs some wavelengths of light and reflects others.

Point near the base of the brain where some fibers in the optic nerve from each eye cross to the other side of the brain.

Theory of color vision that all color perception derives from three different color receptors in the retina (usually red, green, and blue receptors).

The aspect of color that corresponds to names such as red, green, and blue.

Partial or total inability to perceive hues.

The vividness or richness of a hue.

Trichromats	Hertz (Hz)
Monochromats	Pitch
Dichromats	Amplitude
Opponent-process theory	Decibel
Frequency	Overtones

Cycles per second; unit of measurement for the frequency of sound waves.

People who have normal color vision.

Auditory experience corresponding primarily to frequency of sound vibrations, resulting in a higher or lower tone.

Organisms that are totally colorblind.

The magnitude of a wave; in sound, the primary determinant of loudness.

People and animals who are blind to either red-green or yellow-blue.

Unit of measurement for the loudness of sounds.

Theory of color vision that three sets of color receptors (yellow-blue, red-green, black-white) respond to determine the color you experience.

Tones that result from sound waves that are multiple of the basic tone: primary determinant of timbre.

The number of cycles per second in a wave; in sound, the primary determinant of pitch.

Timbre	Place theory
Oval window	Frequency theory
Cochlea	Volley principle
Basilar membrane	Olfactory bulb
Auditory nerve	Pheromone

Theory that pitch is determined by the location of greatest vibration of the basilar membrane.	The quality or texture of sound; caused by overtones.
Theory that pitch is determined by the frequency with which hair cells in the cochlea fire.	Membrane across the opening between the middle ear and inner ear that conducts vibrations to the cochlea.
Refinement of frequency theory; receptors in ear fire in sequence, one group, then another, etc., complete pattern of firing corresponds to the frequence of sound.	Part of the inner ear containing fluid that vibrates which in turn causes the basilar membrane to vibrate.
The smell center in the brain.	Vibrating membrane in the cochlea of the inner ear; it contains sense receptors for sound.
Chemical that communicates information to other organisms through smell.	The bundle of axons that carries signals from each ear to the brain.

Taste buds	Gate control theory
Kinesthetic senses	Perceptual constancy
Stretch receptors	Size constancy
Golgi tendon organs	Shape constancy
Vestibular senses	Brightness constancy

Theory that a "neurological gate" in the spinal cord controls the transmission of pain messages to the brain.

Strucures on the tongue that contain the receptor cells for taste.

Tendency to perceive objects as stable and unchanging despite changes in sensory stimulation.

Senses of muscle movement, posture, and strain on muscles and joints.

Perception of an object as the same size regardless of the distance from which it is viewed.

Receptors that sense muscle stretch and contraction.

Tendency to see an object as the same shape no matter what angle it is viewed from.

Receptors that sense movement of the tendons, which connect muscle to bone.

Perception of brightness as the same, even though the amount of light reaching the retina changes.

Senses of equilibrium and body position in space.

Color constancy	Elevation
Monocular cues	Texture gradient
Binocular cues	Shadowing
Linear perspective	Motion parallax
Aerial perspective	Stereoscopic vision

Monocular cue to distance and depth based on the fact that the higher on the horizonal plane an object is, the farther away it appears.	Inclination to perceive familiar objects as retaining their color despite changes in sensory information.
Monocular cue to distance and depth based on the fact that objects seen at greater distances appear to be smoother and less textured.	Visual cues requiring the use of one eye.
Monocular cue to distance and depth based on the fact that shadows often appear on the parts of objects that are more distant.	Visual cues requiring the use of both eyes.
Monocular distance cue: objects closer than point of visual focus seem to move opposite viewer's moving head, and objects beyond the focus point seem to move same direction as the viewer's head.	Monocular cue to distance and depth based on the fact that two parallel lines seem to come together at the horizon.
Combination of two retinal images to give a three-dimensional perceptual experience.	Monocular cue to distance and depth based on the fact that more distant objects are likely to appear hazy and blurred.

Retinal disparity	Stroboscopic motion
Convergence	Sound
Monaural cue	Sound waves
Binaural cue	Organ of Corti
Autokinetic illusion	Biopsychosocial theory

Apparent movement that results from flashing a series of still pictures in rapid succession, as in a motion picture.

Binocular distance cue based on the difference between the images cast on the two retinas when both eyes are focused on the same object.

A (psychological?) experience created by the brain in response to changes in air pressure that are received by the auditory system.

A visual depth cue that comes from muscles controlling eye movement as the eyes turn inward to view a nearby stimulus.

Changes in pressure caused when molecules of air or fluid collide with one another and then move apart again.

Cue to sound location that requires just one ear.

Structure on the surface of the basilar membrane that contains the receptor cells for hearing.

Cue to sound location that involves both ears working together.

Theory that the interaction of biological, psychological, and cultural factors influence the intensity and duration of pain.

The perception that a stationary object is actually moving.

Placebo effect	Feature detectors
Interposition	
Phi phenomenon	
Receptor cell	
Visual acuity	

Specialized brain cells that only respond to particular elements in the visual field such as movement or lines of specific orientation.	Pain relief that occurs when a person believes a pill or procedure will reduce pain. The actual cause of relief seems to come from endorphins.
	Monocular distance cue in which one object, by partly blocking a second object, is perceived as being closer.
	Apparent movement caused by flashing lights in sequence, as on theater marquees.
	A specialized cell that responds to a particular type of energy.
	The ability to distinguish fine details visually.

4 States of Consciousness

Chapter Focus

The many varieties of human consciousness are introduced in this chapter with special attention to sleep, dreams, drug altered states, meditation, and hypnosis. Conscious experience involves selecting the most important information to attend to and filtering out competing stimuli. Daydreaming and fantasy are normal experiences within consciousness and may be beneficial as long as they do not occur so often as to interfere with human interactions and other behaviors.

Sleep or similar rest states are experienced by most animals although sleep duration varies across species. Sleep may be viewed as an adaptive mechanism with a restorative function. Sleep and waking follow circadian cycles that are regulated by the suprachiasmatic nucleus of the hypothalamus (SCN) in the brain. Sleep is rhythmic and marked by distinct physical changes. A waking state is followed by an initial twilight phase marked by the presence of alpha waves. A brief Stage 1 sleep follows. Stages 2 and 3 are the deeper stages of sleep characterized by sleep spindles (Stage 2) and the emergence of slow, high peaked delta waves (Stage 3). Delta waves pervade Stage 4 sleep. Once a sleeper progresses through the first 4 stages, the cycle ascends back to Stage 1 then REM sleep begins. During REM, measures of brain activity and internal states resemble that of a waking person, but the body is incapable of voluntary movement; vivid dreams occur during this stage.

Inadequate sleep is a national epidemic. Sleep loss negatively impacts attention, memory, reaction times, and behavior while increasing the risks of accidents and errors. Awareness of sleep deprivation is essential for people in certain high-risk occupational roles. New studies have linked sleep deprivation to depression in students. Taking short naps have been suggested as an effective way to reduce sleep debt.

Sleep disorders include sleeptalking, sleepwalking, night terrors, insomnia, apnea, and narcolepsy. Sleeptalking, sleepwalking, and night terrors are experienced during NREM sleep, while nightmares occur during REM sleep. These disorders are more prevalent in children than in adults. Apnea is associated with breathing difficulties at night. Narcolepsy is a hereditary disorder where victims enter spontaneous REM sleep without warning.

Dreams occur in every culture. Several explanations for why dreams occur have been proposed. These include: dreams are manifestations of unconscious wishes; dreams process information gathered during the day; dreams are extensions of the concerns of daily life; dreams are activations of brain regions.

Some altered states of consciousness are induced by the use of psychoactive drugs. Drug use today is primarily for recreational rather than religious purposes and the drugs are newer and more potent. Substance abuse is a leading American health problem and is commonly accompanied by substance dependence. The effects of drugs are often studied using double-blind procedures: neither researchers nor participants are aware who received the drug or a placebo.

Psychoactive drugs can be grouped into depressants, stimulants, and hallucinogens. Depressants retard behavior and include alcohol, barbiturates, and the opiates. Alcohol is America's number one drug problem and can harm almost every organ in the body. Alcohol affects the frontal lobes of the brain impairing reasoning, inhibitions, and judgment. It interferes with memory, and is correlated with increased tendencies toward violence. Barbiturates were first used as sedatives and anticonvulsants but their use has declined. Today they may be prescribed for insomnia but may cause dependence, anxiety, and birth defects if taken chronically. Opiates are derived from the poppy plant common in eastern regions of the world. Opiates resemble endorphins, chemicals that act as natural painkillers.

Stimulants include caffeine, nicotine, amphetamines, and cocaine. Caffeine occurs naturally in coffee, tea, and cocoa and is widely touted as maintaining wake and alert states. Large doses may cause caffeinism and can interfere with the effectiveness of prescribed medications. Nicotine found in tobacco may be considered the most dangerous and addictive stimulant. Nicotine reaches the brain rapidly affecting many neurotransmitters. Nicotine use is especially high amongst teenagers. Amphetamines increase feelings of alertness and cause personality changes. The methamphetamine Ecstasy affects emotions and has detrimental effects on particular neurons, impairs visual memory, and is associated with birth defects. Cocaine derives from cocoa leaves and was once a popular anesthetic for surgery. Powdered cocaine and crystallized crack reach the brain rapidly and act on the neurotransmitter dopamine.

Hallucinogens cause changes in perceptions and experience. A relatively short history of hallucinogen use exists. Effects of LSD vary widely—from mental clarity and intense sensation to confusion and nightmares. Marijuana derives from the hemp plant, is estimated to have a 5,000 year history, and is currently the most widely used illegal drug in the U.S. The active ingredient in marijuana is THC. Marijuana has direct physiological and psychological effects. Debate is controversial over the classification of marijuana as a dangerous drug.

A combination of biological, psychological, social, and cultural factors contribute to the likelihood of drug abuse and addiction. Causes of substance abuse are complex and vary across individuals. Heredity appears to play a prominent role in abuse of certain drugs such as alcohol. But the person's expectations, environment, as well as cultural beliefs and values must also be taken into consideration.

Finally, both meditation and hypnosis can alter consciousness. Different forms of meditation exist and each work to suppress activity of the sympathetic nervous system. Reported benefits of meditation include treatment of medical problems, reduced stress, pain relief, and emotional or spiritual gains. Hypnosis has been difficult to define and people vary markedly in their hypnotic experiences and susceptibility to hypnosis. Hypnosis has become popular among athletes, in combined use with psychotherapy, and to treat some medical conditions.

Learning Objectives and Questions

After you have read and studied this chapter, you should be able to complete the following statements.

LEARNING OBJECTIVES

1. Explain the difference between waking consciousness and altered states of consciousness, providing examples of each.

2. Define daydreaming and explain the basic theories. Discuss different types of daydream themes and which kinds of daydreams may be found in healthy individuals.

3. Explain circadian rhythms and the human biological clock. How is our functioning affected by these rhythms and how can disruptions in these rhythms negatively affect people?

4. Identify the various stages of sleep and describe the physiological changes accompanying each stage. Outline the chronological sequencing and timing of sleep stages throughout the night.

5. Identify at least three sleep disorders and discuss their symptoms.

6. Summarize the research on dreams, how dreams vary among people, and four proposed functions of dreaming.

7. Know the difference between substance abuse and substance dependence, tolerance, and withdrawal.

8. Discuss the differences in drugs and drug use in the past and current drugs and drug use.

9. List the seven signs of substance dependence.

10. Discuss why some people seem to be more susceptible to becoming alcoholics. Consider gender and ethnic group differences.

11. Describe the physical and psychological effects of barbiturates, opiates, caffeine, nicotine, stimulants, cocaine, LSD, and marijuana and problems associated with their use.

12. Define meditation and discuss the positive and negative effects of meditation and its potential use.

13. Discuss the history and uses of hypnosis. Describe how people differ in their hypnotic susceptibility and the possible medical and therapeutic benefits of hypnosis.

SHORT ESSAY QUESTIONS

1. Discuss the research findings in regard to sleep deprivation: its prevalence, symptoms, and the effects of long-term deprivation.

2. List five of the eleven signs of alcoholism.

3. Summarize the trend of 'binge drinking' on college campuses and discuss factors that may contribute to binge drinking as well as its effects.

4. Describe the effect of addictive drugs on neurotransmitters and the brain.

5. Discuss how researchers design and carry out experiments and studies of alcohol and drug use and abuse.

6. Outline the path of alcohol in the brain; list the parts of the brain affected by alcohol chronologically and why some people perceive alcohol as a stimulant.

7. Define insomnia, its prevalence and its causes, and the steps a person can take to overcome this sleep disorder.

Chapter Outline

The following is an outline conveying the main concepts of this chapter.

Multiple Choice Posttest

After studying the text and completing the Study Guide activities, answer these questions to determine if you need to review any areas before the course exam.

1. Daydreaming, meditation, intoxication, sleep, and hypnosis are all types of _____.
   a. self-awareness
   b. waking consciousness
   c. self-absorption
   d. altered states of consciousness

2. While studying for an exam, you gradually look up from your work and begin thinking about the job and lifestyle you want after graduation. This type of thought is called _____.
   a. auto prediction
   b. creative thinking
   c. meditation
   d. daydreaming

3. Our sleeping-waking cycle follows a _____ rhythm.
   a. ultradian
   b. monaural
   c. diurnal
   d. circadian

4. People may be able to adjust their biological clocks to prevent jet lag by taking small amount of the hormone _____.
   a. serotonin
   b. epinephrine
   c. dopamine
   d. melatonin

5. Which of the following is NOT seen in REM sleep?
   a. paralysis of body muscles
   b. periods of REM sleep get shorter as the night continues
   c. rapid eye movement
   d. arousal of brain activity

6. The low voltage brain waves produced during relaxed wakefulness or the twilight stage between waking and sleeping are called _____ waves.
   a. alpha
   b. beta
   c. delta
   d. theta

7. In children and young adults, periods of REM sleep get progressively ____ and periods of Stage 4 sleep get progressively _____ throughout the night.
   a. shorter; shorter
   b. longer; shorter
   c. shorter; longer
   d. longer; shorter

8. Freud believed that sleep and dreams expressed ideas that were free from the _____.
   a. memories of worrisome daily events
   b. instinctive feelings of anger, jealousy, or ambition
   c. conscious controls and moral rules
   d. case study method

9. Which of the following is NOT a suggestion to help overcome insomnia?
   a. establish regular sleeping habits
   b. have a strong alcoholic drink before bed
   c. change bedtime routine
   d. get out of bed and do something until feeling sleepy

10. Most episodes of insomnia are ____ and stem from ____.
    a. temporary; stressful events
    b. chronic; stressful events
    c. temporary; underlying psychological problems
    d. chronic; underlying psychological problems

11. Alice's strange adventures in Wonderland and Dorothy's bizarre journey through the Land of Oz most probably occurred when they were in _____ sleep.
    a. Stage 1
    b. Stage 2
    c. Stage 4
    d. REM

12. Albert is meditating. He is likely to experience each of the following EXCEPT _____.
    a. decreased sensory awareness
    b. a sense of timelessness
    c. a sense of well-being
    d. feelings of total relaxation

13. Drugs, such as heroin, that dull the senses and induce feelings of euphoria and relaxation are called _____.
    a. hallucinogens
    b. opiates
    c. barbiturates
    d. placebos

14. Chemical substances that change moods and perceptions are called _____ drugs.
    a. psychoactive
    b. psychedelic
    c. psychoanalytic
    d. psychoactive

15. In the double-blind procedure, some subjects receive a medication while the control group receives an inactive substance called _____.
    a. control treatment
    b. hawthorne reactor
    c. a placebo
    d. dependent variable

16. Which of the following statements about marijuana is NOT true?
    a. Marijuana interferes with attention and short-term memory.
    b. Marijuana use can lead to cardiovascular and respiratory damage.
    c. Marijuana is the most popular drug among college students today.
    d. Marijuana users experience distortions in time perception.

17. The most common contributing factor to automobile accidents after alcohol use is _____.
    a. other drug use
    b. sleep deprivation
    c. cell phone use while driving
    d. talking to others in the car

18. Which of the following drugs can lead to psychosis similar to paranoid schizophrenia?
    a. nicotine
    b. marijuana
    c. amphetamines
    d. heroin

19. The trancelike state in which a subject responds readily to suggestions is _____.
    a. Stage 4 sleep
    b. hypnosis
    c. meditation
    d. coma

20. Which of the following statements best explains why we need sleep?
    a. It helps with physical restoration.
    b. It helps with mental restoration.
    c. It may enhance creativity and problem solving skills.
    d. all of the above

21. The human biological clock is regulated by the _____ in the brain.
    a. optic chiasm
    b. suprachiasmatic nucleus
    c. retina
    d. none of the above

22. An effective way to reduce sleep debt may be to _____.
    a. take a nap during the day
    b. condition yourself to sleep fewer hours each night
    c. take prescription drugs for insomnia
    d. reduce REM sleep

23. Which of the following is NOT true regarding nightmares?
    a. They are commonly experienced during childhood.
    b. They occur during REM sleep.
    c. They are a sign of underlying psychological problems.
    d. Their occurrence is associated with stress in adults.

24. Which of the following does NOT describe the drug Ecstasy?
    a. High doses may damage dopamine and serotonin neurons.
    b. It is a form of methamphetamine.
    c. Use may lead to an increase in intelligence test scores.
    d. Use during pregnancy may lead to birth defects.

Answers and Explanations to Multiple Choice Posttest

1. d.   All are considered to be altered states of consciousness. p. 119

2. d.   Daydreams are apparently effortless shifts in attention away from the present into an imagined world. p. 120

3. d.   Circadian cycles represent the body's biological clock adapted to a 24-hour sleep/wake cycle. p. 122

4. d.   A small amount of melatonin may prevent jet lag. p. 123

5. b.   Periods of REM sleep get longer, not shorter, throughout the night. p. 124

6. a.   As measured by the EEG, low voltage alpha waves are produced during twilight sleep. p. 123

7. b.   REM sleep gets progressively longer and Stage 4 gets shorter for children and young adults. p. 124

8. c.   Freud believed that dreams were free from conscious control and moral rules (ego and superego). p. 128

9. b.   Alcohol interferes with getting a good night's sleep. p. 127

10. a.   Although some insomnia is part of a larger psychological problem, most insomnia is temporary and grows out of stressful events. p 127

11. d.   Most graphic dreams are reported to occur in REM sleep. p. 128

12. a.   Regular meditators report increased sensory awareness, timelessness, well-being, and total relaxation. p. 146

13. b.   Heroin is an opiate. p. 137

14. d.   Psychoactive drugs are chemical substances that alter moods and perceptions. p. 130

15. c.   A placebo is an inactive substance given to the control group. p. 133

16. c.   Marijuana, the most popularly used illegal drug in the U.S., is only the fourth most popular drug among students after alcohol, caffeine, and nicotine. p. 142

17. b.   Driving while sleepy is just as dangerous as driving while drunk. p. 125

18. c.   Chronic users may develop amphetamine psychosis which resembles paranoid schizophrenia. p. 139

19. b.   Hypnosis is a trancelike state in which a person responds readily to suggestions. p. 146

20. d.   Evidence suggests sleep may be important in all of these factors. pp. 121–122

21. b.   The suprachiasmatic nucleus of the hypothalamus regulates our internal biological clock. p. 122

22. a.   Naps from 20–60 minutes can reduce sleep debt and increase alertness and performance. p. 126

23. c.   Neither nightmares nor night terrors alone indicate psychological problems. p. 127

24. c.   Use of Ecstasy may lead to a decrease in intelligence test scores. p. 140

Language Support

Students identified the following words from the text as needing more explanation. This page can be cut-out, folded in half, and used as a bookmark for this chapter.

A

Abstinence	refrain from certain food, drugs, alcohol, or behavior
Accessible	easy to approach, reach, enter, attain, understand
Accredited	officially accepted, certified, reputable
Aggravate	make worse or more severe; intensify, irritate, or annoy
Appraisal	estimation or judging the nature of value, a considered opinion
At bay	keeping away difficulty or an enemy

B

Banned	to forbid, prohibit or bar, denounce, make illegal
Biopsy	removing living tissue for a diagnostic evaluation
Black market	illegal buying and selling of goods, which violates legal price controls
Bombard	attack vigorously

C

Censored	suppress or delete objectionable material; adversely criticize
Clandestine	conceal or take place in secrecy
Consumption	eat, drink, devour, use
Convivial	friendly, jovial, festive; fond of eating, drinking, and partying
Counterculture	lifestyle of those who reject society's dominant values and behavior
Crave	long for, desire, require

D

Deterrent	discourage or restrain from, prevent
Disillusioned	free from illusion or conviction, disenchanted
Distort	twist out of shape, alter original appearance, misrepresent
Duration	length of time something occurs or exists

E

Epidemic	widespread, rapidly spreading, prevalent; affecting many at once
Episodically	occurring sporadically, loosely connected incident in a course of events
Escalate	increase the intensity or magnitude of
Euphoria	strong feeling of happiness, confidence, or well-being

F

Fend off	resist, ward off, keep away, defend
Fleeting	vanishing quickly, passing swiftly
Folk remedy	traditional cultural medical or health practices
Fraternity	male social organization, usually on college campuses
Frenzied	wildly excited or enthusiastic; violently agitated
Frown upon	to show displeasure or disapproval, scowl

G

Glamorize	glorify or romanticize
Groggy	dazed, weakened, unsteady

H

Harbinger	announce or come before, forerunner, to herald
Hippie movement	1960s youths who rejected established society, advocated free love, expanded consciousness, unconventional dress and behavior

I

Illicit	illegal, unlawful, not permitted for moral or legal reasons
Illogical	contrary to or disregarding the laws of logic
Imbibe	consume by drinking, absorbing, or soaking up
Inebriated	intoxicated, drunk, under the influence of alcohol
Interspersed	scattered or placed at intervals among other things; diversified
Ironically	coincidentally, unexpectedly

K

Kaleidoscopic	continually shifting pattern of colored glass reflected in a mirrored tube

M

Mirroring	reflecting back, faithful representation
Mishap	unfortunate accident
Monotonous	lacking in variety, tedious, boring, repetitive

N

Notion	generalized, vague concept, idea or belief; a foolish whim

O

Off the record	confidential; not to be published or quoted

P

Pacifier	nipple shaped device that babies suck on while teething
Paved the way for	prepare, make possible, lead up to
Peak	highest or maximum level or point
Plagued	trouble, annoy or torment; any widespread affliction
Precaution	taking measures in advance to avoid or avert possible harm or misfortune
Preoccupied	absorbed or engrossed to the exclusion of other things
Profoundly	showing deep insight, significance; beyond the superficial
Profuse	abundant, in great amount

R

Relapse	fall or slip back into previous state or behavior
Repercussion	result or effect of a previous event or action
Retard	slow or delay the development or progress of, hinder
Ritual	established pattern of behavior regularly performed in a set manner
Rouse	awaken, stir or incite to anger

S

Scenario	imagined sequence of events, detailed plans or possibilities
Siesta	midday or afternoon rest or nap usually taken in Latin American countries
Snort	to inhale a drug
Sobriety	state of being sober or not using alcohol
Somnolent	sleepy, drowsy, tending to cause sleep
Sorority	female social organization, usually on college campuses
Spurred	urge to action, proceed hurriedly
Stave off	keep or ward off, stall or prevent from happening
Surge	sudden strong rush or sweep; move forward or rise like a wave
Sustaining	support, hold up, endure without yielding, keep going
Symbolic	representing or pertaining to something else

T

Trance	half conscious state between sleep and waking, dazed, mentally absorbed
Trigger	anything that causes or initiates a reaction; activate

U

Unregulated	not in accord with requirements or standards

W

Watchful eye	carefully observant, alert, vigilant
Wheel and deal	highly profitable transactions by clever, crafty person

Consciousness	Non-REM (NREM) sleep
Waking consciousness	Dreams
Altered state of consciousness	Insomnia
Daydreams	Narcolepsy
REM (paradoxical) sleep	Amphetamines

Non-rapid-eye-movement stages of sleep that alternate with REM stages during the sleep cycle.	Our awareness of various cognitive processes, such as sleeping, dreaming, concentrating, and making decisions.
Vivid visual and auditory experiences that occur primarily during REM periods of sleep.	Mental state that encompasses the thoughts, feelings, and perceptions that occur when we are awake and reasonably alert.
Sleep disorder characterized by difficulty in falling asleep or remaining asleep throughout the night.	Mental state that differs noticeably from normal waking consciousness.
Hereditary sleep disorder characterized by sudden nodding off during the day and sudden loss of muscle tone following moments of emotional excitement.	Apparently effortless shifts in attention away from the here and now into a private world of make believe.
Stimulant drugs that initially produce "rushes" of euphoria often followed by sudden "crashes" and, sometimes, severe depression.	Sleep stage characterized by rapid eye movement and increased dreaming.

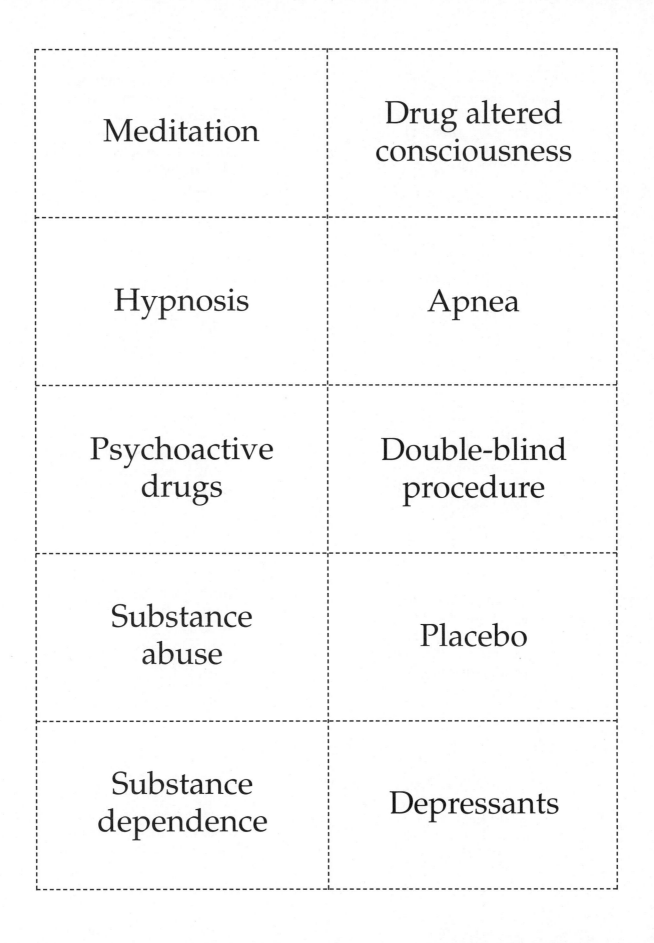

Meditation	Drug altered consciousness
Hypnosis	Apnea
Psychoactive drugs	Double-blind procedure
Substance abuse	Placebo
Substance dependence	Depressants

The use of psychoactive drugs to alter waking consciousness.

Any of various methods of concentration, reflection, or focusing of thoughts undertaken to suppress the activity of the sympathetic nervous system.

Sleep disorder characterized by breathing difficulty during the night and exhaustion during the day.

Trancelike state in which the subject responds readily to suggestions.

Experiment in which neither the subject nor the researcher know which subjects are receiving the treatment.

Chemical substances that change moods and perceptions.

Chemically inactive substance used for comparison with active drugs in experiments on the effects of drugs.

A pattern of drug use that diminishes the user's ability to fulfill responsibilities; that results in repeated use of a drug in dangerous situations, or leads to legal problems.

Chemicals that slow down behavior or cognitive processes.

A pattern of compulsive drug taking that results in tolerance, withdrawal, or other specific symptoms.

Alcohol

Cocaine

Barbiturates

Hallucinogens

Opiates

LSD

Stimulants

Marijuana

Drug derived from cocoa plant that produces sense of euphoria by stimulating the sympathetic nervous system, also produces anxiety, depression, and addictive cravings.	Depressant that is the intoxicating ingredient in whiskey, beer, wine, and other fermented or distilled liquors.
Any of a number of drugs, such as LSD and mescaline, that distort visual and auditory perception.	Potentially deadly depressants, first used for their sedative and anticonvulsant properties, now used only to treat such conditions as epilepsy and arthritis.
Hallucinogen or "psychedelic" drug that produces hallucinations and delusions similar to those occurring in a psychotic state.	Drugs, such as opium and heroin, derived from opium poppy, dull senses, induce feelings of euphoria, and relaxation. Synthetic drugs resembling opium derivatives.
A mild hallucinogen that produces a "high," feelings of euphoria, a sense of well-being, and swings in mood from gaiety to relaxation and may cause anxiety and paranoia.	Drugs, including amphetamines, and cocaine, that stimulate the sympathetic nervous system and produce feelings of optimism and boundless energy.

5 Learning

Chapter Focus

This chapter explores several types of learning, the process by which experience or practice results in a relatively permanent change in behavior. Classical conditioning, operant conditioning, and cognitive learning are all types of learning. Ivan Pavlov first demonstrated classical, or Pavlovian, conditioning with his now famous salivating dog experiments. His work helped to determine the four basic elements of classical conditioning. These are the unconditioned stimulus (US), unconditioned response (UR), conditioned stimulus (CS), and conditioned response (CR). It is important to be able to distinguish these elements in different examples of classical conditioning and to understand that classical conditioning is a passive process in which responses are automatically triggered by a stimulus. Establishing a classically conditioned response typically involves repeated pairings of the US and a cue from the environment before a CR is generated.

Classical conditioning has been established in almost every known animal species and is common in humans. Many phobias are a result of classical conditioning. Phobias may eventually be overcome by repeated pairings of the CS that produces the conditioned fear response with a stimulus that evokes a pleasant emotional response. Joseph Wolpe adapted this technique to treat anxiety and called in desensitization therapy. Classical conditioning has also been used to treat autoimmune disorders by suppressing the activity of the immune system.

The concept of preparedness helps to explain the selective nature of classical conditioning.

Certain things, such as those that involve potential dangers, more readily become conditioned fear responses because our bodies have been programmed to make these associations. Conditioned taste aversion is a prime example of preparedness. Connections between distinct flavors and illness are learned quickly thereby increasing an organisms chances of survival.

First pioneered by E. L. Thorndike, operant, or instrumental conditioning, involves making a certain response to earn rewards or to avoid punishments. Unlike classical conditioning, operant conditioning involves active behaviors that 'operate' on the environment. Two essential elements of operant conditioning are emitted behavior and a consequence following a behavior. Establishing an operantly conditioned response is often achieved through strengthening spontaneous behavior, increasing motivation to perform a desired behavior, or through shaping. To study operant conditioning in animals many researchers use a Skinner box.

Reinforcers increase the likelihood that a behavior will be repeated whereas punishers decrease the likelihood. These concepts are summarized by Thorndike's law of effect, also known as the principle of reinforcement. Two kinds of reinforcers exist: positive reinforcers and negative reinforcers. Using biofeedback, researchers have demonstrated it is possible for individuals to gain control over physiological processes. This technique has been effective in treating a wide variety of disorders in children and adults.

Unlike negative reinforcement that strengthens a behavior, punishment decreases the likelihood that a behavior will occur. To be effective punishment must be swift, sufficient, and consistent. Punishment can be useful in dangerous or self-destructive situations but may be problematic since it only suppresses behavior and can evoke negative feelings. In certain cases when avoidance of a punisher is not possible, learned helplessness results. Learned helplessness was brought to the forefront by Martin Seligman.

Classical and operant conditioning share many common factors. Both involve contingencies. Contingencies involve relationships in which one event depends on another. In classical conditioning contingencies are perceived between the CS and the US. In most cases the CS will precede the US, but in backward conditioning the CS may follow the US. Contingencies in operant conditioning involve making connections between action performance and receipt of reward or punishment. Schedules of reinforcement determine when and how often reinforcers are delivered. Fixed-interval, variable-interval, fixed-ratio, and variable-ratio are all different schedules of reinforcement.

Extinction of conditioned responses in classical conditioning may occur by repeated presentation of the CS without the US, whereas in operant conditioning extinction occurs by withholding reinforcement. In both forms of learning it is not uncommon for extinguished responses to spontaneously recover. In operant conditioning the ability to extinguish a response depends on the strength of the original learning, the pattern of reinforcement, the variety of settings in which the original learning took place, the complexity of the behavior, and whether learning occurred through punishment or reinforcement.

In classical and operant conditioning responses are influenced by environmental cues. Stimulus generalization occurs when the presentation of different but similar stimuli results in performance of the learned response. In contrast, stimulus discrimination involves responding only to a single specific stimulus. Response generalization is specific to operant conditioning and occurs when an organism responds differently to the response originally given to a stimulus.

Original learning can serve as a basis for new learning. In classical conditioning, higher-order conditioning can be established in which the CS serves as an US for additional training. In operant conditioning, secondary reinforcers may become associated with primary reinforcers through classical conditioning to acquire reinforcing properties.

Cognitive learning is learning that depends on mental processes that are not directly observable. Some types of learning do not result in changes in behavior such is the case with latent learning, pioneered by Edward Chace Tolman. Latent learning may involve the formation of cognitive maps that are stored and recalled when needed. Wolfgang Köhler and Harry Harlow demonstrated that insight plays an important role in cognitive learning. Kohler's and Harlow's experiments demonstrated that increasingly complex problems could be solved as new learning sets were established.

Finally, observational, or vicarious, learning is a common type of learning that accounts for many of the behaviors we are capable of demonstrating without previous performance of those behaviors. In observational learning consequences of behaviors are experienced through other people as vicarious reinforcement or vicarious punishment. Social learning theorists study observational learning. Albert Bandura's famous experiments showed that children may imitate aggressive behaviors modeled by adults. Social learning theory emphasizes observation and thought to interpret experiences that influence behavior.

Learning Objectives and Questions

After you have read and studied this chapter, you should be able to complete the following statements.

LEARNING OBJECTIVES

1. Describe the results of Pavlov's classical conditioning studies in terms of the US, UR, CS, CR by describing his famous salivation/dog study.

2. Discuss the development and success of desensitization therapy and how classical conditioning principles apply to human life.

3. Describe the principles of reinforcement by defining primary reinforcers and secondary reinforcers and provide and example of each.

4. Compare and contrast positive reinforcement and negative reinforcement in terms of their methods and effects.

5. Name and briefly discuss the four schedules of reinforcement and provide an example for each schedule and the resulting pattern of behavior for each schedule. Explain the effects of delay of reinforcement.

6. Discuss the requirements for punishment to be effective as well as the dangers and limitations of using punishment to change behavior. Describe the role of avoidance training in using punishment to change behavior.

7. Explain the concepts of preparedness. Summarize research findings on food aversion and how it relates to preparedness.

8. Explain learned helplessness and describe how it developed. Discuss what effects it has on people and animals once established.

9. Briefly discuss the focus of cognitive learning theorists and describe some representative research to support their views.

10. Discuss social learning theory and its implications for human learning.

11. Identify the contributions the following people made to our understanding of the different types of learning: Pavlov, Thorndike, Skinner, Wolpe, Seligman, Köhler, and Harlow.

SHORT ESSAY QUESTIONS

1. Explain Watson's goals and the results of his work with Little Albert. Provide a personal example of classical conditioning in your learning experience.

2. Explain the processes of extinction, spontaneous recovery, shaping, inhibition, stimulus generalization, discrimination, and higher-order conditioning.

3. Compare and contrast classical conditioning with operant conditioning. Discuss which theory appears to explain MOST behavior, and why.

4. Discuss the phenomenon of insight learning and whether it is only applicable for humans.

5. Explain the steps involved in modifying your own behavior.

6. Discuss the process of shaping behavioral change through biofeedback and its popularity and criticism in the research and medical communities.

7. Compare the importance of contingencies in classical and operant conditioning. Discuss backward conditioning and blocking.

Chapter Outline

The following is an outline conveying the main concepts of this chapter.

After studying the text and completing the Study Guide activities, answer these questions to determine if you need to review any areas before the course exam.

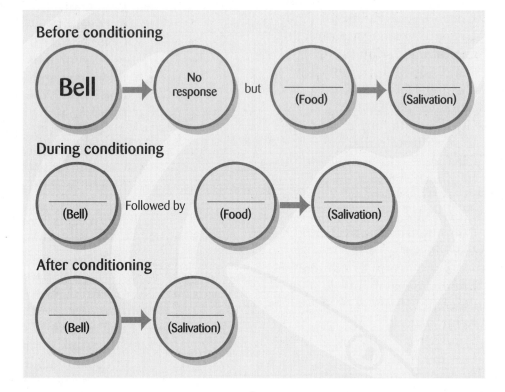

Before conditioning

Bell → No response but (Food) → (Salivation)

During conditioning

(Bell) Followed by (Food) → (Salivation)

After conditioning

(Bell) → (Salivation)

1. In the chart above, provide the correct elements in the three stages of Pavlov's classical conditioning experiment.
   a. conditioned response (CR)
   b. unconditioned stimulus (US)
   c. conditioned stimulus (CS)
   d. unconditioned response (UR)

2. In Watson's experiment with Little Albert, the conditioned response (CR) was _____.
   a. fear of the experimenter (Watson)
   b. fear of the laboratory
   c. fear of the rat
   d. fear of the loud noise

3. The idea that a behavior will increase or decrease based on the consequences that follow the behavior is crucial to ____.
   a. operant conditioning
   b. vicarious learning
   c. classical conditioning
   d. insight learning

4. In classical conditioning the learner is ____, and in operant conditioning the learner is _____.
   a. passive; passive
   b. passive; active
   c. active; passive
   d. active; active

5. Any stimulus that follows a behavior and increases the likelihood that the behavior will be repeated is called a _____.
   a. cue
   b. situational stimulus
   c. reinforcer
   d. higher-order conditioner

6. Any stimulus that follows a behavior and decreases the likelihood that the behavior will be repeated is called a _____.
   a. cue
   b. situational stimulus
   c. reinforcer
   d. punisher

7. Changing behavior through the reinforcement of partial responses is called _____.
   a. modeling
   b. shaping
   c. negative reinforcement
   d. classical conditioning

8. _____ therapy for treating anxiety involves the pairing of relaxation training with systematic exposure to the fearful stimulus.
   a. Operant conditioning
   b. Shaping
   c. Aversive conditioning
   d. Desensitization

9. The process of learning is defined as experience resulting in _____.
   a. amplification of sensory stimuli
   b. delayed genetic behavioral contributions
   c. relatively permanent behavior change
   d. acquisition of motivation

10. A dolphin learns to swim toward a blue platform but not toward a platform of a different color. This shows the concept of _____.
    a. discrimination
    b. modeling
    c. higher-order conditioning
    d. stimulus generalization

11. Reacting to a stimulus that is similar to one that you have already learned to react to is called _____.
    a. response generalization
    b. modeling
    c. higher-order conditioning
    d. stimulus generalization

12. Failure to take steps to avoid or escape from an unpleasant or aversive stimulus that occurs as a result of previous exposure to unavoidable painful stimuli is called _____.
    a. learned helplessness
    b. avoidance learning
    c. aversive conditioning
    d. vicarious learning

13. The process in which a learned response, which has been extinguished suddenly, reappears on its own, with no retraining is called _____.
    a. reaction formation
    b. generalization
    c. spontaneous recovery
    d. shaping

14. A reinforcer that is reinforcing in and of itself is called a _____, and a reinforcer that takes on reinforcing properties only through association with other reinforcers is called a (n) _____ reinforcer.
    a. direct reinforcer/indirect reinforcer
    b. delayed reinforcer/immediate reinforcer
    c. primary reinforcer/secondary reinforcer
    d. secondary reinforcer/primary reinforcer

15. The idea that learning occurs and is stored up, even when behaviors are not reinforced is called _____.
    a. insight
    b. latent learning
    c. placebo learning
    d. innate learning

16. The type of learning that involves elements suddenly coming together so that the solution to a problem is clear is called _____.
    a. latent learning
    b. insight
    c. cognitive mapping
    d. vicarious learning

17. The mental picture of an area, such as a floor plan of a building, is called _____.
    a. a perceptual illusion
    b. a mental set
    c. subliminal perception
    d. a cognitive map

18. Becoming increasingly more effective in solving problems as one experiences solving problems is called _____.
    a. a learning set
    b. a response cue
    c. latent learning
    d. a response set

19. An operant conditioning technique in which a learner gains control over some biological response is _____.
   a. contingency training
   b. preparedness
   c. social learning
   d. biofeedback

20. Which of the following steps is the basic principle of self-modification of behavior?
   a. Decide what behavior you want to acquire.
   b. Define the target behavior precisely
   c Monitor your present behavior.
   d. Provide yourself with a positive reinforcer that is contingent upon specific improvements in the target behavior.

21. Match the correct example with the type of schedule of reinforcement shown on the chart below.
   a. Scott gets paid a salary every two weeks.
   b. Having unannounced psychology pop quizzes
   c. Getting paid a commission for every car sold
   d. Payoff from a Las Vegas slot machine

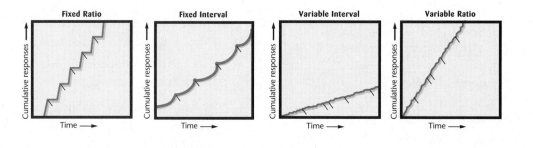

Fixed Ratio · Fixed Interval · Variable Interval · Variable Ratio

_____   _____   _____   _____

Answers and Explanations to Multiple Choice Posttest

1. Before conditioning: B (Food is the unlearned or unconditioned stimulus(US)

   D (Salivation is the unlearned or unconditioned response (UR) to food (S)

   During conditioning: C (Bell is the learned or conditioned stimulus when paired with food (US); B (Food is the US); D (Salivation is an unconditioned response (UR) but becomes a conditioned response (CR) after repeated pairing of the bell and food.)

   After conditioning: C (Bell is the learned or conditioned stimulus (CS); A (Salivation is the learned or conditioned response (CR) to the bell (CS). p. 152, Fig. 5.2

2. c. Albert was conditioned (learned) to fear the rat (CS) because it was paired with a loud noise (US). p. 153

3. a. Operant conditioning is designed on the principle of acting in a way to gain something desired or avoiding something unpleasant. p. 156

4. b. Classical conditioning is passive; operant conditioning is active. p. 156

5. c. Reinforcers increase behavior. p. 157

6. d. Punishment decreases the behavior. p. 157

7. b. Shaping is the process of changing behavior by reinforcing partial responses or successive approximations. p. 158

8. d. Desensitization is a conditioning technique designed to gradually reduce anxiety about a situation or object. p. 154

9. c. Learning is the process by which experience or practice results in a relatively permanent change in behavior or potential behavior. p. 151

10. a. Stimulus discrimination is learning to respond only to one stimulus and inhibit the response to all other stimuli. p. 169

11. d. Reacting to another stimulus is called stimulus generalization. p. 169

12. a. Learned helplessness is the failure to takes steps to avoid or escape an unpleasant or aversive stimulus. p. 162

13. c. Spontaneous recovery is the reappearance of an extinguished response after with passage of time, without training. p. 167

14. c. Primary reinforcers (food) are reinforcing in and of themselves and secondary reinforcers are learned through association with other reinforcers (money). p. 170

15. b. Latent learning is not immediately reflected in a behavior change. p. 173

16. b. Insight is a sudden solution to a problem. p. 174

17. d. A learned mental picture of a spatial environment is a cognitive map. p. 173

18. a. A learning set enables us to learn more effectively with experience. p. 174

19. d. Biofeedback consists of learning control over a biological response. p. 171

20. d. Positive reinforcers as well as consequences for your behavior are the basic principles of self-modification of behavior. p. 158

21. a. Scott gets paid a salary every two weeks. Fixed interval (FI)

    b. Having unannounced psychology pop quizzes. Variable interval (VI)

    c. Getting paid a commission for every car sold. Fixed ratio (FR)

    d. Payoff from a Las Vegas slot machine. Variable ratio (VR) Figure 5–5, p. 166

Language Support

Students identified the following words from the text as needing more explanation. This page can be cut out, folded in half, and used as a bookmark for this chapter.

A

Abstract	thought apart from concrete reality or actuality; not applied or practical; theoretical; difficult to understand
Accidentally	happening unexpectedly or by chance
Anecdotal	based on incidental observations or reports rather than systematic evaluation
Alleviate	get rid of or make less, stop
Attribute	state the cause of; consider resulting from a specific cause, a quality, or characteristic

B

Bully	to intimidate or terrorize; an overbearing person who picks on those smaller or weaker

C

Caliber	degree or level of competence or capacity
Casino	large room or building used for professional gambling
Chore	small routine or task
Clue in	provide with necessary information
"The coast is clear"	nothing is present to impede or endanger one's progress; proceed
Concrete	actual things or realities unlike abstractions, solid form
Confine	enclose within boundaries or limits; restrict
Coincidence	mere chance of two or more events taking place at one time
Congested	overcrowded; overburdened; stuffed up
Consistent	in agreement with; constantly adhering to the same form or principles
Contingent	dependent on chance or fulfilling a condition; uncertainty
Convert	change something into a different form or property or use for another purpose
Crucial	of vital or critical importance to an outcome or decision

D

Devise	to form a plan; create from existing ideas or concepts
Diminishing	returns less improvement or benefit over time; any increase fails to occur
Discontinue	cease to use or produce, terminate, stop
Downplay	represent as unimportant or insignificant; minimize
Drawback	undesirable or objectionable feature; disadvantage
Drool	to water at the mouth in anticipation of food; salivate
Dysfunction	impaired functioning as in a body organ or social system

E

Elapse	passage of time
Encourage	stimulate, approve, foster, inspire, promote, motivate
Entail	involve or cause by necessity or as a consequence of
Eventually	at some later time; finally
Extensive	comprehensive, far-reaching, thorough

F

Fade	to lose strength or dim, disappear or die gradually
Fine-tune	make adjustments to produce improvement or stability
First-hand	directly from the original source

G

Gauge	estimate, judge, conform to a standard, delineate

H

Half-hearted	having or showing little or no enthusiasm
Hard-wired	a built in or intrinsic behavior pattern that is difficult to change
Harsh	unpleasant, severe, uncomfortable
Horror	shocking, strong aversion, overwhelming, terrifying fear
Hurdle	barrier, difficulty to overcome, obstacle

I

Imitate	copy, follow a model, mimic, impersonate
Impede	obstacles or hindrances that retard the movement or progress of an event
Implication	shown to be involved, to imply or suggest
Impose	to establish by authority; to push on others
Inadvertently	unintentional, lack of attention
Inclination	preference or tendency towards, a leaning
Incontinence	inability to restrain or control (i.e., elimination); lacking moderation
Indifferent	apathetic; with little interest or concern; having no bias or preference; neutral
Infraction	violation, breach or break a law or commitment
Inquiry	an investigation that seeks truth, conformation or knowledge; question or ask
Insightful	instant grasping of the true nature of something through intuitive understanding
IRS	Internal Revenue Service
Isolate	set or place apart or detach from others

J

Jackpot	chief prize in a game or contest; an outstanding success

L

Legitimate	according to the law, established rules and principles, authorized
Likelihood	probability or change of something happening
Lisp	defect in speech with s and z pronounced like the th-sound
Listless	having no interest, spiritless

M

Maintain	keep a certain way, continue, preserve
Mallet	hammer-like tool with enlarged head used for repair, music, or games
Marathon	an extended contest or event requiring great endurance
Misbehave	improper conduct
Misdeed	an immoral act

N

NASA	National Aeronautics and Space Administration
Nausea	sick to stomach usually regarding food and often resulting in vomiting
Noxious	harmful to health or well-being, toxic; corrupting influence

O

Onset	beginning or start; assault or attack
Overtly	open to view or knowledge; not secret or hidden
Overwhelmed	overpowered in mind or feelings; excessively burdened

P

Pastime	something that makes time pass enjoyably such as a hobby or sport
Persistent	enduring or lasting, constantly repeated, continuing or permanent
Pop up	something that springs up or out, often unexpectedly
Potentially	capable of becoming; possibility; latent excellence or ability that is undeveloped
Privilege	special right or benefit, entitlement or advantage

Q

Quackery — fraudulent methods or practices; claiming qualifications that are lacking; a phony

R

Reckless — unconcerned about consequences; careless

Rerun — watching film or show again; restating something; rehash

Revulsion — strong feelings of dislike or disgust

Rigorous — rigid, severe, exact, precise, logically valid

Rude — discourteous, without refinement, impolite

S

Scary — frightening or alarming; filling with fear or worry

Scold — find fault with; use loud and abusive speech

Signal — an act or event that causes an action; indication or warning

Significant — having importance

Slot machine — gambling or vending machine operating by inserting money

Spanking — strike with open hand, blow, slap, punishment

Sparingly — economically, provided in small amounts, meager or frugal

Spotlight — intense light focused to pick out something

Stamped in — to record, impress or imprint

Strategy — plan or method for achieving a specific goal

Strut — walk with strong bearing, chest pushed out

Subsequent — occurring or coming later; following in order

Successive — following in order or in an uninterrupted sequence

Swift — move with great speed or velocity, happening quickly without delay, quick to act

T

Tedious — tiresome, wordy

Temptation — enticed to do something considered wrong; to appeal strongly

U

Ultimately — highest, most desirable, fundamental or basic, the outcome

Undergo — to endure, to be subjected to, sustain

Undermine — impair, weaken, destroy by subtle stages

Up to date — keep up with the times in accordance with the latest or newest trends

V

Venture — undertaking involving risk or uncertainty, expose to hazard or risk

Vicious — spiteful, unpleasantly intense, savage, malicious

Victory — triumph; success or superior position achieved against an opponent

Virtually — for the most part; almost totally; just about

W

Withhold — hold back; refrain from giving

Z

Zero gravity — condition in which the apparent effect of gravity is zero; freefalling or in orbit

Key Vocabulary Terms

Cut out each term and use as study cards.
Definition is on the back side of each term.

Learning	Unconditioned response (UR)
Conditioning	Conditioned stimulus (CS)
Classical or Pavlovian conditioning	Conditioned response (CR)
Operant or instrumental conditioning	Desensitization therapy
Unconditioned stimulus (US)	Conditioned taste aversion

Response that takes place in an organism whenever an unconditioned stimulus occurs.	The process by which experience or practice results in a relatively permanent change in behavior or potential behavior.
Originally neutral stimulus that is paired with an unconditioned stimulus and eventually produces the desired response in an organism when presented alone.	The acquisition of specific patterns of behavior in the presence of well-defined stimuli.
After conditioning, the response an organism produces when a conditioned stimulus is presented.	Type of learning in which a response naturally elicited by one stimulus comes to be elicited by a different, formerly neutral stimulus.
Conditioning technique designed to gradually reduce anxiety about a particular object or situation.	Type of learning in which behaviors are emitted (in the presence of specific stimuli) to earn rewards or avoid punishments.
Conditioned avoidance of certain foods even if there is only one pairing of conditioned and unconditioned stimuli.	Stimulus that invariably causes an organism to respond in a specific way.

Operant behavior	Negative reinforcer
Reinforcer	Punishment
Punishers	Avoidance training
Law of effect (principle of reinforcement)	Learned helplessness
Positive reinforcer	Intermittent pairing

Any event whose reduction or termination increases the likelihood that ongoing behavior will recur.	Behavior designed to operate on the environment in a way that will gain something desired or avoid something unpleasant.
Any event whose presence decreases the likelihood that ongoing behavior will recur.	A stimulus that follows a behavior and increases the likelihood that the behavior will be repeated.
Learning a desirable behavior to prevent the occurrence of something unpleasant, such as punishment.	A stimulus that follows a behavior and decreases the likelihood that the behavior will be repeated.
Failure to take steps to avoid or escape from an unpleasant or aversive stimulus that occurs as a result of previous exposure to unavoidable painful stimuli.	Thorndike's theory that behavior consistently rewarded will be "stamped in " as learned behavior and behavior that brings about discomfort will be stamped out.
Pairing the conditioned stimulus and the unconditioned stimulus on only a portion of the learning trials.	Any event whose presence increases the likelihood that ongoing behavior will recur.

Skinner box	Stimulus discrimination
Shaping	Response generalization
Extinction	Higher-order conditioning
Spontaneous recovery	Primary reinforcer
Stimulus generalization	Secondary reinforcer

Learning to respond to only one stimulus and to inhibit the response to all other stimuli.

Box often used in operant conditioning of animals; it limits the available response and thus increases the likelihood that the desired response will occur.

Giving a response that is somewhat different from the response originally learned to that stimulus.

Reinforcing successive approximations to a desired behavior.

Conditioning based on previous learning; the conditioned stimulus serves as an unconditioned stimulus for further training.

Decrease in the strength or frequency, or stopping of a learned response due to failure to continue pairing the US and CS (classical conditioning) or the withholding of reinforcement (operant conditioning).

Reinforcer that is rewarding in itself, such as food, water, and sex.

The reappearance of an extinguished response after the passage of time, without training.

Reinforcer whose value is acquired through association with other primary or secondary reinforcers.

Tendency to respond to cues that are similar to the original learning.

Contingency	Fixed-ratio schedule
Blocking	Variable-ratio schedule
Schedule of reinforcement	Biofeedback
Fixed-interval schedule	Cognitive learning
Variable-interval schedule	Latent learning

Reinforcement schedule in which the correct response is reinforced after a fixed number of correct responses.

A reliable "if-then" relationship between two events such as a CS and a US.

Reinforcement schedule in which a varying number of correct responses must occur before reinforcement is presented.

Process whereby prior conditioning prevents conditioning to a second stimulus even when the two stimuli are presented simultaneously.

A technique that uses monitoring devices to provide precise information about internal physiological processes, such as heart rate or blood pressure, to teach people to gain voluntary control over these functions.

In operant conditioning, the rule for determining when and how often reinforcers will be delivered.

Learning that depends on mental processes that are not directly observable.

Reinforcement schedule that calls for reinforcement of a correct response after a fixed length of time since the last reinforcement.

Learning that is not immediately reflected in a behavior change.

Reinforcement schedule in which a correct response is reinforced after varying lengths of time following the last reinforcement.

Cognitive map	Vicarious reinforcement/ punishment
Insight	Preparedness
Learning set	Stimulus control
Social learning theorists	Neurofeedback
Observational (or vicarious) learning	

The extent to which we imitate behaviors learned through observation that is modified by watching others who are reinforced or punished for their behavior.

A learned mental image of a spatial environment that may be called on to solve problems when stimuli in the environment change.

A biological readiness to learn certain associations because of their survival advantages.

Learning that occurs rapidly as a result of understanding all the elements of a problem.

Occurs when conditioned responses are influenced by surrounding cues in the environment.

Ability to become increasingly more effective in solving problems as more problems are solved.

A biofeedback technique that monitors brain waves using an EEG to teach people to gain voluntary control over their brain wave activity.

Psychologists whose view of learning emphasizes the ability to learn by observing a model or receiving instructions, without firsthand experience by the learner.

Learning by observing other people's behavior.

6 Memory

Chapter Focus

This chapter explores memory, the ability to remember things we have experienced, imagined, and learned. Generally, three stages of memory are recognized—the sensory registers, short-term memory, and long-term memory—that comprise the information processing view of memory. The authors begin this chapter by examining the role of sensory registers in memory. Visual and auditory registers have been extensively studied. Visual information is taken in quickly and fades more rapidly than auditory information. Information is selectively taken in by the sensory registers by means of attention. Attention functions like an automatic filtering device allowing only certain information into short-term memory.

Short-term memory, or working memory, stores a limited amount of information for a brief period of time. The capacity of short-term memory can be increased by grouping information into meaningful units, a process known as chunking. Verbal information is mainly encoded into short-term memory phonologically, but some information may be encoded as images or on the basis of meaning. Dual coding may account for the fact that memory for images is generally better than memory for words. Through the practice of rote rehearsal, or maintenance rehearsal, information can be maintained in short-term memory for greater lengths of time.

Long-term memory is a more permanent form of memory able to store a vast amount of information for a very long time. Most encoding of information into long-term memory is based on meaning. The serial position effect explains the tendency to recall those items on a list that appeared either at the beginning or the end of the list, forgetting the items in the middle. Effective tactics to maintain information in long-term memory include rote rehearsal, elaborative rehearsal, and the use of schemata. It is important to understand the differences between the various types of long-term memories identified. These include: episodic, semantic, procedural, and emotional memories. In addition, researchers draw distinctions between explicit memories that include episodic and semantic memories, and implicit memories that include procedural and emotional memories.

The brain and its neurons play an important role in the biology of memory. As new information is learned, new synaptic connections are formed. In addition, the relearning of old material results in the strengthening of old connections. Long-term potentiation is actively involved in the memory process by increasing the likelihood that electrical potentials will fire from synaptic connections. Memories are not stored in one location in the brain. Rather, many different parts of the brain are specialized for the storage of either short-term or long-term memories. It is important to recognize the roles of the frontal lobe, motor cortex, cerebellum, hippocampus, amygdala, temporal lobe, and prefrontal cortex in memory formation and storage (refer to figure 6–4 of text).

Forgetting may be explained by a number of factors. According to decay theory, memories fade because of the passage of time which may explain some forgetting in short-term memory. Retrograde amnesia may account for some long-term memory loss following head trauma. Severe memory loss may occur from different types of brain damage. Forgetting can also be explained by lack of attention to stimuli or from additional learning that causes either retroactive or proactive interference. In context-dependent memory, or state-dependent memory, recall ability can be improved by providing environmental cues or returning to internal physiological states that were present when information was first learned. Furthermore, forgetting may occur because memories are not recalled just as originally encoded but through a reconstructive process that omits or alters certain details.

A number of tactics can be employed to improve memory. These include: developing motivation; practicing memory skills; being confident in your ability to remember; minimizing distractions; staying focused; making connections between new material and other information already stored in long-term memory; using mental imagery; using retrieval cues; relying on more than memory alone; and being aware that your own personal schemata may distort your recall of events.

Finally, certain factors can influence memories for specific events. For example, the values and customs within a given culture greatly affect what people remember and their recall ability. Early autobiographical memories are harder to recall than more recent ones and most people experience childhood amnesia, an inability to recall events that occurred prior to two years of age. Many researchers interested in flashbulb memories have discovered that these vivid memories for certain events may not be as accurate as once believed. Research into recovered memories suggests new memories for events that never happened can be created by suggestion and that it is proving difficult to separate real memories from false ones.

Learning Objectives and Questions

After you have read and studied this chapter, you should be able to complete the following statements.

LEARNING OBJECTIVES

1. Describe the purpose, capacity, and function of the sensory register including the differences between the visual and auditory registers.

2. Learn about the purpose, capacity, and function of short-term and long-term memory and discuss their similarities and differences.

3. Describe how information is coded in short-term memory and discuss how decay and interference play a role in recalling information from short-term memory.

4. Compare and contrast rote rehearsal with elaborative rehearsal. Give examples of when each is most effectively utilized. Discuss retrograde amnesia and how it relates to rote and elaborative rehearsal.

5. Define schemata and discuss how our schemata may affect what we recall and how it may help to fill in missing information.

6. Define and discuss semantic, procedural, episodic, and emotional memory giving an example for each.

7. Compare and contrast explicit and implicit memories and comment upon the implications of implicit memory for everyday life.

8. Discuss how information is coded in long-term memory and how decay, interference, and retrieval cues play a part in recalling information from long-term memory.

9. Discuss Freud's theory of repressed memories and relate this to the concept of recovered memories.

10. Define autobiographical and flashbulb memories and discuss the accuracy of these kind of memories and what kinds of early memories people may be more likely to have.

11. Learn the 10 steps for improving your memory in school.

12. Define mnemonics, describe at least three mnemonic devices, and discuss their effectiveness.

13. Identify each step in the SQ3R method and explain how each step works.

14. Summarize the research on the biological basis of memory. Know the major brain structures and regions involved in memory and the role of neurotransmitters in storage or loss of memory.

15. Discuss Korsakoff's syndrome and Alzheimer's disease and their causes and effects on brain damage and memory loss.

SHORT ESSAY QUESTIONS

1. Explain Broadbent's filter theory and Treisman's modified filter theory. Which theory best accounts for how people select what they attend to from the massive amount of information entering the sensory register?

2. Define proactive and retroactive interference. Describe reconstructive memory and give two examples of how we utilize it in real-life situations.

3. Discuss the research on the reliability of eyewitness testimony and how this relates to recovered memories. What do scientists currently believe about the accuracy and reliability of recovered memories?

4. Recall your memories of the incidents surrounding September 11th as they relate to the definition of a flashbulb memory. Discuss the events surrounding your learning of the event, the emotions and thoughts you experienced then, and how this event has affected your present life.

5. Make a commitment to yourself to use at least three steps for improving your memory. List them here and describe how you will make them new habits.

Chapter Outline

The following is an outline conveying the main concepts of this chapter.

Multiple Choice Posttest

After studying the text and completing the Study Guide activities, answer these questions to determine if you need to review any areas before the course exam.

1. Label the elements of the information processing model of memory illustrated in Figure 6-1 on page 185. Select from the following terms: a) decay; b) repetition; c) attention; d)sensory register; e) retrieval; f) interference; g) rehearsal; h) long-term memory; i) coding; j) short term memory; k) external stimulus.

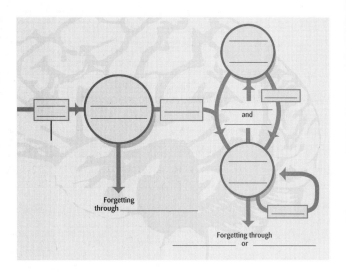

Forgetting through _____

Forgetting through
or _____

2. Our visual impression of our friend walking past us would initially be found in the _____.
   a. sensory registers
   b. short-term memory
   c. long-term memory
   d. hippocampus

3. What we are thinking of at any given moment, or what we commonly know as "consciousness," is _____.
   a. long-term memory
   b. Short-term memory
   c. secondary memory
   d. sensory registers

4. Information is grouped for storage in short-term memory through the process of _____.
   a. categorizing
   b. chunking
   c. rote rehearsal
   d. nonsense syllables

5. The linking of new information in short-term memory to familiar material stored in long-term memory is called _____.
   a. elaborative rehearsal
   b. rote rehearsal
   c. semantic rehearsal
   d. chunking

6. The inability to recall events immediately preceding an accident or injury, but without loss of earlier memory is called _____ amnesia.
   a. psychogenic
   b. retroactive
   c. retrograde
   d. fugue

7. The portion of long-term memory that stores general facts and information is called _____.
   a. eidetic
   b. episodic
   c. semantic
   d. procedural

8. While memorizing a list of words, students were exposed to the scent of chocolate. If the students recall more words when there is the scent of chocolate present, then the effect of chocolate is most likely due to _____ memory.
   a. explicit
   b. implicit
   c. procedural
   d. eidetic

9. Proactive interference of long-term memory means that _____.
   a. old material has eliminated memories of new material
   b. old material interferes with remembering new material
   c. new material represses short-term memories
   d. new material interferes with remembering old material

10. When memories are not lost but are transformed into something somewhat different, it is called _____.
    a. retroactive interference
    b. eidetic memory
    c. proactive interference
    d. reconstructive memory

11. The phenomenon whereby most people cannot recall events that occurred in their life before the age of 2, is called _____.
    a. infantile autism
    b. psychogenic amnesia
    c. fugue amnesia
    d. childhood amnesia

12. Our recollection of events that occurred in our life and when those events took place is called _____ memory.
    a. autobiographical
    b. reconstructive
    c. semantic
    d. procedural

13. Memories that concern highly significant events and are vividly remembered, such as the World Trade Center and Pentagon events of September 11th, 2001, are called _____.
    a. eyewitness images
    b. flashbulb memories
    c. now print images
    d. photographic memories

14. The most important determinant of interference is _____.
    a. similarity of material
    b. complexity of material
    c. decay
    d. rehearsal time

15. Remembering a telephone number because it contains the numbers of the year in which you were born is an example of the use of _____.
    a. a mnemonic device
    b. association
    c. eidetic imagery
    d. chunking

16. The hippocampus is important for _____.
    a. transferring information from short-term to long-term memory
    b. the retrieval of memories from long-term memory
    c. maintaining a constant level of attention
    d. the formation of short-term memory

17. The neurotransmitter that appears to be instrumental in the memory process is _____.
    a. serotonin
    b. dopamine
    c. norepinephrine
    d. acetylcholine

18. In more than 1,000 cases in which innocent people were wrongly convicted of a crime, the single most pervasive element leading to the wrongful conviction was _____.
    a. faulty forensic work by police labs
    b. phony evidence "planted" by the police
    c. faulty eyewitness testimony
    d. misinterpretations of the law by judges and juries

19. Each of the following is a recommended strategy for improving your memory abilities EXCEPT _____.
    a. developing your motivation
    b. practicing memory skills
    c. staying focused and minimizing distractions
    d. learning to rely on your memory alone

20. Which of the following statements is true regarding the role of attention in information processing?
    a. Attention involves selectively recognizing sensations.
    b. Attention is believed to work as a large filter, letting most stimuli through.
    c. Attention is not an automatic process but requires constant monitoring of the environment.
    d. none of the above

21. Which of the following statements is not true regarding mnemonics?
    a. Mnemonics may be useful to help tie new material to information already stored in STM.
    b. Mnemonic techniques may include rhymes and jingles.
    c. Relating personal information to mnemonics may facilitate recall.
    d. All of the above are true.

22. Which of the following statements best reflects the role of long-term potentiation in memory processes?
    a. LTP accounts for why we forget— synaptic connections are lost in the brain.
    b. As new memories are formed, old connections are weakened.
    c. Memory formation involves forming new synaptic connections in the brain or strengthening existing ones.
    d. LTP plays an influential role in STM, but a lesser role in LTM.

23. Which of the following statements is true regarding the storage of memories in the brain?
    a. All memories are stored in one place in the brain.
    b. Short-term memories tend to be stored in the cerebellum.
    c. Damage to the hippocampus greatly impairs short-term memories.
    d. Damage to the amygdala impairs recall of new emotional memories.

24. The theory that memories deteriorate because of the passage of time is known as _____.
    a. interference theory
    b. anterograde amnesia theory
    c. decay theory
    d. childhood amnesia theory

Answers and Explanations to Multiple Choice Posttest

1.

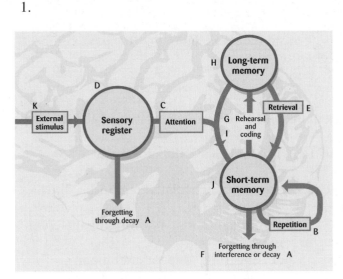

2. a. Visual sensations flow from your senses into the sensory registers. p. 185

3. b. What we are thinking of at any given moment refers to short-term memory. p. 186

4. b. Chunking is grouping information in meaningful units in short-term memory. p. 187

5. a. Elaborative rehearsal relates new information to something we already know. p. 191

6. c. Retrograde amnesia is the inability to recall events preceding an accident or injury, but without loss of earlier memory. p. 198

7. c. Semantic memory stores general facts and information. p. 193

8. b. Implicit memory provides retrieval cues we may not be aware of having made. p. 194

9. b. Old material interfering with remembering new material is called proactive interference. p. 200

10. d. Reconstructive memory changes the original memory. p. 202

11. d. Childhood amnesia refers to the difficulty adults have remembering experiences before age 2. p. 204

12. a. Autobiographical memory is collection of memories for events that took place in our lives. p. 203

13. b. Flashbulb memories are vivid memories of certain events and incidents surrounding them even long after the event occurred. pp. 204–205

14. a. Similarity of material can lead to greater amounts of interference. pp. 198–199

15. a. Mnemonic devices are techniques that make material easier to remember. p. 191

16. a. The hippocampus is important in converting short-term memory into long-term memory. p. 196

17. d. Acetylcholine is the neurotransmitter that is instrumental in memory. pp. 198–199

18. c. Faulty eyewitness testimony was the single most persuasive element leading to false conviction in over 1,000 cases studied. p. 201

19. d. Rely on more than memory alone by using other tools. p. 192

20. a. Attention involves selectively looking, listening, smelling, tasting, and feeling. pp. 184–185

21. a. Mnemonics may be useful to help tie new material to information already stored in LTM. p. 191

22. c. As we learn, new connections are formed in the brain and old connections are strengthened. As the number of connections among neurons increases, firing of electrical charges increases. p. 196

23. d. Damage to the amygdala impairs recall of new emotional memories. pp.196–197

24. c. According to decay theory, memories deteriorate because of the passage of time. p. 198

Language Support

Students identified the following words from the text as needing more explanation. This page can be cut out, folded in half, and used as a bookmark for this chapter.

A

Absentminded	preoccupied with one's thoughts and unaware or forgetful of other matters
Acoustically	related to sound or hearing
Acrostics	written words in which the first, last, or other letters form a word or phrase
Amnesic	complete or partial loss of a large block of interrelated memories due to brain injury or shock
Anagram	word, phrase, or sentence formed from another by rearranging its letters
Analogous	corresponding to or similar in some way
Arbitrary	without restriction or special value, uncertain, dependent on one's judgment or will
Articulate	expressing self readily, clearly, or effectively; intelligible; well spoken
Ascribe	credit or attribute, think of as belonging to a quality or characteristic

B

Barring	keeping out, excluding by exception, to legally object

C

Capture	hold the interest or record in a permanent file, preserve, represent, emphasize
Cluster	group together a number of similar items
Coherent	understandable, having clarity and consistency
Concussion	jarring injury to brain from a sharp blow to the head resulting in disturbed cerebral function
Conspicuous	obvious, easily seen, readily observable, attracting attention
Contention	discord; rivalry or competition
Corroborate	to support with evidence or authority, making more certain, confirm

D

Deed	performance, accomplishment or action
Descent	passing from higher or lower state or degree; ancestry or lineage
Disoriented	loss of bearing, sense of time, place, identify, confused, displaced
Dispersed	move apart in different directions; spread widely
Doggedly	marked by stubborn determination; holding on; not giving up
Durability	capable of lasting or enduring; highly resistant to wear or decay

E

Effortlessly	requiring little or no effort
Elude	avoid; unable to perceive or understand
Enormity	of momentous importance; considerable departure from the unexpected
Exception	excluding; rare instance not conforming to general rule
Extraordinary	going beyond the usual, regular or customary

F

Fanatic	person with extreme enthusiasm or zeal
Fleeting	vanishing or passing quickly
Forge	move ahead with increased speed and effectiveness, progress steadily

G

Going through the motions	seeming to take the appropriate actions

I

Inadequate	insufficient; having a shortcoming or deficiency
Inadvertently	happen by accident, unintentional, not focusing the mind on a matter
Incapable	lacking the capacity or qualification for the purpose, unfit
Indistinguishable	not clearly seen or understood; differences too subtle to be made
Integral	essential part of the whole; necessary for completion
Interrupt	cut off or stop before completion, break continuity or uniformity
Invariably	incapable of being changed, static, constant
Intact	unaltered or unbroken, complete or whole

J

Jingle	short, catchy succession of repetitive sounds, song
Jot	to write down quickly; least amount or briefly; a little bit
Jumble	mentally confused, disordered

L

Larcenous	theft, robbery; wrongful taking of another's goods
Lineage	one's derivation from; common ancestry of a group

M

Mingle	unite, form or mix, blend together
Myriad	innumerable or great number of people, things, variations or aspects

N

Nazi	member of Hitler's political party who controlled Germany from 1933-45, advocated Aryan (white) supremacy, leading to World War II and the Holocaust

O

Oblivious	lacking active, conscious knowledge, awareness or memory of
Odd	different from usual or expected; bizarre; remaining after all are paired
Orator	speaker with great eloquence using appropriate, effective language
Over-learning	continue to study or practice after attaining advanced knowledge or skill

P

Password	secret word or expression used to gain access to restricted information
Pivotal	crucial; vitally important; turning point
Plausible	appearing to be true, reasonable, believable, or credible
Podium	lectern; stand for speaker's notes or books
Prodigious	extraordinary degree, amount or quality; exceeding usual bounds or accepted beliefs
Prompt	without delay; to assist by suggesting, inspiring, reminding
Pronounced	strongly marked; noticeable; free from doubt or wavering

R

Rambling	moving aimlessly; speaking in wandering, long-winded fashion
Recast	rearrange, remodel, or reconstruct
Refresh	stimulate the memory, revive or renew the vigor or energy of
Relevance	related to the matter; ability to retrieve material needed
Rely	depend upon; have confidence based on experience
Reminiscence	recall to mind long forgotten experiences or facts; think about past memories

S

Sabotage	action or procedure that deliberately hurts or defeats
Scramble	to move, collect, or organize things in a hurried, disorganized manner
Secluded	isolate or remove from social contact or activity
Senseless	lacking meaning, foolish, making no sense
Sequence	one thing after another, a continuously connected series
Similarly	having common characteristics; closely resembling

Simultaneously	existing or occurring at the same time; coincidence
Storehouse	place where large supply of facts, knowledge, or other material is stored
T	
Translate	move or change from one state or form to another (i.e., language)
Trivia	unimportant matters, facts or details; quiz game involving obscure facts
U	
Unreliable	not giving the same results on successive trials; can't count on
V	
Verbatim	using the exact same words; word for word

Key Vocabulary Terms

Cut out each term and use as study cards.
Definition is on the back side of each term.

Information-processing model	Rote rehearsal
Sensory registers	Elaborative rehearsal
Attention	Retrograde anmesia
Short-term memory (STM)	Long-term memory (LTM)
Chunking	Semantic memory

Retaining information in short-term memory simply by repeating it over and over.

A computerlike model used to describe the way humans encode, store, and retrieve information.

The linking of new information in short-term memory to familiar material stored in long-term memory.

Entry points for raw information from the senses.

Inability to recall events preceding an accident or injury, but without loss of earlier memory.

Selection of some incoming information for further processing.

Portion of memory that is more or less permanent corresponding to everything we "know."

Working memory; briefly stores and processes selected information from the sensory registers.

Portion of long-term memory that stores general facts and information.

Grouping of information into meaningful units for easier handling by short-term memory.

Episodic memory	Schema
Explicit memory	Flashbulb memory
Implicit memory	Mnemonics
Retroactive interference	Memory
Proactive interference	Serial position effect

Set of beliefs or expectation about something that is based on past experience.	Portion of long-term memory that stores personally experienced events.
A vivid memory of a certain event and the incidents surrounding it even after a long time has passed.	Memory for information that we can readily express in words and are aware of having, and can be intentionally retrieved from memory.
Techniques that make material easier to remember.	Memory for information that we cannot readily express in words and may not be aware of having, these memories cannot be intentionally retrieved from memory.
The ability to remember the things that we have experienced, imagined, and learned.	Process by which new information interferes with old information already in memory.
The finding that when asked to recall a list of unrelated items, performance is better for items at the beginning and end of the list.	Process by which information already in memory interferes with new information.

Procedural
memory

Emotional
memory

Childhood
amnesia

Long-term
potentiation (LTP)

Decay theory

	The portion of long term memory that stores information relating to skills, habits, and other preceptual-motor tasks.
	Learned emotional responses to various stimuli.
	The difficulty adults have remembering experiences from their first two years of life.
	A long-lasting change in the structure or function of a synapse that increases the efficiency of neural transmission, and is thought to be related to how information is stored by neurons
	A theory that argues that the passage of time causes forgetting.

7 Cognition and Mental Abilities

Chapter Focus

This chapter begins with an introduction to cognition, all of the processes used to acquire and apply information. Language, images, and concepts are considered the three most important building blocks of thought. Language is uniquely human. Language consists of phonemes, morphemes, and grammar. Syntax and semantics are parts of grammar and enable listeners to distinguish between the surface structure (words and phrases) and the deep structure (underlying meaning) of sentences. Images play an important role by providing mental representations of sensory experiences that allow nonverbal forms of thought. In addition, concepts may help us to think more efficiently by using mental categories to classify things that relate to one another. One aspect of thinking is the use of prototypes that represent the key features of a concept.

Language may also influence how we think and what we think about. This is expressed in Benjamin Whorf's linguistic relativity hypothesis. Other researchers contend that the influences of language, thought, and culture cannot be separated.

The ability to solve problems plays a large role in cognition. The first step to problem solving is to interpret and define the problem, known as problem representation. Problem solving can include divergent thinking or convergent thinking. Additional steps to problem solving include selecting a solution strategy and evaluating progress. Solution strategies include the use of trial and error, information retrieval, algorithms, and various heuristics. Internal and external factors can help or hinder problem solving, such as a person's mental set, the perception of a problem and the approach used,

or functional fixedness. In many cases brainstorming may be recommended to generate new ideas for review and evaluation.

Decision making requires a person to identify the best solution to a problem. Truly logical decisions are often made using compensatory models in which criteria for a particular choice are weighted in terms of importance. People commonly employ heuristics for decision making, despite the fact that these often lead to poor decisions. Decisions may be influenced by the way information provided to make the decision is framed. Other aspects of decision making are the hindsight bias and the 'if only' construction.

The second half of this chapter explores intelligence and mental abilities. Intelligence refers to the abilities involved in learning and adapting behavior. There are several prominent theories of intelligence. Early intelligence theorists believed intelligence was quite general and flowed through every action. However, L.L. Thurstone believed in seven different kinds of mental abilities: spatial ability, memory, perceptual speed, word fluency, numerical ability, reasoning, and verbal meaning. In contrast, R.B. Cattell identified crystallized and fluid intelligence as two clusters of mental abilities.

Contemporary theorists propose alternative theories of intelligence. Robert Sternberg's triarchic theory of intelligence states that analytical intelligence, creative intelligence, and practical intelligence are the three basic kinds of intelligence. In contrast, Howard Gardner's theory of multiple intelligences proposes eight different kinds of intelligence: logical-mathematical, linguistic, spatial, musical, bodily-kinesthetic, interpersonal, intrapersonal, and naturalistic. Daniel Goleman has proposed emotional intelligence theory. The five traits of emotional intelligence include: knowing one's own emotions; managing one's own emotions; using emotions; to motivate oneself; recognizing the emotions of other people; and managing relationships. It is important to be able to distinguish among these different theories and to draw distinctions among the various intelligence types.

The Stanford-Binet Intelligence Scale was the first individual test to establish a numerical value of intelligence, now known as intelligence quotient (IQ). Four kinds of mental abilities are measured by this test: verbal intelligence, abstract/visual reasoning, quantitative reasoning, and short-term memory. The Wechsler Intelligence Scales are another type of intelligence test. The Wechsler Adult Intelligence Scale (WAIS-III) and the Wechsler Intelligence Scale for Children (WISC-III) are used to test intelligence in individual adults and children. Group tests for intelligence have also been written and are widely used in schools. Performance tests and culture fair tests have been designed to help assess intelligence in people who are not fluent in English or who come from outside the culture in which the test was devised.

A good intelligence test must yield reliability and validity. Split-half reliability is a way to determine reliability by dividing the test into two parts and checking scores on both parts. Measures of validity include content validity and criterion-related validity. IQ tests have been highly criticized for a number of reasons including narrowness of question content, discrimination against minorities, or against people of different social classes and cultures. In addition, critics claim that IQ and intelligence are not the same, and IQ scores are a simplified way of summing up complex abilities. Despite the criticisms, studies have shown that IQ tests do tend to accurately predict school success, occupational success, and job performance.

Individual differences in intelligence may be influenced by both heredity and the environment. Twin studies have revealed that twins reared apart have similar intelligence test scores. In addition, adoption studies revealed a child's IQ score is more similar to the biological mother. Together these types of studies have made a strong case for the heritability of intelligence.

Intellectually stimulating surroundings and good nutrition can increase IQ. Other studies show adoptive children raised by parents of high socioeconomic status may have higher IQs than adoptive children raised by parents of low socioeconomic status. In recognition of the impact of environment on IQ, early intervention programs like Head Start have been created. The Flynn Effect refers to the noted increase in IQ scores that has occurred in recent decades.

Underlying gender differences in mental ability have not been found. Cognitive differences appear to be restricted to specific cognitive skills. The tendency is for girls to display greater verbal ability, and for boys' strengths to lie in spatial and mathematic abilities. Males tend to fall more regularly at the extremes of the intelligence range, having many more extremely high IQ scores, and also scores within the range of mental retardation. Research suggests that environmental factors such as upbringing play a large factor in the gender discrepancies noted in career choice.

Cultural differences in academic achievement are the result of the varied approaches to study and school success found across cultures. An innate superiority in intelligence was not found in a particular culture. The cultures with the strongest ethic for study and most challenging curricula had the highest achievement rates.

The two extremes of intelligence are mental retardation and intellectually gifted. Evaluations of mental retardation involve tests of motor skills, social adaptation, and behavior. People diagnosed with mental retardation may display savant performance. The cause of most mental retardation is unknown, however identifiable contributions stem from environmental, social, nutritional, and other risk factors. The rarer and most severe cases of mental retardation may involve genetic or biological disorders. Genetic diseases include PKU and Down syndrome. Biologically caused mental retardation may be dramatically moderated through interventions and appropriate socialization.

Giftedness appears at the other extreme of the intelligence scale. Most gifted individuals display special talents in only a few areas, and much giftedness is not recognized for this reason. Recent studies suggest that giftedness is an asset for socialization, and does not lead to problems with peer interaction.

Finally, creativity is the ability to produce novel and socially valued ideas or objects. There is no definite link between intelligence and creativity beyond a certain IQ threshold level. The most creative people seek problems to solve and tend to be dedicated, ambitious and curious. The *Torrance Test of Creative Thinking* asks questions relating to pictures, and the *Christensen-Guilford Test* involves listing and responding to open-ended word questions. Test scores interpret the potential for imagination and association. This leads to problems of validity and caution is recommended in this area of assessment.

Learning Objectives and Questions

After you have read and studied this chapter, you should be able to complete the following statements.

LEARNING OBJECTIVES

1. Define cognition. Differentiate between images and concepts and explain the use of prototypes.

2. Explain Whorf's linguistic relativity hypothesis and summarize the evidence regarding links between language and thought.

3. Discuss proper interpretation and categorization in the problem solving process and how conceptual blocks may inhibit effective problem solving.

4. Compare and contrast divergent and convergent thinking and discuss their role in creative problem solving.

5. Identify three heuristics that may lead us to make poor decisions and explain how each one hinders effective decision making.

6. Discuss Spearman's, Thurstone's, and Cattell's models of intelligence and specifically describe the components of each model.

7. Describe Sternberg's and Gardner's theories of intelligence and how they differ from previous models of intelligence. List Sternberg's three types of intelligence and Gardner's seven multiple intelligences.

8. Name the people responsible for the development of intelligence tests for children. Include in your discussion key concepts such as IQ and how the formula for IQ was developed.

9. Distinguish between the Wechsler Adult Intelligence Scale-Revised (WAIS-R) and the Stanford Binet in terms of their focus. Identify the two parts of the WAIS-R.

10. Define performance tests and culture-fair tests. Discuss the necessity of such tests, where they are useful, and their advantages or disadvantages.

11. Define the terms reliability and validity and discuss two types of each.

12. Discuss the research findings on gender differences in mental abilities.

13. Define mental retardation. Identify the various levels of retardation and the necessary criteria for diagnosis. Discuss possible causes of retardation and effectiveness of treatment.

14. Discuss the criterion for giftedness. Summarize the research and criticisms of current techniques to measure giftedness. Discuss the advantages and possible disadvantages of accelerated classes for gifted students.

SHORT ESSAY QUESTIONS

1. Define language, phonemes, morphemes, semantics, syntax, and grammar and briefly discuss the role of each of them in the development of communications and language.

2. Identify and describe four tactics for improving your problem-solving abilities and discuss the advantages of each method.

3. Compare and contrast compensatory and noncompensatory models and discuss the roles of representativeness, availability, and the confirmation bias in decision making. Identify the strengths and weaknesses of each technique.

4. Explain "emotional intelligence." Identify the five traits of emotional intelligence.

5. Name at least three group IQ tests and three individual IQ tests. Explain the advantages and disadvantages of each.

6. Summarize current beliefs and research regarding the role of heredity and environment in intelligence. Include research on the effectiveness of intervention programs aimed at improving the academic performance of disadvantaged children.

7. Define creativity and discuss its relationship to intelligence. Identify four types of creativity tests and how they measure creativity.

Chapter Outline

The following is an outline conveying the main concepts of this chapter.

Cognition
1. Building Blocks of Thought   page 211
   A. Language
      - Phonemes
      - Morphemes
      - Grammar
        - Syntax
        - Semantics
      - Surface structure
      - Deep structure
   B. Images
   C. Concepts
      - Prototypes
2. Language, Thought, and Culture page 214
   A. Linguistic Relativity Hypothesis
3. Problem Solving   page 216
   A. The Interpretation of Problems
      - Problem representation
        - Divergent thinking
        - Convergent thinking
   B. Producing Strategies and Evaluation Progress
      - Trial and error
      - Information retrieval
      - Algorithms
      - Heuristics
        - Hill climbing
        - Subgoals
        - Means-end analysis
        - Working backwards
   C. Obstacles to Solving Problems
      - Set
      - Functional fixedness

UNDERSTANDING OURSELVES: Becoming a More Skillful Problem Solver   page 220
      - Eliminate poor choices
      - Visualize a solution
      - Develop expertise
      - Think flexibly

4. Decision Making   page 222
   A. Logical Decision Making
      - Compensatory
   B. Decision-Making Heuristics
      - Representativeness heuristic
      - Availability
      - Confirmation bias
   C. Explaining Our Decisions
      - Framing
      - Hindsight
      - "If Only"
5. Intelligence and Mental Abilities page 225
   Intelligence
   A. Theories of Intelligence
      - Early theorists
        - Spearman's general intelligence
        - Thurstone's seven kinds of mental abilities
      - Spatial ability
      - Memory
      - Perceptual speed
      - Word fluency
      - Numerical ability
      - Reasoning
      - Verbal meaning
        - Cattell's crystallized and fluid intelligence
      - Crystallized intelligence
      - Fluid intelligence
   Contemporary Theorists
        - Sternberg's Triarchic Theory of Intelligence
      - Analytic intelligence
      - Creative intelligence
      - Practical intelligence
        - Gardner's Theory of Multiple Intelligences
      - Logical-mathematical intelligence
      - Linguistic intelligence
      - Spatial intelligence
      - Musical intelligence
      - Bodily kinesthetic intelligence
      - Interpersonal intelligence
      - Intrapersonal intelligence
      - Naturalistic intelligence (recently added)
        - Goleman's Emotional Intelligence
      - Knowing one's own emotions
      - Managing one's emotions
      - Using emotions to motivate oneself

Multiple Choice Posttest

After studying the text and completing the Study Guide activities, answer these questions to determine if you need to review any areas before the course exam.

1. The three most important building blocks of thoughts are ____, _____, and ____.
   a. semantics, phonemes, and morphemes
   b. cognition, feelings, and language
   c. language, images, and concepts
   d. stream of consciousness, sensory register, and perception

2. Label the terms in correct order in the direction of movement in speech production and comprehension in the figure shown below.
   a. Phenomes
   b. Meaning
   c. Morphemes
   d. Sentences

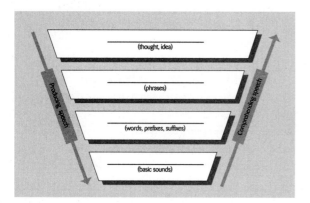

3. _____ consists of the language rules that determine how sounds and words can be combined and used to communicate meaning within a language.
   a. Semantics   c. Morphemes
   b. Syntax   d. Grammar

4. Most concepts that people use in thinking _____.
   a. accurately account for critical differences among various images
   b. depend on the magnitude of sensory memory
   c. allow them to generalize but not to think abstractly
   d. are fuzzy and overlap with one another

5. A mental model containing the most typical features of a concept is called a (n) ___.
   a. algorithm
   b. prototype
   c. stereotype
   d. description

6. The problem-solving methods that guarantee solutions if appropriate and properly followed are called _____.
   a. heuristics
   b. trial and error
   c. hill-climbing
   d. algorithm

7. The technique of ____ encourages people to generate a list of ideas without evaluation of those ideas.
   a. convergent thinking
   b. brainstorming
   c. circular thinking
   d. functional thinking

8. People sometimes make decisions based on information that is most easily retrieved from memory, even though this information may not be accurate. This process of decision making is called _____.
   a. compensatory model
   b. means-end analysis
   c. the availability heuristic
   d. functional analysis

9. The tendency to look for evidence in support of a belief and to ignore evidence that would disprove a belief is called _____.
   a. the confirmation bias
   b. means-end analysis
   c. the representativeness heuristic
   d. functional analysis

10. Spearman believed that specific mental abilities are ____ each other, and Thurstone believed that they are ___ each other.
    a. dependent on; dependent on
    b. dependent on; relatively independent of
    c. relatively independent of; dependent on
    d. relatively independent of; relatively independent of

11. Which of the following is NOT one of the three basic kinds of intelligence that comprises Sternberg's triarchic theory of intelligence?
    a. practical intelligence
    b. analytical intelligence
    c. naturalistic intelligence
    d. creative intelligence

12. Which of the following is NOT one of the types of intelligence described in Gardner's theory of multiple intelligences?
    a. practical intelligence
    b. interpersonal intelligence
    c. linguistic intelligence
    d. spatial intelligence

13. The Binet-Simon scale was originally developed to _____.
    a. identify gifted children
    b. identify children who might have difficulty in school
    c. measure the intelligence of normal children
    d. measure scholastic achievement

14. Wechsler hypothesized that adult intelligence _____.
    a. consists of the ability to solve problems
    b. consists solely of the ability to handle the environment
    c. consists more of the ability to solve problems than of the ability to handle the environment
    d. consists more of the ability to handle life situations than of skill in solving verbal and abstract problems.

15. Performance tests and culture-fair tests are similar in that they ____.
    a. focus on linguistic abilities
    b. are exclusively group tests
    c. minimize or eliminate the use of words
    d. focus only on mathematical and abstraction skills

16. The ability of a test to produce consistent and stable scores is its ____ while the ability of a test to measure what it sets out to measure is its _____.
    A. validity; reliability
    B. standard deviation; validity
    C. reliability; validity
    D. reliability; standard deviation

17. The largest program designed to improve educationally disadvantaged children's chances of school achievement is ____.
    a. the Milwaukee Project
    b. the Perry Preschool Program
    c. the Hobbs and Robinson Program
    d. the Head Start Program

18. Plomin's review of the literature on IQ led him to conclude that a person's IQ is about ___ percent the result of genetic factors and about ___ percent the result of environmental factors.
    a. 80; 20
    b. 70; 30
    c. 50; 50
    d. 30; 70

19. In the majority of cases the cause of both mental retardation and giftedness is _____.
    a. clearly identified genetic abnormalities
    b. unknown
    c. poor prenatal nutrition
    d. financial status of the parents

20. Creative people are ___ than less creative people with equivalent IQ scores.
    a. more intelligent in their actual job performance
    b. perceived as being more intelligent
    c. less intelligent in their actual job performance
    d. perceived as being less intelligent

21. The type of thinking required to solve problems requiring a creative or flexible, or inventive solution is ____, and the type of thinking needed to solve problems requiring one or a few logically thought-out solutions is _____.
    a. functional thinking; circular thinking
    b. convergent thinking; divergent thinking
    c. divergent thinking; functional thinking
    d. divergent thinking; convergent thinking

22. Each of the following is a characteristic of emotional intelligence EXCEPT _____.
    a. knowing your emotions
    b. using your emotions to motivate yourself
    c. expressing your emotions
    d. managing relationships

23. Which of the following statements accurately reflects the Flynn Effect?
    a. Over the last several decades intelligence test scores have risen.
    b. Young children are less cognitively advanced today compared to 30 years ago.
    c. Compared to today's test scores, the gap in intelligence test scores between blacks and whites was narrower 30 years ago.
    d. Televisions, computers, and video games have caused increases in intelligence test scores.

24. Which of the following is true regarding mental retardation?
    a. Mental retardation is not based entirely on IQ.
    b. Savants can display exceptional skills is specialized areas.
    c. Mental retardation encompasses a vast array of mental deficits with a wide variety of causes, treatments, and outcomes.
    d. all of the above

25. Which of the following statements accurately reflects the criticism over IQ tests?
    a. Content of the tests is too broad and attempts to assess too many skills.
    b. Test scores are a very complex way of summing up a simple set of abilities.
    c. IQ tests only measure a person's ability at a certain point in time, but cannot explain reasons for a good or poor performance.
    d. Questions on IQ tests should reflect intelligence as a single entity that should be measured the same for each culture.

Answers and Explanations to Multiple Choice Posttest

1. c. Thoughts are believed to be made up of language, images, and concepts. p. 211

2. Top to bottom: b. meaning; d. sentences; c. morphemes; a. phenomes Fig. 7–1; p. 212

3. d. The language rules that determine how to combine and use sounds and words to communicate are called grammar. p. 212

4. d. Most people use fuzzy, poorly defined, and overlapping concepts. p. 213

5. b. A prototype is a mental model containing representative features of a concept. p. 213

6. d. Algorithms are step-by-step problem-solving methods that guarantee a correct solution. p. 218

7. b. Brainstorming involves generating numerous ideas before evaluating them. p. 221

8. c. The availability heuristic relies on the information most easily retrieved from long-term memory. p. 223

9. a. Confirmation bias causes us to find evidence to support our beliefs. p. 223

10. b. Spearman believed that intelligence is generalized to specific mental abilities; while Thurstone believed they are relatively independent of each other. p. 227

11. c. Naturalistic intelligence is part of the theory of multiple intelligences advanced by Howard Gardner. p. 227

12. a. Practical intelligence is not a type of multiple intelligence. p 227

13. b. The Binet-Simon scale was developed in 1905 to identify children that might have difficulty in school. p. 229

14. d. Wechsler believed that adult intelligence is more concerned with the ability to handle life situations than excel at verbal or mathematical problems. p. 230

15. c. Both performance tests and culture-fair tests were designed to eliminate or minimize words and language. p. 231

16. c. Reliability measures a test's ability to produce stable, consistent scores; and validity effectively measures what a test has been designed to measure. p. 231

17. d. The Head Start Program is the largest program created to enrich disadvantaged children's educational opportunities. p. 236

18. c. Plomin found that heredity and environment almost equally contributed to human differences in intelligence. p. 237

19. b. As with mental retardation, the causes of giftedness are largely unknown. p. 242

20. b. Creative people are perceived as being more intelligent than their less creative but equivalent IQ score counterparts. p. 243

21. d. Divergent thinking reflects original, inventive, and flexible thinking; convergent thinking is directed towards finding one correct solution. p. 216

22. c. Expressing your emotions is NOT one of the five traits of emotional intelligence. p. 228

23. a. According to James Flynn, intelligence test scores have risen about 3 points per decade and increases in IQ may be as high as 6 points per decade. pp. 237–238

24. d. All of the statements are true regarding mental retardation. pp. 239–242

25. c. Tests measure our ability at a certain point in time. Test scores do not tell us why someone performs poorly or well. pp. 232–233

Language Support

Students identified the following words from the text as needing more explanation. This page can be cut out, folded in half, and used as a bookmark for this chapter.

A

Accelerate	cause to move faster, quicken the progress or development of
Accentuate	emphasize, make more prominent or intense, bring attention to
Acne	primarily an adolescent skin disorder marked by pimples on the face
AIDS	acquired immune deficiency syndrome; life threatening disease
Ascent	rise upward, advance in status or reputation

B

Baffled	confused, puzzled, doubt, or become perplexed
Brilliant	unusual mental keenness or alertness; very bright

C

Capitalize on	gain by turning something to advantage, profit from
Circumvent	get around something by using a strategy or cleverness
Civil service	government administrative job determined by competitive exam
Clarify	to make clear or understandable, free from confusion
Clear-cut	completely evident, definite, unambiguous, with clearly defined borders
Collaboration	working jointly with others, especially in an intellectual endeavor
Complacency	self-satisfied state which may lack awareness of danger, unconcerned
Concede	to acknowledge hesitantly or grudgingly
Conceivably	possibly, perhaps, by chance
(In) Conjunction	being in association or union with; combined events or circumstances
Cross-reference	relate information from one source to another, check
Curiosity	desire to know, interest leading to inquiry

D

Deficit	lack or impairment in capacity to function
Deteriorate	make worse, wear away, disintegrate
Detrimental	drawback, harmful or able to cause damage
Dispute	quarrel, debate, verbal argument that persists
Dread	fear greatly or feel reluctant about something

E

Enmeshed	caught up or entangled in
Entity	independent, separate, and distinct existence of a being
Equilateral	having all sides or faces equal
Excel	surpass in achievement or accomplishment, superior performance
Exhausted	extremely tired, used up or empty

F

Figurative	saying one thing normally indicating another regarded as being similar
Flawed	defect in structure or form, imperfection that hinders effectiveness
Fluency	effortless, smooth, rapid, expressed with ease
Foster	promote the growth or development of
Fuzzy	indistinct, lacking in clarity or definition

G

Grapple	struggle or wrestle, try to come to grips with
Guarantee	assert confidently, give security to

H

Hamper	to restrict with obstacles, hold back, restrain or impede
Hierarchy	ranked or graded series, classification or order
Hinder	slow or make difficult the progress of, hold back

I

Inherent	by nature or habit; essential characteristic of something
Innovation	introduce a new idea, method or device
Inquisitive	inclined to ask questions; curious; wanting to examine and learn
Interaction	mutual or reciprocal action or influence

J

Juggle	handle or deal with several things at once to satisfy competing requirements

K

Kinesthetic	having to do with body tension, movement and sensation
Knack	special ability that is difficult to teach or understand

L

Lanky	ungracefully tall and thin
Literally	reproduced word for word; exactly
Lobby	attempt to influence or sway towards a desired action

M

Maladjusted	lacking harmony with one's environment by poor or inadequate adjustment
Malnutrition	faulty or inadequate nutrition
Manifest	make evident by showing or displaying
Marshal	to bring together and order in an effective way
Merit	to be worthy of or entitled to; earn or deserve
Metaphorically	using a word or phase in place of another to suggest their similarity or likeness
Minimize	intentionally reduce or underestimate; play down
Modest	moderately estimating one's worth or ability; limited in size, amount, or scope
Modify	limit or restrict, make less extreme, make basic changes in

N

Negligible	so small or unimportant or of such little consequence so as to warrant little or no attention
Notorious	widely known and discussed, usually unfavorably
Novice	beginner, unexperienced person

O

Obliterate	remove from memory or recognition; cause to disappear
Obscure	hide or conceal; cover or make indistinct; relatively unknown person
Offset	counterbalance or compensate for something else
Orphanage	an institution for the care of children without parents

P

Pantomime	convey a story by bodily or facial movements only
Paraprofessional	trained aide who assists a professional (i.e., a teacher, doctor, or lawyer)
Pictorially	suggesting or conveying visual images
Prototype	standard or typical example; first functional form of a new design or construction

Q

Quantitative	express in terms of amount or measurement

R

Reiterate	state or do over again or repeat, sometimes with tiring effects
Remedial	concerned with correcting faulty study habits and raising a student's general competence; intended as a remedy
Resemblance	be like or similar to
Rule of thumb	general principle based on experience and common sense but not scientifically accurate

S

Shortcoming	lacking some necessary element, having a deficiency or inadequate
Shrewd	clever, perceptive, able to see what's hidden, practical
Signing hands	communicating by using sign language for the deaf
Sort out	examine for clarification, free from confusion, arrange by characteristics
Step-by-step	marked by successive, gradual degrees of limited progression
Stumped	frustrated, baffled, defeated by confusion
Stymied	stand in the way of; present an obstacle
Suspend	defer to a later time or specific condition
Sway	to fluctuate between positions or opinions; go back and forth

T

Tacit	without a stated contract or agreement, implied without verbal expression
Tactic	device, plan or method for accomplishing an end
Tangled	very involved or complex, giving the appearance of disorder

Y

Yearning	feeling tenderness or urgent longing; to desire or miss

Z

Zero in on	close in or focus attention on an objective

Key Vocabulary Terms

Cut out each term and use as study cards.
Definition is on the back side of each term.

Cognition	Concept
Phonemes	Prototype
Morphemes	Linguistic relativity hypothesis
Grammar	Problem representation
Image	Algorithm

A mental category for classifying objects, people, or experiences.

The process whereby we acquire and use knowledge.

According to Rosch, a mental model containing the most typical feature of a concept.

The basic sounds that make up any language.

Whorf's idea that patterns of thinking are determined by the specific language one speaks.

The smallest meaningful units of speech, such as simple words, prefixes, and suffixes.

The first step in solving a problem; it involves interpreting or defining the problem.

The language rules that determine how sounds and words can be combined and used to communicate meaning within a language.

A step-by-step method of problem solving that guarantees a correct solution.

A mental representation of a sensory experience.

Heuristics	Mental set
Hill climbing	Functional fixedness
Subgoals	Divergent thinking
Means-end analysis	Convergent thinking
Working backward	Brainstorming

Tendency to perceive and to approach problems in certain ways.

Rules of thumb that help in simplifying and solving problems, although they do not guarantee a correct solution.

The tendency to perceive only a limited number of uses for an object, thus interfering with the process of problem solving.

A heuristic problem solving strategy in which each step moves you progressively closer to the final goal.

Thinking that meets the criteria of originality, inventiveness, and flexibility.

Intermediate, more manageable goals used in one heuristic strategy to make it easier to reach the final goal.

Thinking that is directed toward one correct solution to a problem.

A heuristic strategy that aims to reduce the discrepancy between the current situation and the desired goal at a number of intermediate points.

A problem-solving strategy in which an individual or a group produces numerous ideas and evaluates them only after all ideas are collected.

A heuristic strategy in which one works backward from the desired goal to the given conditions.

Compensatory model	Framing
Representativeness	Emotional intelligence
Availability	Hindsight
Confirmation bias	Intelligence quotient (IQ)
Intelligence	Wechsler Adult Intelligence Scale

The perspective from which we interpret information before making a decision.

A rational decision-making model in which choices are systematically evaluated on various criteria.

Goleman's theory that one form of intelligence refers to how effectively people perceive and understand their own emotions and the emotions of others, and can regulate and manage their emotional behavior.

A heuristic by which a new situation is judged on the basis of its resemblance to a stereo-typical model.

Thinking about alternative realities and things that never happened.

A heuristic by which a judgment or decision is based on information that is most easily retrieved from memory.

A numerical value given to intelligence that is determined from the scores on an intelligence test; based on a score of 100 for average intelligence.

The tendency to look for evidence in support of a belief and to ignore evidence that would disprove a belief.

An individual intelligence test developed especially for adults; measures both verbal and performance abilities.

A general term referring to the ability or abilities involved in learning and adaptive behavior.

Wechsler Scale for Children	Split-half reliability
Group tests	Validity
Performance tests	Content validity
Culture-fair tests	Criterion-related validity
Reliability	Mental retardation

A method of determining test reliability by dividing the test into two parts and checking the agreement of scores on both parts.

An individual intelligence test developed especially for school-aged children; measures verbal and performance abilities and also yields an overall IQ score.

Ability of a test to measure what it has been designed to measure.

Written intelligence tests administered by one examiner to many people at one time.

Refers to a test's having an adequate sample of the skills or knowledge it is supposed to measure.

Intelligence tests that minimize the use of language.

Validity of a test as measured by a comparison of the test score and independent measures of what the test is designed to measure.

Intelligence tests designed to eliminate cultural bias by minimizing skills and values that vary from one culture to another.

Condition of significantly subaverage intelligence combined with deficiencies in adaptive behavior.

Ability of a test to produce consistent and stable scores.

Giftedness	Counterfactual thinking
Creativity	Triarchic theory of intelligence
Language	Theory of multiple intelligences

Thinking about alternative realities and things that never happened (i.e., "what if"?)	Refers to superior IQ combined with demonstrated or potential ability in such areas as academic aptitude, creativity, or leadership.
Sternberg's theory that intelligence involves mental skills (componential), insight and creative adaptability (experiential), and environmential responsiveness (contextual.)	The ability to produce novel and socially valued ideas or objects.
Gardner's theory that there are many intelligences, each one relatively independent of the others. He lists seven types of multiple intelligence.	A flexible system of communication that uses sounds, rules, gestures, on symbols to convey information.

8

Motivation and Emotion

Chapter Focus

This chapter explores motivation and emotion. The authors begin by describing motives that drive human behavior. Motives are the specific needs or desires that arouse an organism and direct its efforts toward a goal. Instincts motivate many nonhuman animal behaviors, but are not able to explain most aspects of human behavior. Drive-reduction theory contends that behaviors are aimed at reducing tension or returning an organism to homeostasis. Drives are either primary (unlearned), or secondary (learned). Another perspective, arousal theory, states behaviors are motivated by the desire to maintain, reduce, or increase a state of arousal. According to the Yerkes-Dodson law, complex tasks require lower arousal states. Some kinds of behaviors may be explained by viewing sensation seeking as a basic motivation. Distinctions may also be drawn between behaviors that are performed because they are either intrinsically or extrinsically motivating.

Abraham Maslow organized motives into a hierarchy. From lower to higher the needs are: physiological, safety, belongingness, esteem, and self-actualization. According to Maslow, more basic needs must be satisfied before motives emerge. Recent research challenges Maslow's views.

Hunger and thirst are specific motives stimulated by internal and external cues. Biologically, areas within the brain, the hypothalamus in particular, regulate hunger and eating by monitoring levels of glucose and leptin in the blood. The brain also monitors the quantity and type of food ingested. Emotions may influence eating habits by increasing or decreasing hunger drives. Cultural and social factors also affect motivations to eat by influencing when, with whom, and what a person eats. Hunger is a product of complex biological and environmental forces; many people suffer from eating disorders like anorexia nervosa, bulimia nervosa, or obesity. High risk populations include adolescents, particularly white upper- or middle-class adolescent females. Little is known about the predisposing or psychological factors of these eating disorders. Obesity is on the rise in and is viewed as the most pressing health problem in America. Many factors contribute to obesity. Obese individuals are subject to medical problems, ridicule, discrimination, which in turn may lead to behavior problems.

Sex drives motivate reproductive behaviors vital to species survival and are the result of biological and environmental factors. Hormones, pheromones, and the brain have complex interactions that influence sexual drives and behaviors. Sex researchers have identified a sexual response cycle consisting of four phases: excitement, plateau, orgasm, and resolution. In addition to biology, sexual behavior is also influenced by experience and learning. Culture may determine what people find attractive. Research reveals that Americans have fairly conservative sex lives. Sexual orientation refers to the direction of an individual's sexual interest. Individuals may identify themselves being of heterosexual, homosexual, or bisexual orientation. Sexual orientation is most likely to be determined by complex interactions between biological and socialization factors.

Other important motives include those that are responsive to environmental stimuli, collectively called stimulus motives. Exploration, curiosity, manipulation, contact, aggression, achievement, and affiliation are stimulus motives. Exploration and curiosity motives are directed toward finding out about the new and unknown. Curiosity has been linked to creativity and cognition. Manipulation motives are directed toward handling a specific object. Harry Harlow's experiments on baby monkeys demonstrated the importance of contact during early development. Aggressive behaviors intend to inflict harm. Freud considered aggression an innate drive, another perspective views aggression as having evolved. Frustration is linked to aggression, but individuals respond very differently to frustration—not always in aggressive acts. Aggression may be learned by observing aggressive models and is of particular concern among child viewers. In addition, culture and gender play roles in aggression. Some cultures attempt to resolve confrontations peacefully, others use conflict. Boys are more aggressive than girls, but it is not known whether this is due to biological or social factors.

Achievement motive is the desire to excel, to overcome obstacles. Three aspects of achievement-oriented behavior have been described using the Work and Family Orientation scale (WOFO): work orientation, mastery, and competitiveness. High scores in competitiveness have been linked to lower achievement. People with high levels of achievement motivation are likely to have common characteristics, including: they are fast learners, self-confident, energetic, and tense, among others. Affiliation motive is the desire to be around other people. Fear and anxiety influence the affiliation motive; most people wish to be around others when experiencing these states.

The second part of this chapter explores emotions, feelings such as fear, joy, or surprise, that underlie behavior. Plutchik proposed that eight basic emotions exist: fear, surprise, disgust, anger, anticipation, joy, and acceptance (see Figure 8–4 of text). Plutchik's views on emotions have been challenged by anthropologists and other scientists who contend that emotions are defined differently according to language and culture. Distinctions are now drawn between primary and secondary emotions. Primary emotions are universal emotions, whereas secondary emotions are not found in all cultures. It is important to be able to identify and describe each of the different theories of emotion and the challenges to each. These include the James-Lange theory, Cannon-Bard theory, and cognitive theories of emotions.

Emotions may be communicated verbally or nonverbally through voice quality, facial expression, body language, personal space, and gestures. Most facial expressions are innate and may serve an adaptive function. The amount of acceptable personal space varies depending on activities, emotions felt, and on the customs of a particular culture. Explicit acts and gestures are often effective nonverbal ways to communicate emotions. However, care should be taken when interpreting verbal and nonverbal cues as people often overestimate their ability to accurately interpret messages conveyed by others.

Finally, expression of emotions differs between the sexes and among cultures. Men are more likely to inhibit expression of their emotions. Also men and women tend to have different emotional reactions to the same stimuli and differ in their ability to interpret nonverbal cues. Culture shapes emotional experiences. Researchers who take the universalist position believe that facial expressions look similar across cultures when certain emotions are expressed. In contrast, researchers who take the culture-learning position believe that people learn appropriate facial expressions for emotions within their culture. Although research shows more support for the universalist position, display rules that vary across cultures often make it difficult to interpret emotions expressed by people from other cultures.

Learning Objectives and Questions

After you have read and studied this chapter, you should be able to complete the following statements.

LEARNING OBJECTIVES

1. Define motive and emotion and explain the roles of stimulus, behavior, and goals in motivation.

2. Explain the functioning of the primary drive of hunger. Discuss those mechanisms in the brain that regulate this drive and which external and cultural factors affect perceptions of hunger.

3. Define anorexia nervosa, bulimia nervosa, and obesity. Discuss their prevalence, symptoms, who is most likely to develop them, and current treatment.

4. Compare and contrast the sex drive with other primary drives. Describe the biological and psychological factors involved in sexual arousal. Summarize current beliefs about differences in sexual orientation.

5. Summarize the research on aggression in humans in terms of the causes of aggression, methods for modifying aggressive behavior, and cultural and gender differences in aggression.

6. Distinguish between the motives for achievement and affiliation. Explain why these needs are so strong in some people.

7. List and define the five levels of Maslow's hierarchy of motives. Describe how these needs affect people's everyday lives and goals.

8. Compare and contrast the James-Lange, Cannon-Bard, and cognitive theories of emotion.

9. Explain and name the eight parts of the scheme for categorizing emotion created by Plutchik.

10. Discuss gender differences in the experience and expression of emotion. Be certain to dispel any myths about male and female emotional responsiveness.

11. Discuss the similarities and differences in facial expression of emotions across cultures. Name those facial expressions considered to be 'universal' in emotional meaning.

SHORT ESSAY QUESTIONS

1. Discuss Harlow's experiments with infant monkeys and 'surrogate mothers.' Discuss the need for contact and whether or not it is universal and applies to other organisms besides humans. How do Harlow's findings generalize to human infant development of attachment?

2. Discuss the most effective methods for losing weight and maintaining the weight loss. Provide the Five Steps for Losing Weight outlined in the text.

3. Compare and contrast verbal and nonverbal communication in expressing emotion. Give at least three examples of nonverbal communication and how each assists in sending an emotional message. Explain why some people may not be willing or able to report their emotions verbally.

4. Identify and discuss the different types of sexual coercion. Describe what factors contribute to sexual coercion (i.e., motivation of the perpetrator) and the impact it has on the victims.

5. Discuss the characteristics of the stimulus motives of activity, exploration, curiosity, manipulation, and contact. Provide an example of each and discuss how they may contribute to changes in behavior and society.

Chapter Outline

The following is an outline conveying the main concepts of this chapter.

Motive
Emotion

1. Perspectives on Motivation   page 251
   A. Instincts
   B. Drive-Reduction Theory
      • Homeostasis
      • Primary Drives
      • Secondary Drives
   C. Arousal Theory
      • Yerkes-Dodson Law
      • Sensation seeking
   D. Intrinsic and Extrinsic Motivation
   E. A Hierarchy of Motives
      • Maslow's Hierarchical Model
         – Physiological needs
         – Safety needs
         – Belongingness needs
         – Esteem needs
         – Self-actualization needs

2. Hunger and Thirst p. 255
   A. Biological and Emotional Factors
   B. Cultural and Social Factors
   C. Eating Disorders and Obesity
      • Anorexia nervosa
      • Bulimia
      • Obesity

UNDERSTANDING OURSELVES: The Slow (but Lasting) Fix for Weight Gain   page 259
      • Check with your doctor first
      • Increase your metabolism through regular exercise
      • Modify your diet
      • Reduce external cues encouraging you to eat
      • Set realistic goals
      • Reward yourself for small improvements

3. Sex   page 260
   A. Biological factors
      • Testosterone
      • Pheromones
      • Sexual Response Cycle
         – Excitement
         – Plateau
         – Orgasm
         – Resolution
   B. Cultural and Environmental Factors
   C. Sexual Orientation
      • Heterosexual
      • Homosexual
      • Bisexual

4. Other Important Motives   page 264
   Stimulus Motives
   A. Exploration and Curiosity
   B. Manipulation and Contact
   C. Aggression
      • Biological or Learned?
      • Aggression and Culture
      • Gender and Aggression
   D. Achievement
      • Achievement motive
      • Work and Family Orientation Scale (WOFO)
   E. Affiliation
      • Affiliation motive

UNDERSTANDING THE WORLD AROUND US: What Motivates Rape?   page 267

5. Emotions   page 270
   A. Basic Emotions
   B. Theories of Emotion
      • James Lange Theory
      • Cannon-Bard Theory
      • Cognitive Theories of Emotions
      • Challenges

6. Communicating Emotion   page 274
   A. Voice Quality and Facial Expression
   B. Body Language, Personal Space, and Gestures
      • Explicit acts
   C. Gender and Emotion
   D. Culture and Emotion
      • Universalist position
      • Cultural learning
      • Display rules

Multiple Choice Posttest

After studying the text and completing the Study Guide activities, answer these questions to determine if you need to review any areas before the course exam.

1. A (n) _____ is a need that pushes a person to work toward a specific goal.
   a. stimulus   c. incentive
   b. behavior   d. motive

2. A (n) _____ is an inborn, goal-directed behavior that is seen in an entire species.
   a. instinct   c. motive
   b. drive   d. stimulus

3. External stimuli that lead to goal-directed behavior are called _____.
   a. drives   c. needs
   b. incentives   d. reciprocals

4. All of the following are examples of primary drives EXCEPT _____.
   a. hunger   c. thirst
   b. money   d. affiliation

5. A desire to perform a behavior that originates within the individual is known as _____, while a desire to perform a behavior to obtain an external reward or avoid punishment is known as _____.
   a. primary motivation; secondary motivation
   b. intrinsic motivation; extrinsic motivation
   c. secondary motivation; primary motivation
   d. extrinsic motivation; intrinsic motivation

6. Increased _____ is the most effective way to increase the body's metabolism when trying to lose weight.
   a. protein consumption c. reduction of calories
   b. exercise   d. sleep

7. A serious eating disorder that is associated with an intense fear of weight gain and a distorted body image is called _____.
   a. anorexia nervosa c. bulimia
   b. Karposi's anemia d. Huntington's chorea

8. An eating disorder characterized by binges of eating followed by self-induced vomiting or purging is called _____.
   a. anorexia nervosa c. bulimia
   b. Karposi's anemia d. Huntington's chorea

9. In Harlow's classic experiments, when the infant monkeys were frightened, they ran to a "surrogate mother" that offered _____.
   a. food and warmth   c. warmth only
   b. food only   d. warmth and closeness

10. Scents that can be sexually stimulating are called _____.
    a. androgens   c. globulins
    b. corticorsteroids d. pheromones

11. The correct chronological order of the phases of the sexual response cycle is _____.
    a. resolution, excitement, plateau, orgasm
    b. excitement, resolution, orgasm, plateau
    c. plateau, excitement, orgasm, resolution
    d. excitement, plateau, orgasm, resolution

12. _____ are largely unlearned motives that push us to investigate, explore, and often change, the world around us.
    a. Primary drives   c. Secondary motives
    b. Stimulus drives d. Achievement drives

13. Research indicates that _____ factors contribute to gender differences in aggressive behavior.
    a. neither biological nor social   c. social, but not biological
    b. biological, but not social   d. both social and biological

14. Which one of the following is NOT of the three separate, but interrelated aspects of achievement-oriented behavior identified by Helmrich and Spence?
    a. work-orientation   c. mastery
    b. curiosity   d. competitiveness

15. Label the correct sequential order of Maslow's hierarchy of motives from the most primitive to the most complex and human, using the following needs:
    a. belongingness   c. safety
    b. esteem   d. self-
    e. physiological   actualization

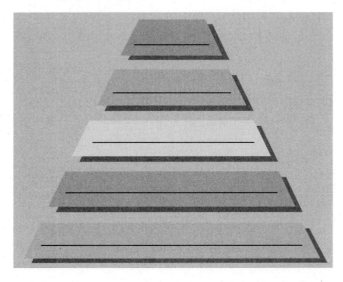

16. The _____ theory of emotion states that the experience of emotion occurs simultaneously with biological changes.
    a. Cannon-Bard   c. Schacter-Singer
    b. James-Lange   d. cognitive

17. The belief that certain facial expressions represent similar emotions across all cultures is known as the _____ position.
    a. universalist   c. culture-learning
    b. fundamentalist   d. unidimensional

18. Recent research indicates that sexual gratification is the predominant motive in rapes about ___ percent of the time.
    a. 30   c. 70
    b. 50   d. 90

19. Which of the following is most likely to describe a high sensation seeker as opposed to a low sensation seeker?
    a. classified as an aggressive individual
    b. prefers team sports
    c. has varied sexual activities
    d. chooses high-paying careers

20. Which of the following statements is NOT true regarding biological factors that influence eating?
    a. Regions of the cerebellum and brainstem regulate eating.
    b. Regions of the hypothalamus, cortex, and spinal cord regulate eating.
    c. Changes in glucose, fats, and other substances in the blood signal the need for food.
    d. Presence of the hormone leptin influences eating.

21. Which of the following factors contributes to overeating and obesity in Americans?
    a. sedentary lifestyle
    b. genetics
    c. food availability
    d.aAll of the above

22. Which of the following statements is true regarding the affiliation motive?
    a. It is aroused when people feel safe or secure.
    b. It is closely tied to fear and anxiety.
    c. It stems from environmental factors alone.
    d. all of the above

Answers and Explanations to Multiple Choice Posttest

1. d. Motives are needs that push people to work toward specific goals. p. 251

2. a. Instincts are inborn, goal-directed behavior seen in an entire species. p. 251

3. c. Incentives are external stimuli that lead to goal-directed behavior. p. 256

4. c. Primary needs are basic needs we are born with, such as hunger, thirst, sexual drive, and comfort. p. 252

5. b. Intrinsic motivation originates with the individual, and extrinsic motivation originates from the desire to obtain an external reward. p. 253

6. c. Exercise is the best way to prevent metabolism from dropping when dieting. p. 259

7. a. Anorexia nervosa is a serious eating disorder associated with intense fear of weight gain and a distorted body image. p. 257

8. c. Bulimia is an eating disorder characterized by eating and purging binges. p. 257

9. d. The surrogate mothers chosen by the infant monkeys offered warmth and closeness. p. 265

10. d. Pheromones are sexually stimulating scents produced by the body. p. 261

11. d. The correct chronological order of the sexual response cycle is: excitement, plateau, orgasm, and resolution. p. 261

12. b. Stimulus drives are unlearned motives that push us to investigate and explore. p. 264

13. d. Both sociological and biological factors contribute to gender differences in aggressive behavior. pp. 265–266

14. b. Curiosity is NOT one of the achievement-oriented behavioral aspects. pp. 268–269

15. Maslow's hierarchy of motives from primitive to complex is: e. physiological; c. safety; a. belongingness; b. esteem, and d. self-actualization. p. 254, Fig. 8–2

16. b. The James-Lange theory of emotions states emotion and biological changes occur simultaneously. p. 273

17. a. The universalist position holds that certain facial expressions represent similar emotions across all cultures. p. 278; Fig. 8-6 on p. 272

18. b. Sexual gratification is the predominant motive in 50 percent of rapes. p. 267

19. c. High sensation seekers are more likely to have more sexual partners and engage in more varied sexual activities. pp. 252–253

20. a. All of the other statements are true. pp. 255–256

21. d. All of the factors contribute to overeating and obesity. pp. 258–260

22. b. Fear and anxiety are closely tied to the affiliation motive. p. 269

Language Support

Students identified the following words from the text as needing more explanation. This page can be cut-out, folded in half, and used as a bookmark for this chapter.

A

Accomplice	one associated with another especially in wrongdoing
Acutely	sudden onset, sharp rise, severe
Adjacent	immediately preceding or following, in close proximity, adjoining
Agile	able to move with grace and ease; quick resourceful, adaptable character
Agitation	to excite or trouble the mind or feelings; attempt to arouse public emotion
Amalgamation	put two or more things together; merge; unite; link or adhere
Aphrodisiac	food or drug that arouses sexual desire; something that excites

B

Beeline	to go quickly in a straight direct course
Bristle	assume an aggressive attitude or appearance when slighted
Bungee jumping	jumping off a high structure attached to a cord so the body springs back before hitting the ground or water

C

Charitable donation	liberal in giving to the needy, generosity in contributing to causes
Cinematic violence	violence portrayed in the movies
Contact sports	any sport that allows physical contact between the players
Consecutive	following one after the other in order
Continuum	progressive sequence or series with no discernable division
Conversely	in reversed order, relation, or action
Counterproductive	tending to hinder the attainment of a desired goal
Courtesy	considerate, cooperative, and polite
Crime ring	gang or group involved in criminal activity

D

Decoding	convert into understandable form; discover underlying meaning
Degrade	lower in rank or status; demote; drop to less effective level; low esteem
Deviate	to depart from norms of society; stray from standard principle or topic
Differentiate	perceive or show a marked difference from other things; distinguish
Discourage	to dissuade or talk out of; hold back by not encouraging, lose confidence
Drastic	extreme or severe action or effect
Drumming fingers	tapping one's fingers rhythmically on a hard surface

E

Emaciated	wasting away physically; very thin or feeble
Embrace	take up readily; welcome or avail oneself of something
Encompass	enclose; envelop; include; form a circle around
Exotic	striking, exciting, or mysteriously different or unusual

F

Fervor	intensity of feeling or expression
Fluctuations	continual change; shift back and forth; irregular movements
Fretting	feel or express worry, annoyance, emotional strain

G

Goosebumps	bristling of hair on skin from cold, fear, or sudden excitement
Gory	unpleasant or sensational; bloody
Graphic	depicted in a realistic or vivid manner, i.e., graphic sex or violence

Gravitate	to be strongly attracted or drawn to; move under gravitational force
Growl	deep guttural sound of anger or hostility; murmur or complain, grumble

H

Hold in check	to stop the movement, rate or intensity of; restrain
Hypothetical	an inference from unproven evidence; conclusion deduced by guessing

I

Impostor	one that assumes false identity for the purpose of deception
Inaccurate	incorrect or untrue
Inconclusive	leading to no clear result
Infallible	unfailing in effectiveness; absolutely trustworthy
Inflict	cause someone to endure something unpleasant
Inordinate	exceeding reasonable limits; excessive
Insignificant	lacking influence; small in stature or quantity
Instantaneous	occurring without delay; presently
Interplay	reciprocal relationship, action or influence from one to another
In the closet	secretly homosexual while appearing heterosexual
In the midst of	in the middle of an action or situation; surrounded by or in proximity to others
Irritability	quick to anger, become annoyed or impatient

L

Limp	lacking firm substance, strength or vigor; spiritless
Lush	plush; fertile; prosperous; plentiful

M

Mundane	commonplace, ordinary, practical

N

Night owl	person who keeps late night hours
Nostalgia	sentimental yearning for return to the past or something lost

O

Optimum	most favorable condition for growth; greatest degree attainable
Orientation	general direction or tendency of one's thoughts, inclinations or acts
Overestimate	overrate, hold in too high esteem or value

P

Pep talk	brief, intense, emotional talk designed to encourage an audience
Pornographic	depicting erotic behavior in art, film, or writing intended to cause sexual excitement
Portrayed	describe in words or picture; enact; play role of; reveal; expose
Predisposition	inclined to; leaning or drawn toward a belief or type of conduct
Premium	exceptional quality or amount; in demand
Presume	take for granted; act without clarity; believe to be true without proof
Prevalent	generally widely accepted, favored or practiced; widespread
Propensity	an intense, natural inclination or preference towards
Provocation	arouse, incite, stimulate, anger, or annoy
Puny	slight or inferior in power, size, or importance

R

Rampant	without restraint; widespread; unchecked
Recrimination	accusation in return; countercharging an accuser
Replenish	fill or rebuild; inspire, make good or powerful again
Revenge	opportunity to get even or satisfaction; retaliate in kind

S

Solicit	approach with request or plea; urge strongly or ask others for
Spectacular	sensational; exceedingly elaborate or grand
Strive	devote serious effort or energy; endeavor; attempt

Strychnine	poisonous plant used in medicine to stimulate the central nervous system
Succumb	yield to superior strength or force; overpowering desire; death
Surrogate	one that serves as a substitute

T

Taunt	tease; provoke; challenge or insult; use of sarcasm
Tendency	inclination or purposeful movement in a particular direction
Trample	crush or step on heavily; be harshly domineering over
Turbulent	causing disturbance, agitation, unrest
Turn one's stomach	to disgust completely; sicken; nauseate

U

| Unmanly | of weak character; cowardly; effeminate |

V

| Vestige | traces; marks or visible signs left by something |
| Vigorous | strong, energetic, forceful mental or physical strength, active force |

W

| Wafting | to move lightly as if by the impulse of wind or waves |
| Wreak havoc | bring about or cause destruction |

Key Vocabulary Terms

Cut out each term and use as study cards.
Definition is on the back side of each term.

Motive	Homeostasis
Emotion	Incentive
Instinct	Intrinsic motivation
Drive	Extrinsic motivation
Drive-reduction theory	Primary drive

State of balance and stability in which the organism functions effectively.

Specific need or desire, such as hunger, thirst, or achievement, that prompts goal-oriented behavior.

External stimulus that prompts goal-directed behavior.

Feeling, such as fear, joy, surprise, and anger that energizes and directs behavior.

A desire to perform a behavior that originates within the individual or the activity itself.

Inborn, inflexible, goal-directed behavior that is characteristic of an entire species.

A desire to perform a behavior to obtain an external reward or avoid punishment.

State of tension or arousal due to biological needs.

An unlearned drive, such as hunger, that is based on a physiological state.

States that motivated behavior is aimed at reducing a state of bodily tension or arousal and returning the organism to homeostasis.

Anorexia nervosa	Yerkes-Dodson law
Bulimia nervosa	James-Lange theory
Stimulus motive	Cannon-Bard theory
Achievement motive	Cognitive theory
Affiliation motive	Display rules

States there is optimal
level of arousal for the best
performance of any task;
the more complex the
task, the lower the
level of arousal that
can be tolerated before
performance deterioration.

A serious eating disorder
that is associated with an
intense fear of weight gain
and a distorted body
image.

States that stimuli cause
physiological changes in
our bodies, and emotions
result from those physio-
logical changes.

An eating disorder
characterized by binges of
eating followed by self-
induced vomiting.

States that the experience
of emotion occurs
simultaneously with
biological changes.

Unlearned motive, such as
curiosity or contact, that
prompts us to explore or
change the world around
us.

States that emotional
experiences depend on
one's perception or
judgment of the situation
one is in.

The need to excel, to
overcome obstacles.

Culture-specific rules that
govern how, when, and
why expressions of
emotion are displayed.

The need to be with
others.

Secondary
drive

Arousal
theory

Aggression

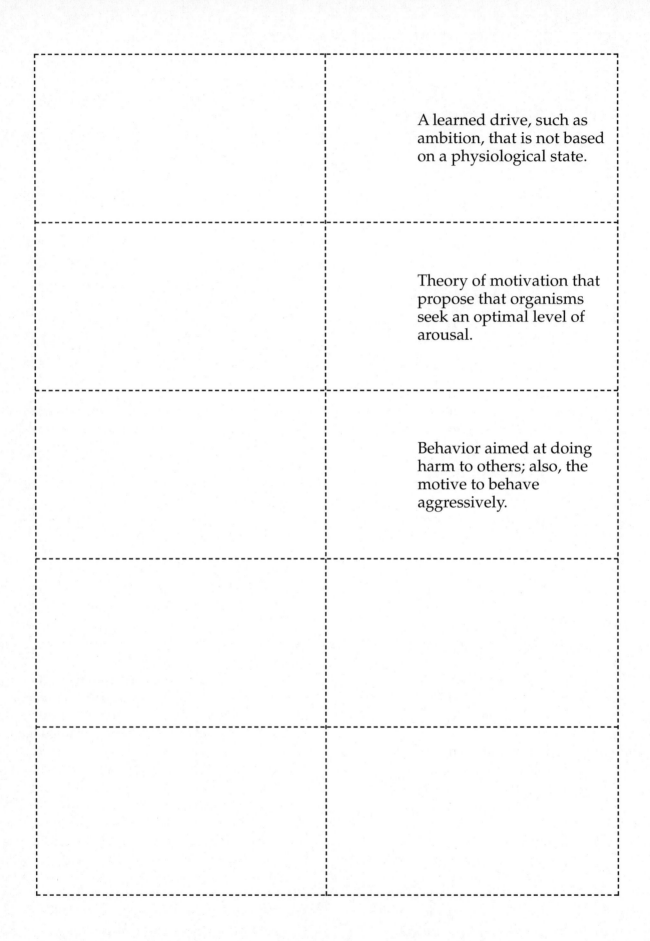

A learned drive, such as
ambition, that is not based
on a physiological state.

Theory of motivation that
propose that organisms
seek an optimal level of
arousal.

Behavior aimed at doing
harm to others; also, the
motive to behave
aggressively.

9 Life-Span Development

Chapter Focus

This chapter examines the changes people undergo from birth to old age. The chapter begins by describing the enduring issues and methods employed by developmental psychologists to study life-span development. Three enduring issues are: individual characteristics vs. shared human traits, stability vs. change, and heredity vs. environment. Developmental psychologists use standard research methods in cross-sectional, longitudinal, and biographical studies.

During prenatal development a fertilized egg develops within the uterus into an embryo and then a fetus. Critical periods in development refer to times when potentially harmful substances are likely to affect the fetus. Following birth, a neonate has several reflexive behaviors such as rooting, sucking, swallowing, grasping, and stepping. Newborns also display individual differences in temperament. Senses such as vision are fairly well developed at birth. Visual cliff studies revealed that depth perception is developed by 6 to 12 months of age. Newborns also experience other senses like hearing, taste, and smell.

Dramatic developmental changes occur throughout infancy and early childhood. Physical development occurs in fits and starts, with the most drastic changes in size and weight occurring in the first year. Motor development is marked by milestones that proceed in a proximodistal fashion. Early motor development arises from a combination of maturation of the nervous system among other internal and external factors. Jean Piaget introduced one of the most influential theories of cognitive

development. According to Piaget, cognitive development is marked by four basic stages: sensory-motor, preoperational, concrete operational, and formal operational. It is important to be able to distinguish the stages, the average age range of children within each stage, and the milestones within each stage such as object permanence, mental representation, egocentrism, and conservation. Moral reasoning develops during childhood and adolescence. Based on his "Heinz dilemma" Lawrence Kohlberg proposed three stages of moral reasoning: preconventional level, conventional level, and postconventional level. Like Piaget's theory of cognitive development, Kohlberg's theory is not without criticism.

Language development follows a pattern marked by babbling at around 2 months followed by gradual acquisition of intonation, word recognition, and understanding. First words usually occur at 1 year and are soon followed by holophrases. Sentence and language production increases dramatically after 3 years of age. One theory of language development proposed by Skinner contends that language is acquired through reinforcement. In contrast, Noam Chomsky argues that inborn language acquisition devices exist to facilitate language learning. Recently, Steven Pinker proposed humans have a language instinct.

Social development is influenced by relationships established with people in various settings. Attachment patterns between infants and their parents develop during infancy. Unlike imprinting which rapidly occurs in some animal species, human attachment patterns form more gradually. Establishment of basic trust is followed by development of autonomy in securely attached children. Autonomy is an essential first step in the socialization process. As the child's social world expands, changes continue to occur in the parent-child relationship. Erik Erikson proposed that children experience an initiative vs. guilt conflict between ages 3 and 6. Four basic parenting styles have been identified that affect a child's outlook and behavior. These are: authoritarian, permissive-indifferent, permissive-indulgent, and authoritative. Social skills needed to play with other children develop gradually. First children engage in solitary play, followed by parallel play, and cooperative play. A child's first peer group is usually comprised of family members until a child begins school. The meaning of friendship deepens as children get older. According to Erikson, children enter a stage of industry vs. inferiority between the ages of 7 and 11, a time when making friends becomes critically important. In addition to peer influences, other environmental factors called the nonshared environment influence development. In addition, children are impacted by the amount and quality of care provided by nonfamily caregivers.

Children develop gender identity by about age 3 and gender constancy by age 4 or 5. Gender-role awareness is acquired at a young age and many children develop gender stereotypes and engage in sex-typed behaviors. Both biology and experience contribute to gender differences in behavior. Child development can also be influenced by television. Among other negative outcomes, television viewing may increase aggression, create a variety of sleep disturbances, and reduce social activity. Some evidence suggests television is correlated with positive outcomes such as learning.

Adolescence is a period characterized by physical, cognitive, and social-emotional changes. Physical changes include a growth spurt and the onset of puberty. The onset of menarche in girls usually occurs around 12 1/2 years. Individuals show vast differences in pubertal development, some develop early and others much later. Adolescence is often a very confusing period marked by the first sexual activity. Teenage pregnancy rates are highest in the U.S. Cognitive development during this period is characterized by abstract reasoning. David Elkind proposed two adolescent thought fallacies: the imaginary audience, and the personal fable. Although adolescents face important tasks in their personal and social lives, the reference to adolescence as a period of "storm and stress" may be an exaggeration for most teens. During this time adolescents form a stable sense of self through a process known as identity formation. James Marcia proposed that identity formation occurs following an identity crisis. Relationships with peers change during this period; many adolescents form cliques that give way to mixed-sex groups in mid-adolescence. Conflicts with parents may occur as teens struggle with the physical changes of puberty and as they strive for independence. Major problems faced by adolescents in our society include declines in self-esteem, depression, suicide, and youth violence.

Developmental changes during adulthood are harder to predict. Most adults seek to form loving partnerships and to experience parenthood. Erikson viewed the biggest challenge of adulthood as intimacy vs. isolation. The vast majority of Americans form heterosexual marriage partnerships, but cohabiting and homosexual relationships are increasing. Adult relationships often end as evidenced by divorce rates. Divorce is viewed as a positive step by some, but can greatly affect children. Adult life is further characterized by educational achievements and selection of career pathways. The number of dual-career families has risen dramatically. This often creates additional burdens for the working woman and requires that children be placed in day care. As adults move into midlife, personality changes are marked by a decrease in self-centeredness and improved coping skills. Erikson viewed the major challenge during this period as generativity vs. stagnation. Stagnation may contribute to a midlife crisis. Levinson preferred the term midlife transition to refer to this period of reevaluation. In adult women, the "Change of Life," or menopause, begins around age 45.

Finally, increases in life expectancy have extended the period of late adulthood. Physical changes include the deterioration of the body, posture, and internal organs. Still, most men and women over 65 have active social and sex lives and report being happy. Many people in this stage retire from their careers. Cognitive abilities remain largely intact in older adults but Alzheimer's disease is a concern with later ages, especially beyond 85. Most elderly people cope well with nearing the end of life. Elisabeth Kübler-Ross identified five distinct stages of dealing with death: denial, anger, bargaining, depression, and acceptance.

Learning Objectives

After you have read and studied this chapter, you should be able to complete the following statements.

OBJECTIVES

1. Define developmental psychology and discuss some limitations of the methods used to study development.

2. Describe prenatal, infancy, and child development.

3. What are the four stages of Piaget's theory of cognitive development?

4. Trace language development from infancy through age 5 or 6.

5. Explain the importance of secure attachments between a caregiver and child.

6. Explain how sex-role identity is formed.

7. Summarize the important physical and cognitive changes that the adolescent undergoes during puberty.

8. Discuss the four problems of adolescence: self-esteem, depression, suicide, and eating disorders.

9. Distinguish between the longitudinal and cross-sectional methods as they relate to the study of adulthood. List the disadvantages of the methods and how the disadvantages can be overcome.

10. Identify the central concerns and crises that characterize the young, middle, and late adulthood stages. Explain moral development.

11. Identify Elisabeth Kübler-Ross's five sequential stages through which people pass as they react to their own impending death.

Chapter Outline

The following is an outline conveying the main concepts of this chapter.

1. Enduring Issues and Methods in Developmental Psychology   page 283
   A. Three Enduring Issues
      1. Individual Characteristics vs. Shared Human Traits
      2. Stability vs. Change
      3. Heredity vs. Environment
   B. Cross-sectional study
   C. Cohort
   D. Longitudinal studies
   E. Biographical study
2. Prenatal Development   page 285
   A. Embryo
   B. Fetus
   C. Placenta
   D. Critical period
3. The Newborn   page 287
   A. Neonates
   B. Reflexes
      • Rooting
      • Sucking
      • Swallowing
      • Grasping
      • Stepping
   C. Temperament
   D. Perceptual Abilities
      • Vision
      • Depth perception
         – Visual cliff
      • Other senses
4. Infancy and Childhood   page 290
   A. Physical Development
   B. Motor Development
      • Maturation
   C. Cognitive Development
      • Piaget's Stages of Cognitive Development
         1. Sensory-Motor Stage (Birth–2 yrs.)
            – Object permanence
            – Mental representation
         2. Preoperational Stage (2–7 yrs.)
            – Egocentric

         3. Concrete Operational Stage (7–11 yrs.)
            – Principles of conservation
            – Formal Operational Stage (11–15 yrs.)
      • Criticisms of Piaget's Theory
   D. Moral Development
      • Kohlberg's Stages of Moral Reasoning
         1. Preconventional Level
         2. Conventional Level
         3. Postconventional Level
   E. Language Development
      • Babbling
      • Holophrases
      • Theories of Language Development
      • Skinner's Reinforcemento Reward
      • Chomsky's Language Acquisition Device
      • Steven Pinker
         – Language instinct
      • Bilingualism and Success in School
   F. Social Development
      • Parent-Child Relationships in Infancy: Development of Attachment
         – Imprinting
         – Attachment
         – Autonomy
         – Socialization
      • Parent-Child Relationships in Childhood
         – Erikson: Initiative vs. guilt
         – Parenting Styles
      • Authoritarian
      • Permissive—indifferent
      • Permissive—indulgent
      • Authoritative
      • Relationships with Other Children
         – Solitary play
         – Parallel play
         – Cooperative play
         – Peer Group
      • Erikson's Industry vs. Inferiority

After studying the text and completing the Study Guide activities, answer these questions to determine if you need to review any areas before the course exam.

1. Times when certain internal and external influences have a major impact on development, whereas at other times those same influences would have little impact, are called _____.
   a. developmental surges
   b. growth stages
   c. critical periods
   d. latency period

2. The term used by psychologists to describe the physical/emotional characteristics of the newborn child and young infant is _____.
   a. cognitive capacity
   b. temperament
   c. maturity
   d. development

3. People born during the same period of historical time are called ____.
   a. a cohort
   b. a cross-sectional group
   c. clique
   d. a peerage

4. Children have developed a capacity for self-recognition by the end of the ___ stage.
   a. concrete operations
   b. preoperational
   c. sensory motor
   d. formal operations

5. A characteristic that first shows up in the formal operations stage is ___.
   a. irreversibility
   b. abstract thinking
   c. egocentrism
   d. logical thinking

6. The _____ process teaches children what behaviors and attitudes are appropriate in their family, friendships, and culture.
   a. attachment
   b. socialization
   c. imprinting
   d. anthropomorphism

7. Authoritative parents are to ____ children as permissive parents are to ____ children.
   a. Distrustful; assertive
   b. Self-reliant; dependent
   c. passive; assertive
   d. distrustful; dependent

8. The onset of sexual maturation in adolescence is known as ____.
   a. the growth spurt
   b. maturation
   c. atrophy
   d. puberty

9. The tendency of teenagers to feel that they are always "on stage" and are constantly being judged about their appearance and their behavior is known as the _____.
   a. personal fable
   b. imaginary audience
   c. idealistic tendency
   d. egocentric distortion

10. According to Erikson, developing a stable sense of self and making the transition from dependence on others to dependence on oneself is called _____.
    a. self-actualization
    b. identity formation
    c. the personal fable
    d. identity diffusion

11. The low point of parent-child relationships usually occurs in _____.
    a. late childhood
    b. early adolescence
    c. mid-adolescence
    d. late adolescence

12. When adolescents are asked what they MOST dislike about themselves, they are most likely to say they dislike their _____.
    a. personality
    b. social status
    c. physical appearance
    d. lack of control over their life

13. Suicide is the ____ leading cause of death among adolescents.
    a. second
    b. third
    c. fourth
    d. fifth

14. Couples who lived together before getting married are ___ satisfied with their marriages and ____ likely to get divorced.
    a. less: less
    b. less; more
    c. more; less
    d. more; more

15. The major turning point in most adults' lives is _____.
    a. getting their first job
    b. buying their first house
    c. dealing with aging parents
    d. having and raising children

16. A time when some adults discover they no longer feel fulfilled in their jobs or personal lives and attempt to make a decisive shift in career or lifestyle is called _____.
    a. empty nest syndrome
    b. midlife transition
    c. midlife crisis
    d. life review

17. The majority of older adults are _____.
    a. impotent and incapable of sexual response
    b. uninterested in sex
    c. sexually active
    d. none of the above

18. Older people who were often labeled as "senile" in the past, were most likely suffering from _____.
    a. normal aging
    b. Parkinson's disease
    c. Huntington's disease
    d. Alzheimer's disease

19. Kübler-Ross describes the sequence of stages of dying as _____.
    a. anger, denial, depression, bargaining, acceptance
    b. denial, anger, bargaining, depression, acceptance
    c. denial, bargaining, depression, anger, acceptance
    d. anger, bargaining, depression, denial, acceptance

20. Studies of teenage killers have found that most of the killers had ____ experience with guns.
    a. virtually no
    b. little
    c. moderate
    d. extensive

Answers and Explanations to Multiple Choice Posttest

1. c. The critical period is when certain internal and external influences have a major impact on development and little impact at other times. p. 285

2. b. Temperament refers to the physical and emotional characteristics of the newborn and infant. p. 287

3. a. Cohort refers to a group of people born during the same historical period of time. p. 284

4. c. By the end of the sensory motor stage, Piaget said most toddlers have a capacity for self-recognition and can identify "myself" in the mirror. p. 293

5. b. Abstract thinking first shows up in the formal operations stage, usually in adolescence. p. 294

6. b. The socialization process teaches children socially appropriate behaviors and attitudes. p. 299

7. b. Authoritative parents are to self-reliant children as permissive parents are to dependent children. p. 300

8. d. Puberty is the onset of sexual maturation in adolescence. p. 305

9. b. The imaginary audience is the term Elkind used to describe the delusion that many adolescent's have about being constantly observed by others. p. 307

10. b. Erikson termed identity formation as the time when young people make the transition from dependence on others to self-dependency. p. 307

11. b. The low point in parent-child relationships is usually in early adolescence when physical changes are occurring. p. 308

12. c. Adolescents tend to dislike their physical appearance more than anything else about themselves, leading to low self-esteem and possible eating disorders. p. 309

13. b. Suicide is the third leading cause of death among teens, after accidents and homicides. p. 309

14. b. Couples who cohabitated before marriage are less satisfied and more likely to divorce. They may have been more tentative about the relationship to begin with. p. 312

15. d. Having and raising children is the major turning point in most adults' lives due to increased duty, obligation, time, and energy involved. p. 312

16. c. The midlife crisis is a time when some adults discover a lack of fulfillment and attempt to make a radical shift in their career or lifestyle. p. 316

17. c. The majority of older adults are sexually active. p. 320

18. d. Alzheimer's disease used to be considered rare; however, now it is considered what was labeled 'senile' in the past. p. 320

19. b. Kubler-Ross's five stages of accepting one's approaching death as: denial, anger. bargaining, depression, and acceptance. p. 321

20. d. Killer kids were found to have extensive experience with guns and easy access to them. p. 310

Students identified the following words from the text as needing more explanation. This page can be cut-out, folded in half, and used as a bookmark for this chapter.

A

Abrupt	action or change without preparation or warning; stop or cut off
Accustomed	adapted to existing conditions; being in the habit of something
Acquisition	new, added, or acquired characteristic, trait or ability; to get as one's own
Animosity	ill will or resentment leading to active hostility
Approach	to make advances in order to create a desired result in a particular manner
Atrophy	decrease in size, arrested development or wasting away; degeneration
Awkward	lacking dexterity or skill, expertness or lacking ease and grace

B

Barrage	vigorous or rapid outpouring; projection of many things at once
Bilingual	expressed in two languages, especially with equal fluency
Broadside	attack attack that is directed or placed sideways

C

Callous	hardened; feeling noemotion or sympathy for others
Candid	honest, sincere without deception; may be frank, blunt, or critical
Chaos	state of utter confusion; unpredictable behavior
Cohabitation	to live in together as or as if a married couple
Coincide	to be in agreement; correspond in nature, character, or function
Colicky	acute abdominal pain usually suffered by babies
Congenital	existing at birth; acquired during development in the uterus; not heredity

D

Defuse	to make less harmful or tense
Depersonalization	deprive of the sense of personal identity; make impersonal
Devastate	reduce to chaos, disorder helplessness; bring to ruin by violent action
Discern	discriminate; see or understand the subtle differences
Disengage	release or detach oneself form something that involves or engages; withdraw
Disparity	different, distinct in quality or character; inharmonious, incompatible elements
Distracted	mentally confused, troubled; may seem distant or aloof
Doleful look	expressing grief or sadness
Dredge up	bring to light by deeply searching
Dutiful	filled with or motivated by a sense of duty

E

Entrust	trust or put confidence in another person
Evidence	something that provides proof; an indication or outward sign

G

Give and Take	making mutual concessions; compromise; usually good natured exchange of ideas or comments
Grievance	complaint; cause of distress or a reason to complain or resist

H

Hair trigger	immediate responsiveness to the slightest stimulus
Hard driving	
Hazard	source of danger or risk

I

Illustrate	make clear by giving an example; clarify
Implement	carry out, accomplish, means of expression; put in action
Incredible	too improbable or extraordinary to be believed
Inclusive	covering all items; broad in scope or orientation
Inevitable	unavoidable; cannot be evaded
Indignity	insult, humiliate; treatment that undermines a person's dignity or self-respect

L

Lament	wail; mourn aloud; strong expression of sorrow or regret

M

Methodology	a discipline's body of rules and procedures
Milestones	significant points in development
Mingle	associate; come in contact with; mix together without losing identity
Mislead	to deliberately lead astray in a wrong direction or action
Modify	make basic changes in or to

O

Odorous	strong distinctive smell whether pleasant or unpleasant
Outrage	arouse anger or resentment usually by a serious offense

P

Palatial house	magnificent; similar to a palace; lavish and stately
Perpetually	valid for all time; lasting and enduring indefinitely
Pervade	to diffuse throughout every part; distribute, spread or scatter
Placid	serenely free of interruption or disturbance; calm
Postpone	put off until a later time; delay

R

Rationale	underlying reasoning or explanation of opinion, belief or practice
Rear	to bring a person to maturity through nurturing care and education
Reserved	restrained in words and actions
Revere	show devotion and honor to
Rudimentary	fundamental or basic principles

S

Sacrifice	to give up or suffer a loss for an ideal, belief, or desired end
Shower	give in abundance; generosity
Shrug off	play down; soft-pedal; minimize; brush aside; underestimate intentionally
Siblings	one of two or more children having common parents or things related by a common tie or characteristic
Silent treatment	completely ignoring a person by silence as a means of expressing contempt or disapproval
Span	extend across an individual's lifetime; a limited time period
Stagnant	not advancing or developing; not moving forward
"Storm and stress"	(sturm und drang) high emotionalism and rousing action; turmoil
Superordinate	superior in rank, class, or status

T

Turmoil	extreme confusion, agitation, or commotion
Tentative	doubt, indecision, uncertainty; hesitant to make a decision
Take stock of	take an inventory of resources or prospects
Taboo	banned, forbidden, not allowed, prohibited

U

Ultimatum	final demand or condition whose rejection will lead another action
Undeniable	unquestionable true; genuine

Uninhibited	expressive, high spirited; boisterously informal
Unpopular	viewed or received unfavorably by the public
Unisex	not distinguishable as male or female; suitable or designed for both sexes
Usher in	mark or observe the beginning of; to bring into being

V

Vanish	pass quickly from sight or completely from existence; disappear
Victimize	subject to deception or fraud; cheat; make a victim of by objecting someone to hardship, oppression, or mistreatment

W

Wail	loud lament; prolonged cry of sound expressing grief, pain, or mourning
Worthwhile	regarded as being worthy of the time or effort spent
Wronged	being injured unjustly

Z

Zest	gusto, keen enjoyment, exciting quality

Key Vocabulary Terms

Cut out each term and use as study cards.
Definition is on the back side of each term.

Developmental psychology	Prenatal development
Cross-sectional study	Fetus
Cohort	Critical period
Longitudinal study	Neonate
Biographical or retrospective study	Temperament

Development from conception to birth.	Study of the changes that occur in people from birth through old age.
A developing human between 3 months after conception and birth.	Method of studying developmental changes by comparing people of different ages at about the same time.
A time when certain internal and external influences have a major effect on development; at other periods, the same influences will have little or no effect.	Group of people born during the same period in historical time.
Newborn baby.	Method of studying developmental changes by evaluating the same people at different points in their lives.
Characteristic patterns of emotional reactions and emotional self-regulation.	Method of studying developmental changes by reconstructing people's past through interviews and inferring the effects of past events that occurred in the past on current behaviors.

Maturation	Egocentric
Sensory-motor stage	Concrete operational stage
Object permanence	Principles of conservation
Mental representation	Formal operational stage
Preoperational stage	Language acquisition device

Unable to see things from another's point of view.	Automatic biological unfolding of development in an organism as a function of the passage of time.
In Piaget's theory, the stage of cognitive development between 7 and 11 years of age, in which the individual can attend to more than one thing at a time and understand someone else's point of view.	In Piaget's theory, the stage of cognitive development between birth and 2 years, in which the individual develops object permanence and acquires the ability to form mental representations.
The concept that the quality of a substance is not altered by reversible changes in its apperance.	The concept that things continue to exist even when they are out of sight.
In Piaget's theory, the stage of cognitive development between 11 and 15 years of age, in which the individual becomes capable of abstract thought.	Mental image or symbol (such as words) used to think about or remember an object, a person, or an event.
A hypothetical neural mechanism for acquiring language that is presumed to be "wired into" all humans.	In Piaget's theory, the stage of cognitive development between 2-7 years, in which the individual becomes able to use mental representations and language to describe, remember, and reason.

Imprinting	Gender identity
Attachment	Gender constancy
Autonomy	Gender-role awareness
Socialization	Gender stereotypes
Peer group	Sex-typed behavior

A little girl's knowledge that she is a girl, and a little boy's knowledge that he is a boy.

In certain species, the tendency to follow the first moving thing (usually its mother) it sees after it is born or hatched.

The realization that gender does not change with age.

Emotional bond that develops in the first year of life that makes human babies cling to their caregivers for safety and comfort.

Knowledge of what behavior is appropriate for each gender.

Sense of independence; desire not to be controlled by others.

General beliefs about characteristics that men and women are presumed to have.

Process by which children learn the behaviors and attitudes appropriate to their family and their culture.

Socially prescribed ways of behaving that differ for boys and girls.

A network of same-aged friends and acquaintances who give one another emotional and social support.

Puberty	Clique
Menarche	Midlife crisis
Identity formation	Midlife transition
Identity crisis	Menopause
Embryo	Alzheimer's disease

Groups of adolescents with similar interests and strong mutual attachment.	The onset of sexual maturation, with accompanying physical development.
A time when adults discover they no longer feel fulfilled in their jobs or personal lives and attempt to make a decisive shift in career or lifestyle.	First menstrual period.
According to Levinson, a process whereby adults assess the past and formulate new goals for the future.	Erikson's term for the development of a stable sense of self necessary to make the transition from dependence on others to dependence on oneself.
Time in a woman's life when menstruation ceases.	Period of intense self-examination and decision making; part of the process of identity formation.
A disorder common in late adulthood that is characterized by progressive losses in memory and changes in personality. It is believed to be caused by a deterioration of the brain's structure and function.	A developing human between 3 months after conception and birth.

Fetal alcohol syndrome (FAS)	Personal fable
Babbling	
Holophrases	
Growth spurt	
Imaginary audience	

	A disorder that occurs in children of women who drink alcohol during pregnancy that is characterized by facial deformities, heart defects, stunted growth, and cognitive impairments.
Elkind's term for adolescents' delusion that they are unique, very important, and invulnerable.	A baby's vocalizations, consisting of repetition of consonant-vowel combinations.
	One-word sentences commonly used by children under 2 years of age.
	A rapid increase in height and weight that occurs during adolescence.
	Elkind's term for adolescents' delusion that they are constantly being observed by others.

10 Personality

Chapter Focus

This chapter examines personality, an individual's unique pattern of thoughts, feelings, and behaviors that persists over time and across situations. Throughout the chapter, different theoretical paradigms of personality are described. Among these are: psychodynamic theories, humanistic personality theories, trait theories, and cognitive-social learning theories. It is important to be able to distinguish between each theory and to know the key people behind each theory and their major contributions.

Psychodynamic theories contend that psychological forces influence personality. Sigmund Freud stressed the influences of the unconscious and advanced his ideas through psychoanalytic theory and therapy. Freud theorized that personality is formed around the id, the ego, and the superego. The id operates through the pleasure principle whereas the ego operates through the reality principle. The superego oversees moral reasoning and sets standards for the ego ideal.

Freud believed personality developed by experiencing and responding to the energy created by sexual instincts, the libido. If libido remains in one part of the body then psychosexual development can stop, a condition known as fixation. Freud identified five psychosexual stages related to personality development: the oral stage (0-18 months), anal stage (18 months to 3 1/2 yrs), phallic stage (after age 3), latency period (5–13), and the genital stage (puberty). During the phallic stage children may experience parental conflicts, known as the Oedipus complex in boys and the Electra complex in girls.

Carl Jung expanded Freud's limited view of libido to represent the psychic energy of all life forces. Jung believed the unconscious consists of the personal unconscious and the collective unconscious that houses special memories shared by all humans. He called these collective experiences archetypes and believed persona was a special archetype that shaped personality. Jung categorized attitudes as extroverted or introverted and people were viewed as either rational or irrational individuals.

Alfred Adler believed personality is shaped by compensation, the efforts put forth to overcome weaknesses or feelings of inferiority. Those unable to overcome these obstacles were at risk of developing inferiority complexes. Another psychodynamic theorist, Karen Horney, contended that environmental and social experiences during childhood are the major factors that shape personality. According to Horney, anxiety originates from both sexual and nonsexual conflicts in childhood. Anxious adults employ one of three neurotic trends to handle problems: submission, aggression, or detachment.

Erik Erikson adopted a psychodynamic view that was more socially oriented and proposed that people experience eight stages of personality development. Erikson's stages are: trust vs. mistrust, autonomy vs. shame and doubt, initiative vs. guilt, industry vs. inferiority, identity vs. role confusion, intimacy vs. isolation, generativity vs. stagnation, ego integrity vs. despair. Success in each stage is dependent upon adjustment during the previous stage.

Psychoanalytic theorists would differ in their analysis and interpretation of the case of Jaylene Smith that was introduced at the beginning of the chapter. Modern psychologists view psychodynamic theories as having limited scientific support but nonetheless attractive for their attempt to explain the origins of human behavior.

Humanistic personality theories differ from psychodynamic theories in that goodness in people and realizing one's potential are seen as the motivating forces toward higher levels of functioning. Carl Rogers believed people develop personalities as they strive toward positive goals. According to Rogers, organisms are driven by actualizing tendencies to fulfill their biological potentials. Humans are also driven by self-actualizing tendencies to fulfill their self-concepts and become a fully functioning person. Unconditional positive regard is more likely to promote full functioning than conditional positive regard. Humanists like Rogers would view Jaylene's case as stemming from a discrepancy between her self-concept and her inborn capacities. Humanistic theories have been criticized for their inability to be scientifically verified.

Trait theorists assert that people differ to the degree to which they possess certain personality traits. Using factor analysis, Raymond Cattell, demonstrated that traits tend to cluster in groups with individuals having about 16 basic traits. Eysenck reduced personality to three basic dimensions: emotional stability, introversion-extroversion, and psychoticism. Contemporary trait theorists contend personality is comprised of five basic dimensions that may represent universal dimensions across cultures. Known as the Big Five, or five-factor model, these are: extroversion, emotional stability, agreeableness, conscientiousness, and openness to experience. Trait theorists would view Jaylene as having certain traits above others. Although trait theories are easier to scientifically examine, they are primarily descriptive and may oversimplify personality.

Cognitive-social learning theories contend that personal and situational factors combine to shape behavior. Albert Bandura stressed that what a person anticipates in a situation, or expectancies, affect behavior and that people conduct themselves according to performance standards. Self-efficacy arises when people meet their internal performance standards. People approach and evaluate situations through expectancies, such as locus of control; individuals either have an internal or external locus of control. Expectancies become part of a person's explanatory style that significantly affects behavior. Cognitive-social theorists believe personalities are fairly stable but behaviors may be less consistent. Jaylene's case would be viewed as a result of learning by observation, reinforcement, and punishment. Although they cannot explain all aspects of personality, cognitive-social learning theories can be scientifically studied, help to explain inconsistent behavior, and have led to useful therapies.

Finally, personality is assessed through tests that are both reliable and valid. Psychologists employ four basic tools: the personal interview; direct observation of behavior; objective tests; and projective tests. Personal interviews may be structured or unstructured. Objective tests include the 16 Personality Factor Questionnaire, the NEO-PI-R, and the Minnesota Multiphasic Personality Inventory (MMPI). Projective tests include the Rorschach test and the Thematic Apperception Test.

Learning Objectives

After you have read and studied this chapter, you should be able to complete the following statements.

OBJECTIVES

1. Define personality.

2. Summarize the interaction of elements of personality according to Freud's theory: id, ego, and superego. Identify Freud's five stages of psychosexual development.

3. Differentiate among the theories of Jung, Adler, and Horney. Identify what these theories have in common.

4. Identify Erik Erikson's eight stages of personality development.

5. Contrast Carl Rogers's humanistic theory with Freudian theory.

6. Explain trait theory.

7. List the five basic traits that most describe differences in personality.

8. Compare cognitive social-learning theories to early views of personality.

9. Describe the four basic tools psychologists use to measure personality. List two objective tests, two projective tests, and their uses.

Chapter Outline

The following is an outline conveying the main concepts of this chapter.

Personality
The Case of Jaylene Smith
1.   Psychodynamic Theories   page 328
   A.   Sigmund Freud
- Unconscious
- Psychoanalysis
- How personality is structured
  - Id
  - Pleasure principle
  - Ego
  - Reality principle
  - Superego
  - Ego ideal
- How Personality Develops
  - Libido
  - Fixation
- Psychosexual Stages
  - Oral Stage
  - Anal Stage
  - Phallic Stage
- Oedipus complex
- Electra complex
  - Latency Period
  - Genital Stage

   B.   Carl Jung
- Personal unconscious
- Collective unconscious
- Archetypes
- Persona
- Extrovert
- Introvert
- Rational individuals
- Irrational individuals

   C.   Alfred Adler
- Compensation
- Inferiority complex

   D.   Karen Horney
- Anxiety
- Neurotic Trends

   E.   Eric Erikson
- Eight Stages of Development
  1. Trust vs. Mistrust
  2. Autonomy vs. Shame and Doubt
  3. Initiative vs. Guilt
  4. Industry vs. Inferiority
  5. Identity vs. Role Confusion
  6. Intimacy vs. Isolation
  7. Generativity vs. Stagnation
  8. Ego Integrity vs. Despair

   F.   A Psychodynamic View of Jaylene Smith

   G.   Evaluating Psychodynamic Theories

2.   Humanistic Personality Theories page 338
   A.   Carl Rogers
- Actualizing tendency
- Self-actualizing tendency
- Fully functioning person
- Unconditional positive regard
- Conditional positive regard

   B.   A Humanistic View of Jaylene Smith

   C.   Evaluating Humanistic Theories

3.   Trait Theories p. 340
   A.   Personality traits
   B.   Factor analysis
   C.   Big Five
- Extroversion
- Emotional stability
- Agreeableness
- Conscientiousness
- Openness to experience

UNDERSTANDING THE WORLD AROUND US: Are the Big Five Personality Traits Universal?   page 342

   D.   A Trait View of Jaylene Smith
   E.   Evaluating Trait Theories

4.   Cognitive-Social Learning Theories   page 344
   A.   Expectancies, Self-Efficacy, and Locus of Control
- Cognitive-social learning theory
- Expectancies
- Performance Standards
- Self-Efficacy
- Locus of Control
  - Internal locus
  - External locus
- Explanatory style
- Self-efficacy

Multiple Choice Posttest

After studying the text and completing the Study Guide activities, answer these questions to determine if you need to review any areas before the course exam.

1. Which of the following is NOT an aspect of personality?
   a. enduring
   b. unique
   c. stable
   d. unpredictable

2. For Freud, the term "sexual instinct" refers to _____.
   a. the personal unconscious
   b. erotic sexuality
   c. any form of pleasure
   d. childhood experiences

3. For Freud, the only personality structure present at birth is the ___.
   a. id
   b. ego
   c. superego
   d. ego ideal

4. The proper chronological order of Freud's psychosexual stages is _____.
   a. oral, anal, phallic, latency, genital
   b. anal, oral, phallic, latency, genital
   c. anal, oral, genital, latency, phallic
   d. oral anal, genital, phallic, latency

5. According to Jung, the memories and behavior patterns inherited from past generations are part of the _____.
   a. persona
   b. alter-ego
   c. personal unconscious
   d. collective unconscious

6. Collective memories of experiences people have had in common since prehistoric times, such as mothers, heroes, or villains are called _____ by Carl Jung.
   a. personas
   b. celebrities' heroes
   c. archetypes
   d. collective

7. Marley is a joiner. She is interested in other people and events going on around her in the world. In Jung's view, she is an _____.
   a. archetype
   b. endomorph
   c. introvert
   d. extrovert

8. Adler's emphasis on people's positive social strivings has caused him to be labeled by many psychologists as the "father" of ____ psychology.
   a. humanistic
   b. Gestalt
   c. cognitive
   d. social

9. Erikson suggested that success in each of the eight life stages he outlined depends upon _____.
   a. resolution of the inferiority complex
   b. cognitive and moral development
   c. resolution of the Oedipus complex
   d. adjustment during the previous stage

10. Erikson's stage of autonomy versus shame and doubt corresponds approximately with Freud's ____ stage of psychosexual development.
    a. oral
    b. anal
    c. phallic
    d. latency

11. Erikson argues that for people to establish a sense of intimacy, they must feel secure in their _____.
    a. identity
    b. initiative
    c. persona
    d. integrity

12. Studies have found that the "Big Five" dimensions of personality _____.
    a. may only represent personality in Western industrial cultures
    b. may only represent personality in North American culture
    c. may only represent personality in non-Western, nonindustrial cultures
    d. may represent universal dimensions of personality across cultures

13. Each of the following is one of the "Big Five" dimensions of personality EXCEPT ____.
    a. neuroticism
    b. agreeableness
    c. emotional stability
    d. extroversion

14. The most widely used objective personality test is the ___.
    a. 16 PF
    b. TAT
    c. Rorschach
    d. MMPI

15. A behaviorist would prefer ____ when assessing someone's personality.
    a. objective tests
    b. observation
    c. interviews
    d. projective tests

16. The Rorschach test relies on the interpretation of ___ to understand personality.
    a. a 16-part questionnaire
    b. cards with human figures on them
    c. 10 cards containing ink blots
    d. sentence completion exercises

17. When explaining personality, cognitive-social learning theorists put ____ at the center of personality.
    a. unconscious processes
    b. emotional stability
    c. mental processes
    d. environmental cues

18. Bill believes he can control his own fate. He feels that by hard work, skill, and training it is possible to avoid punishments and find rewards. Rotter would say that Bill has a(n) ____ locus of control.
    a. internal
    b. external
    c. primary
    d. secondary

19. According to Bandura, the expectancy that one's efforts will be successful is called _____.
    a. self-esteem
    b. locus of control
    c. self-actualizing tendency
    d. self-efficacy

20. Which of the following is NOT one of the four basic types of tools used by psychologists to measure personality?
    a. personal interview
    b. objective tests
    c. projective tests
    d. aptitude tests

21. Which of the following is NOT related to expectancies as described by cognitive-social theory?
    a. performance standards
    b. actualizing tendency
    c. locus of control
    d. explanatory style

Label Drawings

Fill In the Blanks

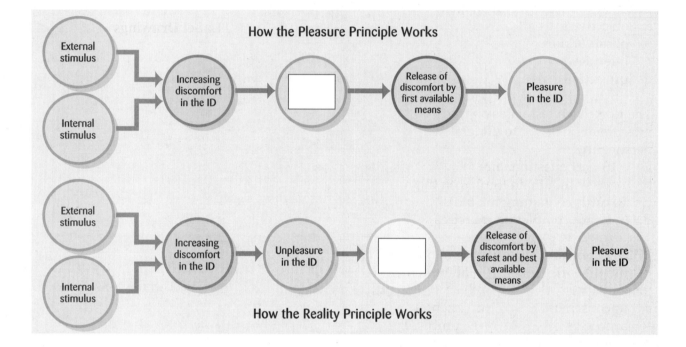

SUMMARY TABLE

Theories of Personality (Supply the roots of personality)

Theory	Roots of Personality	Methods of Assessing
_____ Psychodynamic	a. Relatively permanent dispositions within the individual that cause the person to think, feel, and act in characteristic ways.	Projective tests, personal interviews
_____ Humanistic	b. A drive toward personal growth and higher levels of functioning.	Objective tests and personal interviews
_____ Trait problem from early childhood	c. Unconscious thoughts, feelings, motives, and conflicts; repressed	Objective tests
_____ Social Learning Theories	d. Determined by past reinforcement and punishment as well as by observing what happens to other people.	Interviews, objective tests, observations

Answers and Explanations to Multiple Choice Posttest

1. d. Unpredictability is not an aspect of personality. p. 327

2. c. For Freud, 'sexual instinct' refers to any form of pleasure. p. 329

3. a. For Freud, the id is the only personality structure present at birth. p. 329

4. a. The proper order of Freud's psychosexual stages is: oral, anal, phallic, latency, genital. pp. 330–331

5. d. The collective unconscious consists of inherited memories and behavior patterns. p. 331

6. c. Archetypes are collective memories of common types, such as mothers and heroes. p. 332

7. d. Extroverts are interested in being with other people and in the world. p. 332

8. a. Adler is considered by many to be the "father" of humanistic psychology. p. 332

9. d. Success in Erikson's eight life stages depends on adjustment during the previous stage. p. 334

10. b. Erikson's autonomy versus shame and doubt stage corresponds with Freud's anal stage. p. 334

11. a. For Erikson, people must feel secure in their identity to establish a sense of intimacy. p. 335

12. d. The "Big Five" dimensions of personality may represent universal dimensions across cultures. p. 341

13. a. Neuroticism is not one of the Big Five dimensions. p. 341

14. d. The MMPI is the most widely used objective personality test. p. 348

15. b. Behaviorists prefer observation when assessing personality. p. 347

16. c. The Rorschach test uses 10 cards containing inkblots. p. 350

17. c. Cognitive-social learning theorists put mental processes at the center of personality. p. 344

18. b. Bill has an external locus of control. p. 344

19. d. Self-efficacy is the expectancy that one's efforts will succeed. p. 344

20. d. Aptitude tests are not one of the four basic types of personality tests. p. 337

21. b. Actualizing tendency was proposed by Carl Rogers, a humanist. p. 338

Label Drawings

Fill in the Blanks

Fig. 10.2 p. 330

Pleasure Principle: Unpleasure in the Id

Reality Principle: Rational thought of Ego

Summary Table p. 347

Roots of Personality p. 347

___C.__ Psychodynamic
___B.__ Humanistic
___A.__ Trait
___D.__ Social Learning Theories

Language Support

Students identified the following words from the text as needing more explanation. This page can be cut-out, folded in half, and used as a bookmark for this chapter.

A

Alliance	a bond or connection between people
Altercation	a noisy, heated, angry dispute
Amiable	friendly, sociable, agreeable, congenial
Amoral	lacking moral sensibility; neither moral nor immoral
Assail	attack violently with blows or words
Attain	achieve, carry out successfully, gain possession of, obtain
Autonomous	self-contained; existing independently

B

Belittle	minimize or degrade; claim something is less than it seems
Bicker	engage in a petty quarrel

C

Consensus	general agreement arrived at by most of those concerned
Constellation	gathering of related people, qualities or things; pattern or arrangement
Conviction	strong persuasion or belief or opinion
Cordially	warmly, genuinely, cheerfully, or graciously
Craving	intense, urgent, or abnormal desire or longing

D

Descriptors	something that describes or identifies
Disheartening	to cause to lose one's spirit or morale
Disposition	prevailing tendency, mood or inclination; temperamental makeup
Dovetail	to fit together into a whole
Drab	characterized by dullness and monotony

E

Embodied	to make concrete and perceptible; represent as a person or with human qualities
Encode	convert from one communication system to another; specify the genetic code for
Endanger	create a dangerous situation or expose to a peril

F

Fruition	realization, attainment, or enjoyment of anything desired

G

Gullibility	easily deceived or cheated; naive

H

Hindsight	perception of the nature of an event after it has happened
Hostility	conflict; opposing or resisting in thought or principle; aggressive action

I

Imperatives	unavoidable obligation or requirement; absolutely necessary or required
Indebted	being obliged for a favor, owing gratitude or recognition to; owing money
Intangible	incapable of being felt, touched, or discerned by the senses or mind
Intuitive	immediate knowing without apparent use of rational thought
Invisible	imperceptible by the senses or mind; subtle; hidden

J

Jock	an athlete (person active in sports); usually a college student

L

Lofty rising to a great height; elevated in character or status

M

Magnitude importance, quality, or caliber of something; great size or extent

Mediocre of moderate or low quality or value; ordinary, so-so

Millennia period of 1,000 years

Mysticism vague speculation; belief without sound basis

O

One-dimensional shallow, superficial, lacking depth

Outbursts violent expression or feeling; a surge of activity or growth

P

Per se as such, essential nature; in, of, by or for itself

Proposition proposal, something offered for consideration or acceptance

Prowess extraordinary ability

R

Reconcile restore friendship and harmony; resolve a disagreement

Recruit seek to enroll or enlist; newcomer to a field or activity

Redundancy needless repetition; part of a message that can be eliminated without losing the essential meaning

Retort answer by a counter argument or sharp response

S

Salient of notable significance; prominent; noticeable

Self-preservation natural or instinctive tendency to protect one's own existence

Spawn bring forth or generate; bring to bear; produce; bring into existence

Stifle repress; withhold from expression; deprive of oxygen

Subordinate lower rank or position; treat with less value or importance

Superficial concerned with the obvious or apparent; shallow; lacking substance or depth

Surmount overcome barriers or obstacles; surpass or exceed in accomplishment

T

Tactfully keen sense of what is appropriate and considerate to say or do in order to maintain good relations with others or avoid offense

Tenet principle, belief, or doctrine generally held to be true

Truant one who shirks duty; staying out of school without permission

U

Unbridled free from restraint; spontaneous; set loose or free

Undermine weaken gradually so as to be well established before becoming apparent

V

Vanity inflated pride in oneself or one's appearance; conceit

W

Watchdog one that guards against loss, waste, theft, or undesirable practices

Key Vocabulary Terms

Cut out each term and use as study cards.
Definition is on the back side of each term.

Personality	Pleasure principle
Psychodynamic theories	Ego
Unconscious	Reality principle
Psychoanalysis	Superego
Id	Ego ideal

According to Freud, the way in which the id seeks immediate gratification of an instinct.	An individual's unique pattern of thoughts, feelings, and behaviors that persist over time and across situations.
Freud's term for the part of the personality that mediates between environmental demands (reality), conscience (superego), and instinctual needs (id); now often used as synonym for "self."	Personality theories contending that behavior results from psychological forces that interact within the individual, often outside conscious awareness.
According to Freud, the way in which the ego seeks to satisfy instinctual demands safely and effectively in the real world.	In Freud's theory, all the ideas, thoughts, and feelings of which we are not and normally cannot become aware.
According to Freud, the social and parental standards the individual has internalized; the conscience and the ego ideal.	The theory of personality Freud developed as well as the form of therapy he invented.
The part of the superego that consists of standards of what one would like to be.	In Freud's theory of personality, the collection of unconscious urges and desires that continually seek expression.

Libido	Oedipus and Electra complexes
Fixation	Latency period
Oral stage	Genital stage
Anal stage	Personal unconscious
Phallic stage	Collective unconscious

According to Freud, a child's sexual attachment to the parent of the opposite sex and jealousy toward the parent of the same sex: generally occurs in the phallic stage.	According to Freud, the energy generated by the sexual instinct.
In Freud's theory of personality, a period in which the child appears to have no interest in the opposite sex; occurs after the phallic stage.	According to Freud, a partial or complete halt at some point in the individual's psychosexual development.
In Freud's theory of personality development, the final stage of normal adult sexual development, which is usually marked by mature sexuality.	First stage in Freud's theory of personality development in which the infant's erotic feelings center on the mouth, lips, and tongue.
In Jung's theory of personality, one of the two levels of the unconscious; it contains the individual's repressed thoughts, forgotten experiences, and undeveloped ideas.	Second stage in Freud's theory of personality development, in which a child's erotic feelings center on the anus and on elimination.
In Jung's theory of personality, the level of the unconscious that is inherited and common to all members of a species.	Third stage in Freud's theory of personality development, in which erotic feelings center on the genitals.

Archetypes	Humanistic personality theory
Persona	Actualizing tendency
Compensation	Self-actualizing tendency
Inferiority complex	Fully functioning person
Neurotic trends	Unconditional positive regard

Any personality theory that asserts the fundamental goodness of people and their striving toward higher levels of functioning.	In Jung's theory of personality, thought forms common to all human beings, stored in the collective unconscious.
According to Rogers, the drive of every organism to fulfill its biological potential and to become what it is inherently capable of becoming.	According to Jung, our public self, the mask we put on to represent ourselves to others.
According to Rogers, the drive of human beings to fulfill their self-concepts, or the images they have of themselves.	According to Adler, the person's effort to overcome imagined or real personal weaknesses.
According to Rogers, an individual whose self-concept closely resembles his or her inborn capacities or potentials.	In Adler's theory, the fixation on feelings of personal inferiority that results in emotional and social paralysis.
In Rogers's theory, the full acceptance and love of another person regardless of that person's behavior.	In Horney's theory, irrational strategies for coping with emotional problems and minimizing anxiety.

Personality traits	Locus of control
Factor analysis	Self-efficacy
Big Five	Performance standards
Cognitive-social learning theories	Objective tests
Expectancies	16 Personality Factor Questions

According to Rotter, an expectancy about whether reinforcement is under internal or external control.

Dimensions or characteristics on which people differ in distinctive ways.

According to Bandura, the expectancy that one's efforts will be successful.

A statistical technique, used by Cattell, that demonstrates that various traits tend to cluster in groups.

In Bandura's theory, standards that people develop to rate the adequacy of their own behavior in a variety of situations.

Five traits or basic dimensions currently thought to be of central importance in describing personality.

Personality tests that are administered and scored in a standard way.

Personality theories that view behavior as the product of the interaction of cognition, learning and past experiences, and the immediate environment.

Objective personality test created by Cattell that provides scores on the 16 traits he identified.

In Bandura's view, what a person anticipates in a situation or as a result of behaving in certain ways.

MMPI	Introvert
Projective tests	Conditional positive regard
Rorschach test	NEO-PI-R
Thematic Apperception Test (TAT)	
Extrovert	

According to Jung, a person who usually focuses on his or her own thoughts and feelings.	The most widely used objective personality test, originally intended for psychiatric diagnosis.
In Rogers's theory, acceptance and love that are dependent on behaving in certain ways and on fulfilling certain conditions.	Personality tests, such as the Rorschach inkblot test; consisting of ambiguous or unstructured material that do not limit the response to be given.
An objective personality test designed to assess the Big Five personality traits.	A projective test composed of ambiguous inkblots, the way a person interprets the blots is thought to reveal aspects of his or her personality.
	A projective test composed of ambiguous pictures about which a person writes a complete story.
	According to Jung, a person who usually focuses on social life and the external world instead of on his or her internal experience.

11 Stress and Health Psychology

Chapter Focus

This chapter examines the adjustments people make to cope with stress, a state of psychological tension or strain. Stress is often studied within the subfield of psychology called health psychology; health psychologists aim to understand the relationship between psychological factors and physical health and illness. The chapter begins with an introduction to the sources of stress, followed by coping with stress, how stress affects health, sources of extreme stress, and ends with consideration of the well-adjusted person.

Sources of stress include life changes, everyday hassles, pressure, frustration, and conflict. The College Life Stress Inventory (CLSI) is a questionnaire used to measure the amount of change present in a student's life. Five common sources of frustration have been identified: delays, lack of resources, losses, failure, and discrimination. Kurt Lewin proposed three basic types of conflict: approach/approach conflict, avoidance/avoidance conflict, and approach/avoidance conflict. Self-imposed stress may come from within an individual who holds irrational, self-defeating thoughts. Individual differences in stress result from differences in interpretation of a potentially stressful situation, levels of self-confidence, and overall world view. Optimists tend to see events as challenges to overcome, whereas pessimists are more likely to dwell on failure. People with an internal locus of control see themselves as being empowered to affect their situations and have increased confidence in difficult situations. Those with an external locus of control tend to feel helpless and view events negatively, perceiving themselves as victims of circumstances.

Certain individuals possess hardiness, the ability to tolerate and even thrive on stressful situations and change. Resilience is the ability to regain confidence, a hopeful attitude, and good spirits after periods of extreme stress or adverse circumstances. Mentor programs and after-school activities appear to build resilience in high-risk children.

Cognitive or behavioral adaptations must be made to cope with psychological stress. Direct coping and defensive coping are two types of adjustment. Direct coping is problem oriented and seeks to intentionally change the stressful situation in one of three manners: confrontation, compromise, or withdrawal. There may be dangers to coping by withdrawal.

Defensive coping involves deceiving oneself about the causes of a stressful situation that may otherwise be unbearable. The self-deception may be unconscious, as Freud concluded, or consciously realized. Defense mechanisms include denial, repression, projection, identification, regression, intellectualization, reaction formation, displacement, and sublimation. Such defense mechanisms can allow for high levels of adaptation to stressful situations, and in some cases may be necessary to maintain a person's feelings of adequacy and self-worth when coping with severe stress. However, defenses can hinder successful adaptation, and may interfere with a person's ability to face a problem directly, causing complications to the original feelings of stress.

Stress depends to a significant degree on the environment in which a person lives. Feelings of hopelessness, hostility, anxiety, and depression all increase when the socioeconomic status falls. This appears due to the lack of means, support, and resources on which to draw in times of hardship.

Gender differences have been found in stress-related studies. Women report greater experiences of stress than men under similar circumstances. Coping strategies for men and women have been found to be similar in many aspects, but men may be more likely to turn to alcohol when depressed, while women tend to revisit the negative emotions surrounding an event or mood. Gender differences in response to stress may be evolutionary adaptations from hunter/gatherer ancestors.

Stress can negatively impact health. Walter Cannon first described the fight-or-flight response, a physiological response to stress. Hans Selye proposed a 3-stage response to stress known as the General Adaptation Syndrome (GAS). Stage 1 is alarm reaction, stage 2 is resistance, and stage 3 is exhaustion. Each stage has distinct physical and psychological components. Prolonged stress may lead to physical illness.

Coronary heart disease (CHD) may be contributed to by stress. Frequent or chronic stress can damage heart and blood vessels, causing arrhythmias and arteriosclerosis. Mental stress at work is linked with CHD, as are negative emotions, especially those exhibited by people with Type A behavior patterns. Such personalities have much higher heart rate and blood pressure levels when under stress, and both contribute to CHD. Depression may also increase the risk of heart disease and premature death. Low-fat diets and stress-management techniques have proven effective treatments.

Psychoneuroimmunology (PNI) studies the effects of chronic stress on the body's immune system. PNI has established a link between stress and cancer in animals. Stress impairs the immune system so that cancerous cells may become established and then spread more quickly around the body. There has been no definite link found between stress and cancer in humans. Stress management and therapy play a vital role in improving the life of cancer patients, who experience high levels of depression, hostility, insomnia, and mental stress.

Stress can be reduced by regular aerobic exercise and relaxation training. A strong social support network is another factor in maintaining good health. Religious commitment has been shown to reduce high blood pressure and depression in the elderly. Altruism may also channel negative emotions into constructive actions. Proactive coping is the anticipation of stressful events and planning so that their impact is minimized. Positive reappraisal involves seeking an insight or 'bright side' to otherwise stressful and negative situations. Humor is a highly effective form of positive reappraisal.

Health psychologists are exploring ways to reduce stress, improve coping, and to promote a healthier lifestyle. To maintain good health it is suggested that a person eat a well-balanced diet, exercise regularly, avoid smoking, and avoid high-risk behaviors.

A person may never fully recover from extreme stress. Major sources of extreme stress include unemployment, divorce and separation, bereavement, catastrophes, combat, and other threatening attacks. Wortman identified four myths about bereavement: people should be distressed when a loved one dies; people need to work through their grief; people who find meaning in death cope better than those who do not; and people should recover from a loss within a year or so. Reactions to catastrophes follow a common pattern. First the victim enters the shock stage, followed by a suggestible stage, and finally a recovery stage. Extreme stress can cause posttraumatic stress disorder (PTSD). Although rare, PTSD is of special concern in war veterans and witnesses to terrorism. Individual characteristics may predispose certain people to PTSD more than others.

Finally, what does it mean to be a well-adjusted person? Unfortunately, there is no clear view on what constitutes good adjustment. Some psychologists contend it is the ability to live by social norms, others contend it is the ability to enjoy the difficulties and ambiguities of life. Yet other psychologists propose adjustment can be measured by how a person responds to certain criteria. Abraham Maslow believes the well-adjusted person attempts to self-actualize.

Learning Objectives and Questions

After you have read and studied this chapter, you should be able to complete the following statements.

LEARNING OBJECTIVES

1. Compare and contrast the terms stress, adjustment, pressure, and frustration in terms of their causes and effects. Also describe the roles of change and hassles in contributing to stress.

2. Identify, define, and discuss each of the three types of conflict described by Lewin. Discuss how people tend to react to these conflicts.

3. Summarize Kosaba's findings on hardiness, resilience, and individual differences on stress.

4. Compare and contrast direct coping methods with defensive coping methods. Provide examples of each.

5. Identify, define, and discuss Freud's defense mechanisms. Give one example for each defense mechanism discussed.

6. Summarize the research regarding socioeconomic and gender differences in coping with stress and discuss who experiences the most stress.

7. Explain the "flight or fight" response. Also, describe the stages of Selye's General Adaptation Syndrome, pointing out relevant research.

8. Discuss the research on the relationship between stress and coronary heart disease.

9. Discuss the research on the relationship between stress and the immune system. Include information about the relationship between stress and cancer.

10. Summarize the information about the well-adjusted person. List Morriss' three criteria for evaluating healthy adjustment.

11. Discuss the relatively new fields of health psychology and psychoneuroimmunology and their contributions to the topic of stress and health.

12. List and describe the evidence for four habits that are important to maintain health.

ESSAY QUESTIONS

1. Discuss the role of irrational thinking on stress and how some stress is self-imposed.

2. Identify and describe five sources of extreme stress and outline some of the physical and/or psychological problems caused by each source presented. Include the three myths of bereavement and the three reactions to natural catastrophes.

3. Summarize the article on why some people are happier than others.

4. List the four steps for staying healthy. Detail specific suggestions for improvement and include definitions of altruism, proactive coping, and positive reappraisal.

5. Define the psychological disorder, posttraumatic stress syndrome. Discuss possible causes, symptoms, and the 'normal' responses to a traumatic event. Include suggestions for recovery.

Chapter Outline

The following is an outline conveying the main concepts of this chapter.

Adjustment
Health Psychology

Multiple Choice Posttest

After studying the text and completing the Study Guide activities, answer these questions to determine if you need to review any areas before the course exam.

1. The College Life Stress Inventory (CLSI) measures _____.
   a. how much stress and change a student has undergone in a given period
   b. how effective a student's coping mechanisms are
   c. the extent to which a student has resolved stress effectively
   d. the degree to which a student's stress reaction is genetically determined

2. Henry's term paper is due and he hasn't finished it. He can turn it in unfinished and receive a failing grade or he can hand it in later and lose so many points that he will also fail. Henry's dilemma is described by Lewin as a (n) _____ conflict.
   a. approach/approach
   b. approach/avoidance
   c. avoidance/avoidance
   d. multiple approach/avoidance

3. Ken wants to go to law school but he is concerned that he will be rejected if he applies or will fail if he is admitted. Ken is faced with what Lewin calls a (n) _____ conflict.
   a. approach/approach
   b. approach/avoidance
   c. avoidance/avoidance
   d. double approach/avoidance

4. Kobasa's work on hardiness and resilience has linked people's self-confidence to _____.
   a. their sense of having some control over events
   b. their levels of intelligence
   c. adopting and internalizing traditional sex roles
   d. the tendency to be extroverted

5. Acknowledging a stressful situation directly and attempting to find a solution to the problem or attain a difficult goal is called _____.
   a. sublimation
   b. compromise
   c. confrontation
   d. aggression

6. After weeks of being taunted by her so-called "friends" at school, Alyssa begins actively avoiding them whenever possible. Her coping style is best described as _____.
   a. confrontation
   b. withdrawal
   c. compromise
   d. rationalization

7. John refuses to admit he has a problem with procrastination, even though his procrastination is creating many problems in his life. John is using _____ to cope with his problem.
   a. denial
   b. sublimation
   c. repression
   d. intellectualization

8. A corporate executive who feels guilty about the way she rose to power accuses her colleagues of ruthless ambition. Her behavior typifies _____.
   a. sublimation
   b. projection
   c. displacement
   d. identification

9. A student, angry that he failed what he felt was an unfair test, goes back to his dormitory and slams the door violently. This student is using the defense mechanism of _____.
   a. sublimation
   b. reaction formation
   c. projection
   d. displacement

10. The proper order in which Selye's stages of the General Adaptation Syndrome (GAS) occur is _____.
    a. resistance, alarm stage, exhaustion
    b. exhaustion, resistance, alarm stage
    c. resistance, exhaustion, alarm stage
    d. alarm stage, resistance, exhaustion

11. People who respond to life events in an intense, time urgent manner are exhibiting a _____ behavior pattern.
    a. Type A
    b. Type B
    c. Type C
    d. hyperactive

12. Prolonged stress has _____ cancer.
    a. been shown to decrease vulnerability to
    b. been found to be unrelated to one's vulnerability to
    c. been shown to increase vulnerability to
    d. been shown to cause

13. When recent or past highly stressful events result in anxiety, sleeplessness, and nightmares, a psychological disorder called _____ might be occurring.
    a. generalized anxiety disorder
    b. panic disorder
    c. posttraumatic stress disorder
    d. panic disorder

14. Which of the following accurately lists in order the stages of reactions to natural catastrophes?
    a. suggestible stage, shock stage, recovery stage
    b. shock stage, suggestible stage, recovery stage
    c. rage, confusion, recovery
    d. confusion, rage, recovery

15. Kobasa described hardiness as a trait in which _____.
    a. our experience of stress is affected by heredity
    b. people adhere to rigid actions and won't compromise
    c. people react to conflict in a hard way
    d. people experience difficult environmental demands as challenging rather than threatening

16. When people are well-adjusted they probably have ____.
    a. learned to get what they need regardless of what others want
    b. learned to balance conformity and nonconformity as well as self-control and spontaneity
    c. few problems
    d. none of the above

17. In addition to avoiding and coping better with stress it is also important to ____ in order to maintain health.
    a. exercise regularly
    b. eat a well-balanced diet
    c. avoid high-risk behaviors
    d. quit smoking
    e. all of the above

18. According to Wortman, which of the following statements in NOT a myth about the bereavement process?
    a. People should recover from a loss within a year or so.
    b. People who do not seek greater understanding for their loss are the best adjusted and the least depressed.
    c. People should be intensely distressed when a loved one dies.
    d. People need to work through their grief
    e. All of the above are myths about bereavement.

19. A subfield of psychology concerned with the relationship between psychological factors and physical health and illness is called _____.
    a. positive psychology
    b. abnormal psychology
    c. health psychology
    d. physiological psychology

20. Which of the following statements is true regarding resistance to stress?
    a. Pessimists tend to cope better with stress than optimists.
    b. People with an external locus of control tend to cope better with stress than people with an internal locus of control.
    c. Self-confident people tend to feel less stress than people who lack self-assurance.
    d. There are little differences in the way individuals react to and cope with stress.

Answers and Explanations to Multiple Choice Posttest

1. a. The CLSI measures how much stress and change a student has undergone in a given period. p. 356

2. c. Henry's dilemma is an avoidance/avoidance conflict because both outcomes are undesirable. p. 358

3. b. Ken is faced with an approach/avoidance conflict because he is both attracted to and repelled from his goals. p. 359

4. a. Kosaba links people's self-confidence to their sense of having some control over events. p. 359

5. c. Confrontation acknowledges a stressful situation directly and attempting to find a solution. p. 361

6. b. Alyssa is using the coping style of withdrawal by avoiding the situation. p. 361

7. a. John is using denial by refusing to acknowledge his problems with procrastination. p. 363

8. b. The female executive is using projection by attributing her repressed guilt about her success to her colleagues. p. 364

9. d. The student is using displacement by redirecting his anger to a substitute object. p. 367

10. d. The proper order in Seyle's stages of GAS are: alarm, resistance, exhaustion. p. 367

11. a. One characteristic of the Type A personality is intense time urgency. p. 368

12. c. Prolonged stress has been shown to increase vulnerability to cancer. p. 369

13. c. Posttraumatic stress disorder is characterized by episodes of anxiety, sleeplessness, and nightmares resulting from a disturbing past event. p. 376

14. b. The order of the states of reaction to natural catastrophes is: shock, suggestible, and recovery. p. 375

15. d. Hardiness is described as a trait in which people experience difficult environmental demands as challenging rather than threatening. p. 359

16. b. Well-adjusted people have learned to balance conformity and nonconformity as well as self-control and spontaneity. p. 378

17. e. Exercise, diet, avoiding smoking, and avoiding high risk behaviors are all elements of a healthy lifestyle. p. 370

18. b. It is a myth that people who find meaning in death cope better. In reality, people who do not seek greater understanding are the best adjusted and the least depressed. p.

19. c. Health psychology is a subfield of psychology concerned with the relationship between psychological factors and physical health and illness. p. 355

20. c. Self-confident people tend to feel less stress than people who lack self-assurance. pp. 359–360

Language Support

Students identified the following words from the text as needing more explanation. This page can be cut-out, folded in half, and used as a bookmark for this chapter.

A

Abandon	leave without intending to return; give oneself over fully to something, withdraw support or protection
Accommodating	helpful, bring into agreement, provide with something needed, make room for, give consideration or adapt to
Adversary	having opposing interests; enemy
Aerobic exercise	sustained exercises to stimulate, strengthen, and oxygenate the heart
Albeit	even though; acknowledging the fact that
Ambivalent	fluctuating among simultaneous, contradictory, or opposing feelings or attitudes toward something; uncertain of which approach to take
Anniversary	yearly (annual) recurring of a date marking a notable event
Annoyance	source of irritation; nuisance; unpleasant; bothersome; disturbing

B

Blown up	built up to an unreasonable extent; expanded to reasonable proportions
Bolster	support or give a boost to; reinforce
Breakdown	failure to function, progress or be effective; classify into categories

C

Cherish	hold dear; nurture; feel or show affection for
Common denominator	a common or shared trait or theme
Component	an essential part or element
Composite	made up of distinct parts; typical or essential characteristics of a group
Congestion	clog; concentrated in a small, narrow place; something that impedes
Consumed	use up; engage or engross fully in; eat or drink in great quantity
Conventionally	based on customary conditions; lacking originality or individuality
Crass	without refinement; gross; vulgar
Cynical	distrustful of human nature and motives; pessimistic

D

Dazed	stunned, groggy, dizzy; overcome with astonishment or disbelief
Desperate	having lost hope; using extreme measure to overcome defeat; suffering extreme need or anxiety
Detonate	explode with sudden violence; set off in a burst of activity
Dissect	separate into pieces; analyze and interpret in detail or scientifically
Dissipate	to spread thin or scatter and gradually vanish
Down-sized	reduce in size; cut back (i.e., labor force); design or make smaller version
Dramatic	striking in appearance or effect; exaggerated emotionalism
Drift	general underlying meaning or tendency
Dual-earner couple	two paycheck family; both parties work and contribute to family income
Dwell	stay for a time; a resident; speak or write persistently (stay on theme)

E

Endeavor	to strive or achieve; exert effort; work with a set purpose
Endorse	approve openly, express support
Extravagantly	exceeding reasonable or necessary limits; lacking moderation, balance, restraint; excessively elaborate

F

Fatality	causing death or destruction; destined for disaster
Fatigue	weariness or exhaustion from labor, exertion, or stress
Forbidden	not allowed by authorities; hinder or prevent
Free-fall	rapid and continuing drop or decline
Frozen	unable to be changed or moved; fixed; drained or incapable of emotion

G

Gracious	kind, courteous, tactful, charming, generous, with good taste
Gratifying	giving pleasure or satisfaction to; indulging
Gregarious	a liking for companionship; sociable

H

Hanging out	hang around in one's company; spend time aimlessly, loitering around
Hand-in-hand	closely associated; in cooperation with
Head-on	in direct opposition; facing forward
Hostage	one held against their will or controlled by an outside influence

I

Incompatible	not able to blend into a harmonious co-existence
Irreparable	unable to be fixed or repaired

L

Lavish	marked by excess, abundant
Looms	appear impressively great or exaggerated; take shape as an impending event

M

Mirage	an optical effect looking like water or a mirror; illusory and unattainable
Mixed blessing	having incompatible or contrary elements; both positive and negative
Mobilize	put into motion or circulation; assemble or make ready for action

N

Natural disaster	a sudden weather event bringing great damage, loss, or destruction
Network	interconnected or interrelated chain, group or system
No-exit	no way or passage out; can't leave
Numb	lacking or devoid of physical sensation or emotion; indifferent

O

Obstacle	hinder or block; something that impedes progress or achievement

P

Perch	resting place or vantage point; prominent position
Petty annoyance	minor or insignificant; unimportant source of irritation, small nuisance
Preexisting	precede; exist before or earlier
Premonition	anticipate an event without conscious reason; previous notice or warning
Preponderance	excessive quantity, weight, power, importance or strength
Procrastination	intentionally or habitually putting off a task; delay

Q

Queasy	causing nausea; full of doubt or uneasiness; ill at ease

R

Radical departure	set out on new course; extreme change in existing conditions or methods
Restraint	control over expression of emotions or thoughts; restrict movement
Ruminate	contemplate, reflect, ponder; go over repeatedly in thought
Rundown	item-by-item report or review; summary
Ruthless	cruel; devoid of humane feelings; causing pain or injury; aggressive

S

Substandard	below legal standards; falling short of normal quality
Suspicious	mistrust of something with evidence; mental uneasiness and uncertainty
Survivor	one who continues to function or prosper; one who remains alive

T

Terrorism	systematic use of fear tactics to dominate by force or threat
Toll	cost in life or health; extent of loss, damage, or suffering
Totem pole	carved, painted pole with symbolic animal images of N.W. Indians
Transfixed	motionless; give permanent or final form; make firm, stable, stationary
Triumphant	victorious, successful; showing a sense of fulfillment and harmony
Turnover	movement of people or goods through a place; shift in personnel

U

Ubiquitous	being everywhere at the same time; widespread; constantly encountered
Unrealistic	inappropriate or not resembling reality or fact
Utterly	carried to the utmost point or highest degree; totally; absolutely

V

Vacillation	indecision; unable to take a stand; wavering between possible choices
Veterinarian	qualified doctor of animal medicine
Vicarious	enjoyed through imagined participation in another's experience

W

Winner-take-all	the victor claims the full reward
Wrestle	struggle or contend with; grapple

Key Vocabulary Terms

Cut out each term and use as study cards.
Definition is on the back side of each term.

Stress	Conflict
Adjustment	Approach/ approach conflict
Health psychology	Avoidance/ avoidance conflict
Pressure	Approach/ avoidance conflict
Frustration	Confrontation

Simultaneous existence of incompatible demands, opportunities, needs, or goals.	A state of psychological tension or strain or any environmental demand that creates a state of tension or threat and requires change or adaptation.
According to Lewin the result of simultaneous attraction to two appealing possibilities, neither of which has any negative qualities.	Any effort to cope with stress.
According to Lewin, the result of facing a choice between two undesirable possibilities, neither of which has any positive qualities.	A subfield of psychology concerned with the relationship between psychological factors and physical health and illness.
According to Lewin, the result of being simultaneously attracted to and repelled by the same goal.	A feeling that one must speed up, intensify, or change the direction of one's behavior or live up to a higher standard of performance.
Acknowledging a stressful situation directly and attempting to find a solution to the problem or attain the difficult goal.	The feeling that occurs when a person is prevented from reaching a goal.

Compromise	Projection
Withdrawal	Identification
Defense mechanisms	Regression
Denial	Intellectualization
Repression	Reaction formation

Attributing one's own repressed motives, feelings, or wishes to others.

Deciding on a more realistic solution or goal when an ideal solution or goal is not practical.

Taking on the characteristics of someone else to avoid feeling incompetent.

Avoiding a situation when other forms of coping are not practical.

Reverting to childlike behavior and defenses.

Self-deceptive techniques for reducing stress, including denial, repression, projection, identification, regression, intellectualization, reaction formation, displacement, and sublimation.

Thinking abstractly about stressful problems as a way of detaching oneself from the problem.

Refusal to acknowledge a painful or threatening reality or not experiencing fully the intensity of the event.

Expression of exaggerated ideas and emotions that are the opposite of one's repressed beliefs or feelings.

Excluding uncomfortable thoughts, feelings, and desires from consciousness.

Displacement	Stressor
Sublimation	
General adaptation syndrome	
Psychoneuro-immunology	
Posttraumatic stress disorder	

Any environmental demand that creates a state of tension or threat and requires change or adaptation.	Shifting repressed motives and emotions from an original object to a substitute object.
	Redirecting repressed motives and feelings into more socially acceptable channels.
	According to Selye, the three stages the body passes through as it adapts to stress: alarm reaction, resistance, and exhaustion.
	A new field of medicine that studies the interaction between stress on the one hand and immune, endocrine, and nervous system activity on the other.
	Psychological disorder characterized by episodes of anxiety, sleeplessness, and nightmares resulting from some disturbing past event.

12 Psychological Disorders

Chapter Focus

This chapter examines psychological disorders. Mental health professionals identify a psychological disorder as a behavior that exhibits maladaptive personality traits, psychological discomfort, or prevents the person from functioning well in life.

Views of psychological disorders have changed dramatically over time. The biological model suggests that hereditary or physiological malfunctions cause psychological disorders. The psychoanalytic model, developed most famously by Freud, holds that behavior disorders are expressions of unconscious early developmental conflicts. The cognitive-behavioral model suggests that maladaptive behaviors are the result of both internal and external learning processes. The diathesis-stress model attempts to integrate the three traditional models to discover specific causes and treatments for psychological disorders. The systems approach, or biopsychosocial model, examines how risk factors from biological, psychological and social areas combine to produce psychological disorders. This chapter studies abnormal behavior following the systems approach.

Psychological disorders are classified by the American Psychological Association (APA) in *The Diagnostic and Statistical Manual of Mental Disorders* (DSM). Now in its fourth edition, it is the most widely accepted classification manual of psychological disorders. According to an APA study, 15 percent of the U.S. population has a mental disorder, and 6 percent has a problem with substance abuse. Anxiety disorders are the most common. Worldwide, the prevalence of psychological disorders varies widely.

A mood disorder, or affect, refers to a disturbance of mood or prolonged emotional state. Depression is the most common mood disorder. Among other symptoms, a person with clinical depression feels overwhelmed by sadness. Major depressive disorder is an episode of extreme sadness lasting for several months. Dysthymia involves less intense sadness that persists for two years or more. Suicide may be a direct result of a depressive episode. Older white males take their own lives most frequently, yet adolescents make up a growing proportion of suicide attempts.

Mania is a mood disorder involving excessive euphoria, activity, or distractibility. A manic person may display a greatly inflated self-esteem, talk of unrealistic hopes and schemes, and/or show aggression and hostility. Mania and depression are alternately present in bipolar disorder. Bipolar disorder appears to have a stronger biological component than depression. Mood disorders result from a combination of biological, psychological, and social factors.

Anxiety disorders are inappropriate or unidentifiable feelings of fear. This fear may be a specific phobia, a panic disorder, or one of many anxiety disorders. Phobias may be learned after exposure to only a single fearful event. A social phobia is anxiety when in public or social situations. Agoraphobia involves many intense fears of such things as crowds, or busy places where escape is difficult. A panic disorder is characterized by recurring episodes of sudden and unpredictable fear often accompanied by physical symptoms.

A person with generalized anxiety disorder

has difficulty relaxing, is tense, apprehensive, and seems constantly alert to potential threats. Obsessive-compulsive disorder (OCD) is considered an anxiety disorder because the obsessive or compulsive behavior is an adaptation designed to control an underlying anxiety. Specific traumatic events may lead to acute stress disorder, in which a person experiences episodes of fear and terror even after an event is over. Posttraumatic stress occurs if the fear remains long after the event has occurred.

Anxiety disorders may be caused by biological predispositions that protect from realistic threats. Cognitive psychologists suggest that a person's perception of a situation will influence the fear experienced when dealing with it. The psychoanalytical method emphasizes the role that internal conflict plays in anxiety, disorders, suggesting that phobias are a defense mechanism. Modern medicine accepts that to some degree, all physical illnesses are psychosomatic. Stress, anxiety and emotional arousal alter body chemistry, the immune system, and the functioning of body organs.

Somatoform disorders display physical symptoms without an identifiable physical cause. Conversion disorders are dramatic forms of somatoform disorders and remain a theoretical and diagnostic challenge to medical science. In hypochondriasis, a person interprets a slight symptom as a sign of a serious disease. People with body dysmorphic disorder unrealistically evaluate their looks as ugly or disfigured.

Dissociative disorders affect the personality, either through amnesia or a change in identity. Dissociative amnesia occurs when a person selectively forgets a situation that was particularly traumatic or stressful. Dissociative identity disorder, or multiple personality disorder, is much rarer than popularly imagined, and evidence suggests it is a response to childhood abuse. Sufferers of the less severe depersonalization disorder feel strange to themselves, as though their actions are being performed mechanically or by someone else. All dissociative disorders involve unconscious processes. Psychological factors and biological processes play a role in dissociative disorders.

Sexual disorders are grouped into three categories: sexual dysfunction, paraphilias, and gender-identity disorders. In males, sexual dysfunction may take the form of erectile disorder (ED); females may experience female sexual arousal disorder.

Paraphilias involve the use of unconventional sex objects or situations to gain sexual arousal. Fetishism is a form of paraphilia that may stem from adolescent sexual experimentation. Pedophilia is a serious paraphilia, most commonly found in males under age 40 who have not adjusted to adult sexual roles and responsibilities.

Gender-identity disorders occur when people have the desire to become, or feel they already are, members of the other sex. Children who are uncomfortable with their genders may be diagnosed with gender-identity disorder. Both prenatal hormonal imbalances, family dynamics, and learning experiences contribute to gender-identity disorders.

Personality disorders are characterized by odd or eccentric behaviors. Schizoid personality disorder is the inability to form social relationships or warm feeling towards others. People with paranoid personality disorder are hypersensitive, suspicious, and mistrustful, and refuse to accept blame. Other personality disorders include dependent personality disorder, avoidant personality disorder, and narcissistic personality disorder.

A borderline personality disorder sufferer has a tendency to act impulsively and in self-destructive ways. Studies of borderline personality disorder show the cause to be dysfunctional relationships with parents. People with antisocial personality disorder tend not to accept responsibility for their actions, and are likely to blame society or their victims for the antisocial actions they commit. This may be a result of emotional deprivation in early childhood.

Schizophrenic disorders are severe conditions identified by bizarre behavior, disordered thoughts and communications, and inappropriate emotions which last for months or years. People with schizophrenia are psychotic. Insanity is an often misused legal term. Sufferers of schizophrenia often have auditory hallucinations and delusions. Several kinds of schizophrenia exist, such as disorganized schizophrenia, catatonic schizophrenia, paranoid schizophrenia, and undifferentiated schizophrenia.

Specific psychological disorders are diagnosed in children. Attention-deficit/hyperactivity disorder (ADHD) is more commonly diagnosed in boys, and is treated with psychostimulant drugs in the short term. Autistic disorder describes a condition where the child does not form normal attachments to parents and caregivers. Theories strongly suggest autistic disorder has a genetic cause.

Finally, although it has been suggested that women exhibit higher instances of psychological disorders, it is extremely difficult to obtain reliable data. Women are more likely than men to admit to having emotional difficulties and seek help. Men tend to resort to alcohol and aggressive actions. Culture does play a role in disorders with a psychological and environmental dependency, such as ADHD.

Learning Objectives

After you have read and studied this chapter, you should be able to complete the following statements.

OBJECTIVES

1. Distinguish among the standards for defining abnormal behavior from the view of society, the individual, and the mental health professional.

2. Summarize historical attitudes toward abnormal behavior.

3. State the four current models of abnormal behavior and explain the diathesis-stress model. Explain how the DSM-IV classifies mental disorders.

4. Distinguish between the two basic kinds of mood disorders and how they may interact with each other.

5. Describe the differences between depression and a normal reaction to negative life events.

6. Discuss the possible causes of mood disorders including biological and psychological factors.

7. Describe the anxiety disorders.

8. Describe the characteristics of the psychophysiological disorders and the somatoform disorders.

9. Characterize three different types of dissociative disorders.

10. Define and give examples of the sexual disorders.

11. Define gender-identity disorders.

12. Define personality disorders. Describe four kinds of personality disorders.

13. Describe four types of schizophrenic disorders and identify possible causes of the disorder.

14. Discuss attention-deficit/hyperactivity disorder (ADHD).

15. Discuss the complex factors that contribute to different rates of abnormal behavior in men and women.

Chapter Outline

The following is an outline conveying the main concepts of this chapter.

Multiple Choice Posttest

After studying the text and completing the Study Guide activities, answer these questions to determine if you need to review any areas before the course exam.

1. The person whose naturalistic views of mental illness first encouraged a system search to uncover its causes, and implied that disturbed people should be treated with care and sympathy was _____.
   a. Hippocrates
   b. Galen
   c. Voltaire
   d. Descartes

2. The turning point year in the history of treatment of the mentally ill was _____, when Phillipe Pinel became director of the Bicetre Hospital in Paris and argued for pleasant living conditions for the patients.
   a. 1379
   b. 1793
   c. 1894
   d. 1937

3. The basic reason for the failed, and sometimes abusive, treatment of mentally disturbed people throughout history has been _____.
   a. fear of retribution by supernatural forces
   b. a lack of understanding of the causes and treatments of psychological disorders
   c. political and legal restrictions placed on treatment by insensitive authorities.
   d. lack of money to provide adequate care for disturbed people.

4. The _____ model of mental illness holds that abnormal behavior is caused by physiological malfunction that is often attributable to hereditary factors.
   a. biological
   b. cognitive-behavioral
   c. psycho-dynamic
   d. naturalistic

5. The view that people biologically predisposed to a mental disorder will tend to exhibit that acute stress disorder when particularly affected by stress is known as the ____ model of abnormal behavior.
   a. multimodal
   b. pluralistic model
   c. psychoneuro-immunological
   d. diathesis-stress

6. The _____ model believes that fears, depression, and self-defeating beliefs are caused by learning and negative thinking and can be unlearned with appropriate reinforcement.
   a. obsessive-compulsive
   b. delusional-compulsive
   c. passive-aggressive
   d. diathesis stress

7. An affective/mood disorder that includes both depression and mania is known as ____.
   a. biological
   b. cognitive-behavioral
   c. psycho-analytic
   d. diathesis-stress

8. An intense, paralyzing fear of a specific situation, object, person, or thing in the absence of any real danger is a ____.
   a. histrionic
   b. bipolar
   c. dual process
   d. obsessive-compulsive

9. An anxiety disorder in which a person feels driven to think disturbing thoughts and/or to perform senseless rituals is ____ disorder.
   a. panic
   b. phobic
   c. conversion
   d. compulsive

10. Mental disorders are categorized according to ___ in the DSM-IV.
    a. family histories
    b. biological causes of disruptive behavior
    c. significant behavior patterns
    d. specific theoretical approaches

11. The disorder previously known as "multiple personality disorder" is now known as
    _____.
    a. dissociative amnesia
    b. dissociative identity disorder
    c. dissociative fugue
    d. depersonal-ization disorder

12. The most widely accepted explanation for dissociative identity disorder is that it is a response to _____.
    a. neurotransmitter imbalances
    b. childhood abuse
    c. role diffusion
    d. extreme loneliness

13. Sexual arousal as a result of fantasizing about or engaging in sexual activity with prepubescent children is _____.
    a. infantile sexual regression
    b. sadomasochistic immaturity
    c. pedophilia
    d. transvestism

14. Rejection of one's biological gender and persistently desiring to become a member of the opposite sex is known as _____.
    a. sexual orientation disorder
    b. bisexuality
    c. cender identity disorder
    d. hermaphroditism

15. John is a pathological liar. He takes things from others, takes advantage of them, and never exhibits any remorse after he is done. John has ____ personality disorder.
    a. paranoid
    b. narcissistic
    c. antisocial
    d. borderline

16. _____ disorders are marked by disordered communication and thoughts, inappropriate emotions, and bizarre behaviors.
    a. Psychosexual
    b. Neurotic
    c. Somatoform
    d. Schizophrenic

17. The psychological term for someone who is mentally disturbed to the point of not being in contact with reality and not being legally responsible for his or her action is _____.
    a. schizophrenia
    b. split personality
    c. insanity
    d. psycho-pathology

18. Research suggests that a biological vulnerability to schizophrenia may lie in excess amounts of ____.
    a. thyroxin
    b. epinephrine
    c. vasopressin
    d. dopamine

19. Currently the cause of attention deficit/hyperactivity disorder and autism is thought to be ____.
    a. arrested emotional development
    b. biological and/or genetic abnormalities
    c. over-demanding and emotionally detached parents
    d. prenatal maternal alcohol use

20. Women are more likely to suffer from ___than men, and men are more likely to suffer from _____ than women.
    a. depression, substance abuse disorders
    b. antisocial personality; anxiety disorder
    c. substance abuse disorders; depression
    d. paranoid disorders; histrionic disorders

Answers and Explanations to Multiple Choice Posttest

1. a. Hippocrates maintained that mental illness was a natural event arising from natural causes and should be treated the same as people with physical illnesses. p. 385

2. b. In 1793, Philippe Pinel was made Director of the Bicetre Hospital in Paris and drastically reorganized the care and treatment for the mentally ill. p. 385

3. b. Lack of understanding of the nature and causes of psychological disorders is the basic reason for the failed and sometimes abusive treatment of the mentally ill. p. 385

4. a. The biological model holds that psychological disorders have a biochemical or physiological basis. p. 386

5. d. The diathesis-stress model sees people who are biologically predisposed to a mental disorder will exhibit that disorder when affected by extreme stress. p. 387

6. b. The cognitive-behavioral model views psychological disorders as resulting from learning maladaptive ways of thinking and behaving. p. 386

7. b. Bipolar disorder alternates between periods of mania and depression, along with period of normal moods. p. 391

8. a. Phobic disorders are characterized by an intense, paralyzing, and irrational fear of something. p. 393

9. a. A person with obsessive/compulsive disorder feels driven to think disturbing thoughts or to perform senseless rituals to reduce anxiety. p. 394

10. c. The DSM-IV lists mental disorders in terms of significant behavior patterns. p. 387

11. b. Dissociative identity disorder was formerly called multiple personality disorder. p. 398

12. b. Clinicians report a history of child abuse in more than three-fourths of their dissociative identity disorder cases. p. 399

13. c. Pedophilia is the desire to have sexual relationships with children. p. 401

14. c. Gender identity disorder is the desire to become a member of the other biological sex. p. 401

15. c. Some individual with antisocial personality disorder lie, steal, cheat, and show little or no sense of responsibility or remorse. p. 403

16. d. Schizophrenia is marked by disordered communications and thoughts and inappropriate emotions and bizarre behavior. p. 405

17. c. Insanity is a legal term for mentally disturbed people not considered responsible for their criminal actions. p. 405

18. d. Recent research suggests that schizophrenia may be related to excessive amounts of dopamine in the central nervous system. p. 406

19. b. We don't yet know the cause of either ADHD or autism, but most theorists believe that they result almost entirely from biological or genetic factors. p. 408

20. a. Men drink or abuse drugs more when they have psychological problems, and women are more likely to become depressed and helpless. p. 409

Language Support

Students identified the following words from the text as needing more explanation. This page can be cut-out, folded in half, and used as a bookmark for this chapter.

A

Alienated	withdrawn or diverted; unfriendly or hostile with a former attachment; estranged
Ambitious	having a desire to achieve a particular goal; aspiring
Animated	full of movement, activity, spirit; lively
Apathetic	having or showing little or no feeling or emotion; indifferent
Apprehensive	anxiety or alarm about the future; showing quick insight or understanding
Arrested	bring to a stop; make inactive

B

"The blues"	low spirits; melancholy, sad

C

Causative	operating or effective as a cause or agent
Chastity	abstaining from sexual intercourse; pure intention and conduct; personal integrity
Coexist	live in peace with each other; exist together at the same time
Cold-blooded	emotionless; acting without consideration or mercy; matter of fact
Con man	swindler; person who robs others after gaining their trust

D

Debilitating	impaired strength; weaken or reduce in intensity or effectiveness; crippling or disabling; loss of health of power
Definitive	final solution or ending; solution; serving as a perfect example
Deviance	stray from a standard, principle, or topic; depart from established norms
Devious	deceptive; deliberately leading astray into mistaken belief, action, or direction
Dismaying	at a loss as to how to deal with something; loss of courage due to pressure, fear, or anxiety
Disobedient	refusing to follow directions or guidance; refuse to conform or comply with
Disparage	degrade; speak slightingly about; demote or lower rank or reputation
Distress	mentally or emotionally worried or troubled; make ill or cause a physical disorder in
Dubious	doubtful; causing uncertainty; questionable or suspect as to true nature or quality

E

Eccentric	deviating from established style; unconventional; strange
Entitlement	having grounds for seeking or claiming something
Erratic	lack of consistency, regularity, or uniformity; having no fixed course
Euphoria	feeling of well-being or elation; high spirits
Exemplify	embody; be typical of or represent; serve as an example
Exorcism	act of removing or expelling something menacing or troublesome
Exploit	to use unfairly for one's own advantage

F

Facsimile	exact copy, reproduction, duplicate
Fake	something that is not what it seems to be; worthless imitation

Fanciful	unrestrained imagination lacking factual reality
Feign	give false appearance; pretend; assert as if true
Fidgety	uneasiness or restlessness shown by nervous movements
"In a Fog"	in a state of mental confusion or unawareness; in a daze
Fragile	easily broken or destroyed; delicate; lacking physical vigor
Frantic	emotionally out of control, marked by fast and nervous, disordered or anxiety driven activity
Fruitful	great resourcefulness of thought or imagination; abundant possibilities for development
Full-blown	having attained complete status; fully developed or mature

G

Genuine	sincerely and honestly felt or experiences; sincere, true, authentic
Gesture	movement or position of body or part of body that expresses an idea, opinion, or emotion
"Get off"	to experience with great pleasure
Grandiose	absurd exaggerations; grand display
Grimace	a facial expression usually of disgust or disapproval

H

Horrifying	feel shock, distaste; to distress greatly
Hot line	direct phone line constantly available to the public for some specific purpose
Humiliating	extremely destructive to one's self-respect or dignity
Hyper vigilance	excessively watchful, especially to danger

I

Ideology	systematic body of concepts and theories, usually about human life or culture
Impassive	no sign or feeling of emotion, pain, or physical feeling; expressionless
Inappropriate	not suitable or compatible with
Incoherence	unintelligible; lacking clarity, order, cohesion, or relevance
Incompetence	inadequate or unsuitable for a particular purpose; lacking the qualities needed for the effective action
Incomprehensible	impossible to understand
Intended	have in mind a purpose or goal; direct the mind on a future plan
Invulnerable	incapable of being injured or harmed; immune to attack

J

Jargon	the language of a particular trade, profession, or group
Jittery	continuous, fast repetitive movements; to be nervous or act nervously

L

Lethal	gravely damaging or destructive; capable of causing death
Lifestyle	typical way of life of an individual, group, or culture reflecting attitudes and preference

M

Maladaptive	unable to adjust or fit
Malfunction	fail to operate normally
Mannerisms	characteristic, often unconscious actions that may be exaggerated or affected
Melancholy	depressed spirits, dejected, sad mood
Misconception	to interpret incorrectly, misunderstand
Momentum	driving force; strength gained by motion or through the development of events
Mutually exclusive	relationship where the presence of one factor prevents the appearance of the other

N

Nurture	to foster the development of; provide with nourishment

O

Onset	the point at which something begins; early stage or period

P

Painstakingly	extremely careful or precise about details; making great effort
"Possessed"	influenced or controlled by something, such as an evil spirit or passion
Promiscuity	having numerous casual sexual partners; indiscriminate

Q

Qualitative	relating to or involving the quality or kind

R

Rat race	exhausting and usually competitive routine activity
Readily	without hesitation; willing; easily
Revert	go back to a former habit, action, or belief; go back in thought or discussion
Rival gang	competing group of people usually involving criminal behavior
Robot-like	an efficient, insensitive person who functions automatically; human-like machine that performs complex human actions

S

Savagely	enraged or furiously angry; fierce or cruel person; criticize or assault brutally
Scarcity	lack of provisions for the support of life
Scheming	making sly and underhanded plans; calculating; devious
Spectrum	continuous or connected sequence, series or range
Stew	state of suppressed agitation, worry, or resentment
Stewardess	female airline flight attendant
Sweeping conclusions	outcome or final result with wide range or force

T

Theoretical	existing only in theory, not practical; speculative
Timid	lacking courage, confidence, boldness, or determination; shy
Tiptoe	strain upwards, on balls of feet and toes or tips of toes; moving secretly
Tyrannical	unjustly cruel or severe; oppressive; exerting absolute power or control

U

Ugliness	offensive or unpleasant to the sight
Unconventional	not bound by established customs; out of the ordinary

V

Vague	indefinite; not clearly expressing one's thoughts or feelings; hazy
Venture	an undertaking involving chance, risk or danger
Vignette	short, descriptive literary sketch; brief incident
Vindictiveness	intending to seek revenge; causing anguish or hurt; spiteful

W

Wild	strongly passionate, emotion or eager; marked by turbulent agitation; without regulation or control; off an intended course
Wrenching	causing mental or emotional anguish

Key Vocabulary Terms

Cut out each term and use as study cards.
Definition is on the back side of each term.

Biological model of psychological disorders	Systems approach of psychological disorders
Psychoanalytic model of psychological disorders	Mood disorders
Cognitive-behavioral model of psychological disorders	Depression
Diathesis-stress model of psychological disorders	Mania
Autistic disorder	Bipolar disorder

View that biological, psychological, and social risk factors combine to produce psychological disorders. Also known as the biopsychosocial model of psychological disorders.	View that psychological disorders have a biochemical or physiological basis.
Disturbances in mood or prolonged emotional state.	View that psychological disorders are the result from unconscious internal conflicts.
A mood disorder characterized by overwhelming feelings of sadness, lack of interest in activities, and perhaps excessive guilt or feelings of worthlessness.	View that psychological disorders result from learning maladaptive ways of thinking and behaving.
A mood disorder characterized by euphoric states, extreme physical activity, excessive talkativeness, distractedness, and sometimes grandiosity.	View that people biologically predisposed to a mental disorder (those with a certain diathesis) will tend to exhibit that disorder when particularly affected by stress.
A mood disorder in which periods of mania and depression alternate, sometimes with periods of normal mood intervening.	A childhood disorder characterized by lack of social instincts and strange motor behavior.

Cognitive distortions	Panic disorder
Anxiety disorders	Generalized anxiety disorder
Specific phobia	Obsessive-compulsive disorder
Social phobia	Psychosomatic disorders
Agoraphobia	Somatoform disorders

An anxiety disorder characterized by recurrent panic attacks in which the person suddenly experiences intense fear or terror without any reasonable cause.

A maladaptive response to early negative life events that leads to feelings of incompetence and unworthiness that are reactivated whenever a new situation arises that resembles the original events.

An anxiety disorder characterized by prolonged vague but intense fears that are not attached to any particular object or circumstance.

Disorders in which anxiety is a characteristic feature or the avoidance of anxiety seems to motivate abnormal behavior.

An anxiety disorder in which a person feels driven to think disturbing thoughts and/or to perform senseless rituals.

Anxiety disorder characterized by an intense, paralyzing fear of something.

Disorders in which there is real physical illness that is largely caused by psychological factors such as stress and anxiety.

An anxiety disorder characterized by excessive, inappropriate fears connected with social situations or performances in front of other people.

Disorders in which there is an apparent physical illness for which there is no organic basis.

An anxiety disorder that involves multiple, intense fear of crowds, public places, and other situations that require separation from a source of security such as the home.

Conversion disorders	Dissociative identity disorder
Hypochondriasis	Sexual dysfunction
Body dysmorphic disorder	Paraphilias
Dissociative disorders	Fetishism
Depersonalization disorder	Pedophilia

(Formerly multiple personality disorder) Disorder characterized by the separation of the personality into two or more distinct personalities.	Somatoform disorders in which a dramatic specific disability has no physical cause but instead seems related to psychological problems.
Loss or impairment of the ordinary physical responses of sexual function.	A somatoform disorder in which a person interprets insignificant symptoms as signs of serious illness in the absence of any organic evidence of such illness.
Sexual disorders in which unconventional objects or situations cause sexual arousal.	A somatoform disorder in which a person becomes so preoccupied with his or her imagined ugliness that normal life is impossible.
A paraphilia in which a nonhuman object is the preferred or exclusive method of achieving sexual excitement.	Disorders in which some aspect of the personality seems separated from the rest.
Desire to have sexual relations with children as the preferred or exclusive method of achieving sexual excitement.	A dissociative disorder whose essential feature is that the person suddenly feels changed or different in a strange way.

Gender-identity disorders	Dependent personality disorder
Gender-identity disorder in children	Avoidant personality disorder
Personality disorders	Narcissistic personality disorder
Schizoid personality disorder	Borderline personality disorder
Paranoid personality disorder	Antisocial personality disorder

Personality disorder in which the person is unable to make choices and decisions independently and cannot tolerate being alone.	Disorders that involve the desire to become, or the insistence that one really is, a member of the other biological sex.
Personality disorder in which the person's fears of rejection by others lead to social isolation.	Rejection of one's biological gender in childhood, along with the clothing and behavior that society considers appropriate to that gender.
Personality disorder in which the person has an exaggerated sense of self-importance and needs constant admiration.	Disorders in which inflexible and maladaptive ways of thinking and behaving learned early in life cause distress to the person or conflicts with others.
Personality disorder characterized by marked instability in self-image, mood, and interpersonal relationships.	Personality disorder in which a person is withdrawn and lacks feelings for others.
Personality disorder that involves a pattern of violent, criminal, or unethical and exploitative behavior and an inability to feel affection for others.	Personality disorder in which the person is inappropriately suspicious and mistrustful of others.

Schizophrenic disorders	Disorganized schizophrenia
Psychotic (Psychosis)	Catatonic schizophrenia
Insanity	Paranoid schizophrenia
Hallucinations	Undifferentiated schizophrenia
Delusions	Attention-deficit/ hyperactivity disorder (ADHD)

Schizophrenic disorder in which bizarre and childlike behaviors are common.

Severe disorder in which there are disturbances of thoughts, communications, and emotions, including delusions and hallucinations.

Schizophrenic disorder in which disturbed motor behavior is prominent.

Behavior characterized by a loss of touch with reality.

Schizophrenic disorder marked by extreme suspiciousness and complex, bizarre delusions.

Legal term for mentally disturbed people who are not considered responsible for their criminal actions.

Schizophrenic disorder in which there are clear schizophrenic symptoms that don't meet the criteria for another subtype of the disorder.

Sensory experiences in the absence of external stimulation.

A childhood disorder characterized by inattention, impulsiveness, and hyperactivity.

False beliefs about reality that have no basis in fact.

13 Therapies

Chapter Focus

This chapter introduces the different types of treatments available to people who suffer from psychological disorders. Insight therapies have a common goal of giving people better awareness and understanding of their feelings, motivations, and actions in the hope that this will help them to adjust. Three major insight therapies are: psychoanalysis, client-centered therapy, and Gestalt therapy. Psychoanalysis was popularized by Sigmund Freud who used free association to tap into the unconscious mind. The client may experience positive or negative transference before the analyst interprets messages to gain insight into problems. Carl Rogers founded client-centered, or person-centered, therapy with the goal of helping clients to become fully functioning. Client-centered therapists express unconditional positive regard to get clients to accept themselves; they take a nondirective approach to problem solving. Gestalt therapy was brought to the forefront by Fritz Perls. It emphasizes the wholeness of the personality and attempts to reawaken people to their emotions in the here and now. Gestalt therapy sessions may be conducted with individuals or with encounter groups. The empty-chair technique is a popular Gestalt tactic.

Hundreds of variations of insight therapies are in practice today. Recent developments include short-term psychodynamic therapy that is more symptom-oriented to help clients deal with immediate problems in their lives.

Behavior therapies concentrate on changing maladaptive behaviors that result from learning. Behavior therapists employ techniques based on classical conditioning, operant conditioning, or modeling. Systematic desensitization is one of the oldest behavior therapy techniques. Often the therapist will develop a hierarchy of fears, and using relaxation techniques will tackle each fear from the bottom up until the fear response is extinguished through exposure. Sometimes unpleasant techniques such as flooding or aversive conditioning may be employed to treat debilitating anxiety disorders or undesirable behaviors. Therapies based on operant conditioning work on the principle that certain behaviors are a result of reinforcement. In behavior contracting, the client and therapist write and sign a contract outlining specific goals and reinforcements. In token economies, people are rewarded with tokens or points for appropriate behaviors. In modeling therapies, desired behaviors are learned by watching others.

Cognitive therapies are based on changing ideas people have about themselves and the world in an effort to also change undesirable behaviors. Cognitive-behavior therapists combine both cognitive and behavior therapies. In stress-inoculation therapy, clients are taught to suppress negative thoughts and replace them with positive ones. In rational-emotive therapy (RET), developed by Albert Ellis, clients are taught how to confront irrational, self-defeating beliefs using a variety of cognitive tactics. Beck's cognitive therapy helps clients examine dysfunctional thoughts in an objective, scientific manner and has proven effective at treating depression.

Group therapies allow therapists to observe behaviors in the presence of others and provide opportunities for social support, learning new behaviors, and may decrease financial costs. Self-help groups, family therapy, and couple therapy are just a few of the many kinds of group therapies. Empathy training is a technique commonly employed in couple therapy to improve listening and understanding of a partner's problem before responding to it.

Although researchers generally agree that psychotherapy is effective, the value of treatment depends on many factors. Psychotherapy tends to work best for mild psychological problems, in people who want to change, and in participants of long-term therapy. One type of therapy does not seem to be more effective than another. All psychotherapies tend to provide clients with explanations for their problems, offer hope, and engage the client in a therapeutic alliance. Today's psychotherapies employ broad treatment programs rather than one particular form of therapy, a concept called eclecticism.

In addition to psychotherapy, biological treatments may be used to treat psychological disorders. Biological treatments include drug therapies, electroconvulsive therapy (ECT), and psychosurgery. Drugs used to treat psychological disorders include antipsychotics for severe disorders, antidepressants for depression and other anxiety-related disorders. Lithium, a natural salt, helps manage bipolar disorder. Other medications include psychostimulants, antianxiety medications, and sedatives.

ECT may be used in cases of prolonged and severe depression. Results from psychosurgery are difficult to predict making it a drastic treatment option. Although rare, prefrontal lobotomies are viewed as a desperate attempt to control intractable psychoses.

Caring for the seriously disturbed is a delicate issue. In the U.S. hospitalization has been the treatment of choice. Hospital types include general, private, and Veterans Administration hospitals. Large state-run institutions acquired a reputation for providing inadequate care. In the 1950s, drug therapies made deinstitutionalization possible, but serious problems have arisen in recent years. Among the many alternative forms of treatment available today are: training people living at home to cope with daily activities; assigning people to a homelike facility; placing clients in a hostel with therapy; offering counseling combined with medication. Prevention is another approach to mental illness. Primary prevention seeks to improve the environment so that new cases of mental disorders do not develop. Secondary prevention involves identifying groups at high risk for mental disorders and intervening early on. Tertiary prevention seeks to help people adjust to community life following release from a mental hospital.

Finally, gender and cultural differences affect the treatment of psychological disorders. Psychotherapy is more socially accepted for women compared to men. Gender differences in treatment for disorders are controversial. Critics contend that male therapists encourage female clients to adopt male-oriented views of normal behavior. In response, the number of feminist therapists is increasing and the APA has established guidelines for treating women in psychotherapy. Efforts to treat mental illness must also be sensitive to cultural differences. Psychotherapy is more effective when the client and therapist share a similar cultural background.

Learning Objectives

After you have read and studied this chapter, you should be able to complete the following statements.

OBJECTIVES

1. Differentiate among insight therapies, behavior therapies, cognitive therapies, and group therapies.

2. Discuss the criticisms of psychoanalysis.

3. Explain how client-centered and rational-emotive therapists interpret causes of emotional problems. Describe the therapeutic techniques of these approaches.

4. Summarize the behavioral therapist's interpretation of disorders. Describe aversive conditioning, desensitization, and modeling.

5. Describe stress-inoculation therapy, Beck's cognitive therapy, and Gestalt therapy.

6. List the advantages and disadvantages of group therapies. Identify five current approaches to group therapy.

7. Discuss the effectiveness of insight therapy and behavior therapy.

8. Outline the available biological treatments and discuss the advantages and disadvantages of each.

9. Summarize the inadequacies of institutionalization. List the alternative to institutionalization.

10. Explain the differences among primary, secondary, and tertiary prevention.

11. Discuss gender and cultural differences in relationship to treatment of psychological problems.

Chapter Outline

The following is an outline conveying the main concepts of this chapter.

1. Insight Therapies   page 415
   A. Psychoanalysis
      - Sigmund Freud
      - Free association
      - Transference
      - Insight
   B. Client Centered (Person-Centered) Therapy
      - Carl Rogers
      - Unconditional positive regard
      - Nondirective
   C. Gestalt Therapy
      - Fritz Perls
      - Encounter groups
        - Empty chair technique
   D. Recent Developments
      - Short-term psychodynamic therapy
        - Immediate problems
2. Behavior Therapies   page 420
   A. Using Classical Conditioning Techniques
      - Desensitization, Extinction and Flooding
        - systematic desensitization
        - hierarchy of fears
      - Extinction
      - Flooding
      - Aversive conditioning
   B. Therapies Based on Operant Conditioning
      - Behavior contracting
      - Token economy
   C. Therapies Based on Modeling
      - Modeling
3. Cognitive Therapies   page 423
   Cognitive Behavior Therapists
   A. Stress-Inoculation Therapy
   B. Rational-Emotive Therapy
      - Albert Ellis
   C. Beck's Cognitive Therapy
4. Group Therapies   page 425
   A. Family Therapy
   B. Couple Therapy
      - Empathy training
   C. Self Help Groups

UNDERSTANDING OURSELVES: How to Find Help   page 427

5. Effectiveness of Psychotherapy page 429
   A. Therapist Alliance
   B. Eclecticism
6. Biological Treatments   page 431
   A. Drug Therapies
      - Antipsychotic drugs
      - Antidepressant drugs
      - Lithium
      - Other medications
        - Psychostimulants
        - Antianxiety medications
        - Sedatives
        - Antidepressant medications
   B. Electroconvulsive Therapy (ECT)
      - Unilateral ECT
   C. Psychosurgery
      - Prefrontal lobotomy
7. Institutionalization and Its Alternatives   page 436
   A. Past treatment
   B. Deinstitutionalization
   C. Alternative Forms of Treatment
   D. Prevention
      - Primary prevention
      - Secondary prevention
      - Tertiary prevention
8. Client Diversity and Treatment page 439
   A. Gender and Treatment
   B. Culture and Treatment

UNDERSTANDING THE WORLD AROUND US: Access to Mental Health Care—Who Gets Treatment?   page 440

After studying the text and completing the Study Guide activities, answer these questions to determine if you need to review any areas before the course exam.

1. Insight therapies focus on giving people _____.
   a. skills to change their behaviors
   b. clearer understanding of their feelings, motives, and actions
   c. an understanding of perceptual processes
   d. an understanding of biological influences on behavior

2. Neo-Freudians differ from traditional Freudian approaches to therapy in that they encourage clients to focus on the _____ and they favor _____ their clients.
   a. past; face-to-face discussions with
   b. present; face-to-face discussions with
   c. past; sitting behind and passively listening to
   d. present; sitting behind and passively listening to

3. The cardinal rule in client-centered therapy is for the therapist to express _____ for the client.
   a. unconditional positive regard
   b. conditional positive regard
   c. positive transference
   d. psychological congruence

4. Gestalt therapy emphasizes _____.
   a. the here and now
   b. face-to-face confrontations
   c. becoming more genuine in daily interactions
   d. all of the above

5. The main task of behavioral therapy is to _____.
   a. get the patient to look past the problem
   b. provide a warm atmosphere for discussing problems
   c. teach clients to behave in more effective ways
   d. provide insight into the causes of problems

6. The technique of _____ trains a client to remain relaxed and calm in the presence of a stimulus that he or she formerly feared.
   a. reciprocal inhibition
   b. free association
   c. systematic desensitization
   d. operant conditioning

7. Making someone who is afraid of snakes handle dozens of snakes in an effort to get him to overcome his fear is called _____.
   a. systematic desensitization
   b. flooding
   c. paradoxical intent
   d. aversive conditioning

8. In what type of therapy is a contract drawn up, binding both client and therapist as if they were involved in a legal agreement?
   a. behavioral contracting
   b. reciprocal inhibition
   c. transactional analysis
   d. a token economy

9. Showing a client how his or her irrational and self-defeating beliefs are causing problems is MOST characteristic of _____ therapy.
   a. psychoanalytic
   b. behavioral
   c. stress-inoculation
   d. rational-emotive

10. Alcoholics Anonymous is an example of a (n)_____ group.
   a. encounter
   b. desensitization
   c. self-help
   d. structured behavior therapy

11. The psychotherapeutic approach that recognizes the value of a broad treatment package over a rigid commitment to one particular form of therapy is _____.
    a. situationalism
    c. interactionism
    b. existentialism
    d. eclecticism

12. In 1988, the new drug ___ was put on the market as the first of a new class of antidepressant drugs.
    a. Ecstasy
    c. Prozac
    b. Lithium
    d. Thorazine

13. Drugs that combat depression work by ____.
    a. increasing the amount of serotonin in the brain
    b. blocking dopamine receptors in the brain
    c. inhibiting the function of the hypothalamus
    d. increasing acetylcholine in the brain

14. Most antipsychotic drugs work by _____.
    a. increasing acetylcholine in the brain
    b. increasing the amount of serotonin in the brain
    c. blocking dopamine receptors in the brain
    d. inhibiting the function of the hypothalamus

15. Electroconvulsive therapy is most often used to alleviate ____.
    a. anxiety
    c. schizophrenia
    b. somatoform disorders
    d. severe depression

16. Which of the following treatments is LEAST likely to be used today?
    a. electroconvulsive therapy
    c. prefrontal lobotomy
    b. drug treatment
    d. behavioral therapy

17. Educating young people about AIDS through TV ad campaigns is a form of ___ prevention.
    a. basic
    c. tertiary
    b. primary
    d. secondary

18. Suicide hot lines and crisis intervention centers are all involved in ___ prevention.
    a. basic
    c. tertiary
    b. primary
    d. secondary

19. Halfway houses and other places where ex-patients can be supported in their efforts to return to normal life after release from institutions are forms of _____ prevention.
    a. basic
    c. tertiary
    b. primary
    d. secondary

20. Which of the following is NOT a type of group therapy?
    a. couple therapy
    b. family therapy
    c. cognitive therapy
    d. self-help group

21. Which of the following statements does NOT describe aspects that are common in the various forms of psychotherapy?
    a. Clients are provided with explanations for their problems.
    b. Most psychotherapies offer people hope.
    c. Clients are engaged in a therapeutic alliance.
    d. Clients are treated with medication.

Answers and Explanations to Multiple Choice Posttest

1. b. Insight therapies are designed to give people better awareness and clearer understandings of their feelings, motivations, and actions. p. 415

2. b. Many Neo-Freudian therapists encourage dealing with current situations and having face-to-face discussions. p. 417

3. a. The cardinal rule in client-centered therapy is for the therapist to express unconditional positive regard or true acceptance. p. 418

4. d. Gestalt therapy emphasizes the here and now, face-to-face confrontations and becoming more genuine in the client's daily life. p. 418

5. c. Behavior therapy's main task is to teach clients new and more satisfying ways of behaving. pp. 420–421

6. c. Systematic desensitization gradually reduces fear and anxiety by association relaxation with the fearful stimuli. p. 421

7. b. Flooding involves full intensity exposure to a feared stimulus. p. 421

8. a. Behavioral contracting is a signed agreement between client and therapist regarding therapeutic goals and reinforcements. p. 422

9. d. Rational-emotive therapy (RET) is based on the idea that irrational and self-defeating beliefs cause psychological problems. p. 424

10. c. AA is the best-known self-help group. p. 428

11. d. Eclecticism recognizes the value of a broad treatment package over one form of therapy. p. 430

12. c. In 1988, Prozac was the first antidepressant drug to be introduced. p. 432

13. a. Antidepressant drugs, like Prozac, work by increasing the amount of serotonin in the brain. p. 432

14. c. Most antipsychotic drugs work by blocking dopamine receptors in the brain. p. 432

15. d. ECT is most often used for prolonged and severe depression when no other treatment is effective. p. 433

16. c. Prefrontal lobotomies are rarely performed today. pp. 434–435

17. b. Programs that educate people about illness are forms of primary prevention. p. 438

18. d. Suicide hotlines and crisis intervention are forms of secondary prevention. p. 438

19. c. Halfway houses are a form of tertiary prevention. p. 438

20. c. Couple therapy, family therapy, and self-help groups are all types of group therapies. Cognitive therapy is not a type of group therapy. pp. 423-425

21. d. Medications may be used to treat a number of different psychological problems, but their prescription is not common to all psychotherapies. p. 430

Language Support

Students identified the following words from the text as needing more explanation. This page can be cut-out, folded in half, and used as a bookmark for this chapter.

A

Accurate	correct; free from error; conforming exactly to truth or a standard
Advent	coming into being or use
Ambulatory	capable of moving from place to place; not bedridden
Aspiring	seeking to attain or accomplish a particular goal

C

Cardinal rule	the most important principle or procedure
Clam up	to become silent
Common sense	sound and wise but unsophisticated judgment; unreflective opinions of ordinary people
Constrictions	inhibit, prohibit, or discourage spontaneous activity; restrain

D

Debilitating	weaken; impair the strength of; reduce in intensive or effectiveness
Demoralized	weaken the morale; discourage; upset the normal function
Derogatory	speak poorly of; degrade; lower rank or reputation
Dialogue	conversation between two or more people; an exchange of ideas and opinions
Dire	disastrous; extreme; desperately urgent
Discharge	release from confinement, custody, or care
Discount	to minimize the importance of; view with doubt
Disproportionate	mismatch; disparity or lack of balance or relationship with
Doomed	to make certain something fails; to fix the fate of
Duration	time during which something exists or continues

E

Edgewise	sideways; with one edge pointed forward
Engaged	having attention occupied; busy; greatly interested in activity; interlock
Emphatically	emphasize; express forcefully in speech or decisive action
Entrench	establish solidly; place self in strong defensive position
Enviable	highly desirable
Erroneous	wrong; straying from truth; containing errors
Escalate	increase in extent, volume, number, amount or scope; expand
Exemplify	serve as an example; embody; typify; make concrete and perceptible

F

Face to face	in direct contact or confrontation; in each other's sight or presence
Feasible	capable of being carried out successfully; likely; doable
Fraught	filled with or accompanied by something specific; emotional distress or tension

H

Halfway house	residence for formerly institutionalized people as they transition to private life
Herald	signal the approach of; greed with enthusiasm or announce
Hodgepodge	jumble; mixture of parts of different elements
Hostel	supervised lodging usually for young travelers

I

Inconsistent	behavior or standards that aren't in agreement
Infantile	very immature; characteristic of an infant
Inhibit	discourage from free or spontaneous activity often through inner psychological impediments or social controls
Intractable	not easily managed, relieved, cured, or removed

L

Last resort	final source of help or protection
Loathsome	disgusting, repulsive, or having an aversion to
Lurk	waiting in a concealed place suggesting an evil purpose

M

Magnify	increase or intensify in significance; enlarge
Makeshift	usually crude and temporary substitute as a means to an end
Masquerade	acting or appearing as mere disguise or show
Meek	submissive or compliant, humbly patient
Mere	nothing more nor better than what something is; only
Modality	form of treatment with certain conditions for implementation
Money-grubber	preoccupied with making and accumulating money
Monopolize	assume complete possession or control of
Morbid	unhealthy mental attitude; excessively gloomy; horrified or intensely afraid

O

Overbearing	domineering; of overwhelming or critical importance; rudely arrogant

P

Penny wise/pound foolish	careful in dealing with small matters and reckless in dealing with important matters
Perverse	corrupt; willfully determined not to do what is expected or desired
Predicament	difficult or trying situation
Prey	helpless or unable to resist attack; victim
Proliferate	increase in number or spread rapidly; multiply

R

Rebuttal	to refute; expose falseness of; contradict or oppose; offer opposing data
Refugee	a person who flees to a foreign country to escape danger or persecution
Restore	put back into use or former or original state; renew
Revelation	striking disclosure; something communicated or discussed; enlightening
Rigidity	stiff; inflexible; set in one's opinion or devoid of flexibility
Romantic	responsive to the idealized, heroic, adventurous or expressions of love or affection

S

Self-perpetuating	capable of indefinitely continuing or renewing itself
Stigma	discredited or shamed; specific diagnostic sign of a disease
Spiral	a continuously spreading and accelerating increase or decrease
Status quo	the existing state of affairs or conditions

T

Tarantula	a large, hairy American spider with a painful but not fatal bite
Terminal illness	fatal illness leading to death
Testify	give evidence, declare; acknowledge openly
Tongue-tied	unable or not inclined to speak freely; may be from shyness
Transition	change, movement, development, or evolution from one form or stage to another

U

Under funded	provide insufficient funding for
Underlie	support; form the foundation or basis of

| Underscore | stress, emphasize, make evident, underline |
| Unpredictable | uncertain or unable to indicate in advance on the basis of observation, experience or scientific reason |

V

| In a vacuum | a state of isolation from outside influences |
| Vehemently | intensely emotional, passionate; forcibly expressed |

W

Ward	a large room in a hospital where patients requiring similar treatment are accommodated
Warehousing	confine or house a person in conditions suggestion of a room for storing merchandise
Wary	cautious; watchful, especially in detecting and escaping from danger
Wonder drug	miracle drug; relatively newly discovered drug that elicits a dramatic response in a patient's condition

Psychotherapy	Psychoanalysis
Insight therapy	Client-centered or person-centered therapy
Free association	Gestalt therapy
Transference	Short-term psycho-dynamic therapy
Insight	Behavior therapies

The theory of personality Freud developed as well as the form of therapy he invented.

The use of psychological techniques to treat personality and behavior disorders.

Nondirectional form of therapy developed by Carl Rogers that calls for unconditional positive regard of the client, by the therapist with the goal of helping the client become fully functioning.

A variety of individual psychotherapies designed to give people a better understanding of their feelings, motivations, and actions in the hope that this will help them adjust.

An insight therapy that emphasizes the wholeness of the personality and attempts to reawaken people to their emotions and sensations in the here and now.

A psychoanalytic technique that encourages the patient to talk without inhibition about whatever thoughts or fantasies come to mind.

Insight therapy that is time-limited and focused on trying to help clients correct the immediate problems in their lives.

The client's carrying over to the analyst feelings held toward childhood authority figure.

Therapeutic approaches that are based on the belief that all behavior, normal and abnormal, is learned, and that the objective of therapy is to teach people new, more satisfying ways of behaving.

Awareness of previously unconscious feelings and memories and how they influence present feelings and behavior.

Systematic desensitization	Cognitive therapies
Aversive conditioning	Stress-inoculation therapy
Behavior contracting	Rational-emotive therapy (RET)
Token economy	Cognitive therapy
Modeling	Group therapy

Psychotherapies that emphasize changing clients' perceptions of their life situations as a way of modifying their behavior.

A behavioral technique for reducing a person's fear and anxiety by gradually associating a new response (relaxation) with stimuli that have been causing the fear and anxiety.

A type of cognitive therapy that trains clients to cope with stressful situations by learning a more useful pattern of self-talk.

Behavior therapy techniques aimed at eliminating undesirable behavior patterns by teaching the person to associate them with pain and discomfort.

A directive cognitive therapy based on the idea that clients' psychological distress is caused by irrational and self-defeating beliefs and that the therapist's job is to challenge such dysfunctional beliefs.

Form of operant conditioning therapy in which the client and therapist set behavioral goals and agree on reinforcements the client will receive on reaching those goals.

Therapy that depends on identifying and changing inappropriately negative and self-critical patterns of thought.

An operant conditioning therapy in which patients earn tokens (reinforcers) for desired behaviors and exchange them for desired items or privileges.

Type of psychotherapy in which clients meet regularly to interact and help one another achieve insight into their feelings and behavior.

A behavior therapy in which the person learns desired behaviors by watching others perform those behaviors.

Family therapy	Electroconvulsive therapy (ECT)
Tertiary prevention	Psychosurgery
Eclecticism	Deinstitutionalization
Biological treatments	Primary prevention
Antipsychotic drugs	Secondary prevention

Biological therapy in which a mild electrical current is passed through the brain for a short period, often producing convulsions and temporary coma; used to treat severe, prolonged depression.

A form of group therapy that sees the family as at least partly responsible for the individual's problems and seeks to change all family members' behaviors to the benefit of the family unit as well as the troubled individual.

Brain surgery performed to change a person's behavior or emotional state; a biological therapy rarely used today.

Programs to help people adjust to community life after release from a mental hospital.

Policy of treating people with severe psychological disorders in the larger community, or in small residential centers such as halfway houses, rather than in large public hospitals.

Psychotherapeutic approach that recognizes the value of a broad treatment package over a rigid commitment to one particular form of therapy.

Techniques and programs to improve the social environment so that new cases of mental disorders do not develop.

Group of approaches, including medication, electroconvulsive therapy, and psychosurgery, that are sometimes used to treat psychological disorders in conjunction with, or instead of, psychotherapy.

Programs to identify groups that are at high risk for mental disorders and to detect maladaptive behavior in these groups and treat it promptly.

Drugs used to treat very severe psychological disorders, particularly schizophrenia.

14 Social Psychology

This chapter explores social psychology, the scientific study of how people's thoughts, feelings, and behaviors are influenced by the real, imagined, or inferred behavior or characteristics of other people. The chapter begins with an introduction to social cognition. Three aspects related to social cognition are the forming of impressions, attribution theory, and the role of interpersonal attraction.

Schemata, the primacy effect, and stereotypes greatly influence impression formation. Schemata are often applied to categories of people and influence people's expectations about behavior. The primacy effect is a result of early experiences that later influence impression formation. A stereotype is a special type of strongly held schema. Expectations about behavior may take the form of a self-fulfilling prophecy.

People often make attributions regarding the causes of behavior. How such attributions are made forms the basis of attribution theory. According to Fritz Heider, behaviors are attributed to either internal or external causes. Harold Kelley proposed that people rely on three kinds of information to explain behavior: distinctiveness, consistency, and consensus. Causal attributions are often biased. Examples of biases include the fundamental attribution error and defensive attribution. The just-world hypothesis is a type of defensive attribution error that originates from thinking that good things happen to good people, and bad things happen to bad people. The principles of attribution theory do not always apply to people in other cultures. Studies have shown that some cultures exhibit the reverse of the self-serving bias and may be less likely to commit the fundamental attribution error.

Interpersonal attraction is another aspect of social cognition. Social psychologists have found that attraction is linked to factors such as proximity, physical attractiveness, similarity, exchange, and intimacy. Typically, proximity is the most important factor in determining attraction. Physically attractive people tend to be liked more than less attractive people. Research has failed to confirm the notion that 'opposites attract'; rather, similarity and complementarity underlie attraction. Exchange is the basis for the reward theory of attraction; equitable relationships are more likely to sustain exchange. Intimacy is based on self-disclosure, a process in which personal experiences are shared with friends but likely concealed from strangers.

Attitudes refer to the relatively stable organization of beliefs, feelings, and tendencies toward something or someone. An attitude has three major components: evaluative beliefs, feelings, and behavior tendencies. Attitudes do not always accurately predict behavior. People who rate highly on self-monitoring are likely to override personal attitudes and observe a situation for cues on behavior. Many attitudes originate from early, direct personal experiences or by imitating the behavior of others. Mass media also impacts attitude formation.

Prejudice is an attitude whereas discrimination is a behavior that expresses prejudice. Prejudicial beliefs are often negative stereotypes. The frustration-aggression theory contends that prejudice results when people direct their anger away from the proper target and toward less powerful targets. Another theory contends prejudice stems from an authoritarian personality pattern. Other influences on prejudice include oversimplification, conformity, and racism. Racism can lead to an in-group bias, the belief that members of a group of people are superior to members of out-groups. Recategorizing, or expanding a schema of a particular group, often reduces prejudice. In addition, prejudicial beliefs can be suppressed through controlled processing or if certain conditions are met.

Attitudes can be changed. Persuasion can result in attitude change through a three-step process of attention to a message, comprehension of the message, and then acceptance of the message. The communication model of persuasion proposes four key elements to attitude change: the source, the message itself, the medium of communication, and characteristics of the audience. Cognitive dissonance exists when two contradictory beliefs are held at the same time. According to cognitive dissonance theory, attitudes are changed to reduce the discomfort of dissonance. Dissonance may also be reduced by increasing the number of thoughts consistent with one another.

Social influences affect people's perceptions, attitudes, and actions. Culture is a major form of social influence that dictates such norms as proper dress, eating habits, and personal space. People may be influenced to conform, or yield voluntarily to social norms at the expense of one's preferences. Large group size, unanimity, and difficult or ambiguous tasks increase the likelihood that a person will conform. A universal tendency to conform may exist but conformity is often greater in collectivist societies.

Compliance refers to behavior change as a result of an explicit request. The foot-in-the-door effect, the lowball procedure, and the door-in-the-face effect are common techniques for inducing compliance.

Obedience is compliance with a command. In his famous studies, Stanley Milgram demonstrated people's willingness to obey a perceived authority figure. It is important to understand the nature of these studies, the role of the teacher and learner, and the outcomes. Factors that influence obedience include the perceived power of the person giving commands, surveillance, and the presence of others.

People often behave differently in the presence of others. Of particular concern is the social action of deindividuation, a loss of personal sense of responsibility when part of a group. Deindividuation, the snowball effect, and belief in protection in large groups help to explain mob behavior. Other social forces promote helping behavior. Some helpful behaviors are linked to personal gain, yet others may be altruistic in nature. Situational and individual factors influence helping behavior. Known as the bystander effect, helping tendencies decrease as the number of passive bystanders increases. Helpful behavior is less likely in ambiguous situations. Personal characteristics such as empathy, mood, fear of embarrassment, and need for approval affect helping behavior. Again, collectivist cultures are more likely to express helping behavior, especially in cases of minor need.

Western society tends to trust group decisions (jury, committee, cabinet, etc.) more strongly than those made by an individual, yet research has found that group decisions are sometimes less sound. This may be due to polarization, where group members join with others of the same opinion to form a more extreme position than thought personally. The risky shift is an aspect of polarization.

Group interaction is important in determining the effectiveness of making decisions. High-status individuals exert more influence on decisions, but may not possess the best problem-solving skills. Also, social loafing may make the group members less likely to exert their best efforts. A cohesive group has strong morale and motivation, but may lead to groupthink, where valid individual doubts are not expressed for fear of upsetting the group mood.

The great person theory states that group leaders were simply 'born leaders' able to shape the times or places in which they found themselves. However, modern theories contend that social and economic factors play a crucial role in leadership. The transactional view holds that a leader's personal traits, the specific situation, and the group's response determine leadership ability. Fred Fiedler's contingency model suggests that leaders are either relationship or task oriented. In collectivist cultures, both the task-orientated and relationship-orientated approaches are combined for greatest effectiveness. The leader works and socializes with the group members, which increases group morale and the social climate. Some evidence suggests women have better leadership styles and make better managers.

Industrial organizational (I/O) psychology examines behavior in the workplace. The Hawthorne effect, first seen in the 1920s, suggested that workers will increase efficiency if they feel attended to, regardless of the nature of the attention. Productivity, motivation, and morale can be increased by giving workers jobs with a variety of skills, or by grouping workers into smaller units. A sense of autonomy is also important for worker satisfaction and product quality.

Finally, centralized systems of communication typically can solve simple problems well. Decentralized systems allow group members to communicate freely and solve more complex problems. Shared responsibility for decision making benefits group satisfaction but not productivity.

Learning Objectives

After you have read and studied this chapter, you should be able to complete the following statements.

OBJECTIVES:

1. Describe the process by which we form first impressions of other people. Identify three factors that influence personal perception.

2. Explain three aspects of attribution and explain attribution errors.

3. Explain the dynamics of interpersonal attraction.

4. Identify the components of attitudes. Explain how attitudes are acquired and how they change.

5. Explain the origin of prejudice and discrimination and how prejudice can be reduced.

6. Discuss the dynamics of attitude change and the process of persuasion.

7. Explain the theory of cognitive dissonance.

8. Explain how culture, conformity, compliance, and obedience exert social influence.

9. Identify the four types of social action.

10. Define risky shift and polarization. Summarize the conditions under which groups are effective and ineffective in solving problems.

11. Identify at least two theories of leadership.

12. Identify the focus and goals of industrial/organizational psychology.

Chapter Outline

The following is an outline conveying the main concepts of this chapter.

1. Social Cognition   page 447
   A. Forming Impressions
      - Schemata
        – Schema
        – Self-fulfilling prophecy
      - Stereotypes
   B. Attribution
      - Explaining Behavior
        – Attribution Theory
      - Biases
        – Fundamental attribution error
        – Defensive attribution
        – Just-world hypotheses
      - Attribution across Cultures
   C. Interpersonal Attraction
      - Proximity
      - Physical attractiveness
      - Similarity
      - Exchange
      - Intimacy
2. Attitudes p. 454
   A. The Nature of Attitudes
      - Attitudes and behaviors
        – Self-monitoring
        – Attitude development
   B. Prejudice and Discrimination
      - Prejudice
      - Discrimination
      - Sources of Prejudice
        – Frustration-aggression theory
        – Authoritarian personality
        – Racism
        – Strategies for Reducing Prejudice and Discrimination
        – Recategorize
        – Controlled processing
        – Conditions

UNDERSTANDING THE WORLD AROUND US: Ethnic Conflict and Violence   pages 458–459

   C. Changing Attitudes
      - The process of persuasion
      - The communication model
      - Cognitive dissonance theory
      - Propaganda
      - Shared collective memories
      - Personal and social identity
      - Societal beliefs
3. Social Influence   page 464
   A. Cultural Influences
      - Norm
   B. Conformity
      - Size of group
      - Unanimity
      - Nature of the task
      - Conformity across Cultures

UNDERSTANDING OURSELVES: Beliefs and Binge Drinking   page 466

   C. Compliance
      - Foot-in-the-door effect
      - Lowballing
      - Door-in-the-face
   D. Obedience
      - Milgram's experiments
4. Social Action   page 469
   A. Deindividuation
   B. Helping Behavior
      - Altruistic behavior
      - Bystander effect
      - Helping behavior across cultures
5. Groups and Decision Making   page 470
   A. Polarization in group decision making
      - Risky shift
      - polarization
   B. Effectiveness of groups
   C. Leadership
      - Great person theory
   D. Leadership across cultures
   E. Women in leadership
   F. Organizational behavior
      - Industrial/organizational (I/O) psychology
      - Hawthorne effect
   G. Communication and responsibility

Multiple Choice Posttest

After studying the text and completing the Study Guide activities, answer these questions to determine if you need to review any areas before the course exam.

1. The process by which others individually or collectively affect one's perceptions, attitudes, and actions.
   a. group dynamics
   b. social influence
   c. conformity
   d. culture

2. Whenever a person has two contradictory cognitions at the same time, a state of _____ exists.
   a. cognitive congruence
   b. nonreciprocity
   c. cognitive dissonance
   d. creative conflict

3. The person who conducted the most well-known research on obedience is _____.
   a. Asch
   b. Milgram
   c. Luchens
   d. Kelley

4. _____ behavior is helping other people with no expectation of personal gain.
   a. Reciprocal
   b. Deindividuated
   c. Diffused
   d. Altruistic

5. The _____ effect is that people are more likely to comply with a second, larger request after complying with a first, small request.
   a. response cue
   b. bait and switch
   c. foot-in-the-door
   d. primacy

6. _____ is a process by which people feel anonymous in a large group.
   a. Deindividuation
   b. Identity moratorium
   c. Identity diffusion
   d. Groupthink

7. The tendency for an individual's helpfulness in an emergency to decrease as the number of bystanders increases is called _____.
   a. the risky shift phenomenon
   b. groupthink
   c. the bystander effect
   d. social loafing

8. In a mob, one dominant person can often convince people to act due to the _____ effect.
   a. lowball
   b. snowball
   c. primacy
   d. door-in-the-face

9. The poor decisions made in the Watergate cover-up, the Challenger disaster, and the Bay of Pigs invasion were due primarily to _____.
   a. groupthink
   b. deindividuation
   c. risky shift
   d. polarization

10. The focus of industrial/organizational psychology is _____.
    a. strategies for founding an economically successful business
    b. behavior in organizational settings
    c. the effects of industrialization on the environment
    d. personal problems of employed persons

11. Most of us associate _____ with good personality traits, intelligence, and happiness.
    a. youth
    b. attractiveness
    c. old age
    d. wealth

12. The most important factor in interpersonal attraction is _____.
    a. proximity
    b. similarity
    c. attractiveness
    d. reciprocity

13. Rebecca consistently expresses her beliefs with a little regard for the constraints imposed by the situation. She is probably a _____ self-monitor.
    a. reactive
    b. nonreactive
    c. low
    d. high

14. According to attribution theory, people ___ for good situations and ____ for bad ones.
    a. take credit; take credit
    b. deny responsibility; deny responsibility
    c. take credit; deny responsibility
    d. deny responsibility; take credit

15. Bad things happen to bad people and good things happen to good people, according to _____.
    a. the self-serving bias
    b. the just-world hypothesis
    c. the self-fulfilling prophecy
    d. the reciprocity model

16. Each of the following is a promising strategy for reducing prejudice and discrimination EXCEPT _____.
    a. recategorization
    b. controlled processing
    c. improving contact between groups
    d. increased competition between groups

17. The number one health hazard for college students is _____.
    a. binge drinking
    b. AIDS and other STDs
    c. smoking
    d. illegal drug use

18. If a man is wearing a blue uniform with a badge and gun holster, we might categorize him as a policeman. We may also have expectations that he will enforce the law and be helpful to people. This process plays a role in impression formation and refers to _____.
    a. creating norms
    b. applying schema
    c. the primacy effect
    d. stereotyping

19. Which of the following statements is NOT true about attitudes?
    a. Attitudes about objects can be changed.
    b. Attitudes may not accurately predict behavior.
    c. Discrimination is a type of unfavorable attitude.
    d. All of the above are true.

Answers and Explanations to Multiple Choice Posttest

1. b. Social Influence is the process by which others individually or collectively affect one's perceptions, attitudes, and actions. p. 464

2. c. Cognitive dissonance occurs when a person has two contradictory cognitions at the same time. p. 462

3. b. Milgram has conducted the most well-known research on obedience. p. 467

4. d. Altruistic behavior seeks no personal gain. pp. 469–470

5. c. The foot-in-the-door effect occurs when people comply with a second larger request after complying first with a small request. pp. 466–467

6. a. Deindividuation is the process by which people feel anonymous in a large group. p. 469

7. c. The bystander effect occurs when an increase in the number of bystanders decreases the likelihood than an individual in the group will be helpful. p. 470

8. b. The snowball effect occurs when a dominant person in a mob is able to convince people to act. p. 469

9. a. Groupthink occurs when there is so much pressure from the group to conform that people don't feel free to express critical ideas. p. 471

10. b. The focus of industrial/organizational psychology is behavior in organized settings. p. 473

11. b. Most people associate attractiveness with good personality traits, intelligence, and happiness. p. 452

12. a. Proximity, or how close people live to each other, is the most important factor in interpersonal attraction. p. 451

13. c. Rebecca is a low self-monitor. p. 455

14. c. People take credit for good situations and deny responsibility for bad ones, according to attribution theory. p. 450

15. b. The just-world hypothesis holds that bad things happen to bad people and good things happen to good people. p. 451

16. d. Increased competition between groups is not a promising strategy for reducing prejudice and discrimination. pp. 458–460

17. a. Binge drinking is the number one health hazard for college students. p. 466

18. b. Schema refers to a set of beliefs and expectations based on past experience that is presumed to apply to all members of that category. p. 448

19. c. Discrimination is a behavior, not an attitude. p. 456

Language Support

Students identified the following words from the text as needing more explanation. This page can be cut-out, folded in half, and used as a bookmark for this chapter.

A

Acquiesce	to go along with, comply or submit, usually after thoughtful consideration
Ally	one that's associated with another as a helper
Ambiguity	having more than one interpretation or meanings
Astray	away from what is desired; in error

B

Bigoted	stubbornly and intolerantly devoted to one's own opinions and prejudices
Blatantly	obvious, in a noisy, offensive, crude manner
Bribe	something that influences or causes behavior to occur

C

Candor	free from prejudice or malice; fair, impartial, honest
Chalk up	to attribute or credit as a cause
Chance encounter	to come upon unexpectedly
Concerted effort	mutually agreed upon, planned, or devised
Conspire	plot; act in harmony toward a common end
Credibility	quality or power of inspiring belief

D

Decipher	to interpret or figure out meaning although indistinct
Deep-rooted	firmly implanted or established
Dissenter	one who differs in opinion
Door-to-door	going to each house in a neighborhood

E

Eloquent	marked by forceful and fluent expression; articulate communicator
Endorsement	to approve of by expressing support or approval, often publicly
Entice	tempt; to attract by arousing hope or desire
Ethos	distinguishing character, sentiment, moral nature, or guiding beliefs of a person, group, or institution

F

Flattery	insincere or excessive praise
Flesh out	make fuller or more nearly complete
Fuss over	show of flattering attention

G

Gamut	whole series or entire range or scope
Genocide	the deliberate and systematic destruction of a racial, political, or cultural group
Gist	essence, main point, or part
Gossip	rumor or report about others; usually personal or sensational

H

Harbor	hold persistently in the mind; provide refuge for
Hardheaded	stubborn, willful; realistic; concerned with practical considerations
Holocaust	mass slaughter of Europeans, especially Jews, by the Nazis in WWII

I

Illegitimate   not recognized as lawful offspring; born of parents who aren't married to each other

Inculcate   teach and impress by repetition, counsel, advice, or caution

Idolize   love or admire to excess; to worship

Indecisive   uncertain how to act or proceed; indefinite

L

Lenient   mind and tolerant disposition

M

Mumble   utter words in a low, confused, indistinct manner

Malign   to give misleading or false reports about

Mandated   by formal order; directed or required by the court

Malevolent   having or showing intense, often vicious, ill will, spite, or hatred

Mar   detract from the perfection or wholeness of

N

In a nutshell   in a very brief statement

Naïve   lacking wisdom or informed judgment; with unaffected simplicity

O

Old standby   something which one can rely on; a favorite and available choice

Oppress   exercise harsh authority or power over; subdue, restrain; weigh heavily on the mind

Ostensibly   to all outward appearances; apparently; open to view

P

Paramount   prevailing over others; dominant; having superior position

Pegged   identified

Polite   showing correct social usage; considerate; tactful; courteous

Plight   unfortunate, difficult, uncertain, or dangerous situation

Put-downs   humiliating remark; degrade or belittle

R

Rally   mass meeting intended to arouse group enthusiasm

Rhetoric   art of speaking or writing effectively; skillful communication

S

Scare tactics   gaining an advantage by spreading alarm or fear

Scenarios   hypothetical or imagined sequence of events; account or summary of possible courses of actions or events

Single file   a row of people or things arranged one behind the other

Solidarity   unity; based on common interests, objectives and standards

Speculation   ponder on a subject; review something casually and often without conclusions

Steeped in   subject thoroughly in some strong or dominating influence

Stethoscope   instrument used to detect and study sounds produced in the body

Stranger   unknown person who one is not acquainted with

T

Truism   undoubted or self-evident truth; one too obvious to mention

U

Unforeseen   not seen or known in advance; not predicted or discerned

V

Vent   to give vigorous or emotional expression to

Vested   special concern or stake in maintaining or influencing something for selfish ends

Violate   to do harm to, especially sexually; fail to show respect for

W

Wanton   hard to control, playfully mean or cruel; inhumane

Social psychology	Fundamental attribution error
Primacy effect	Defensive attribution
Self-fulfilling prophecy	Just-world hypothesis
Stereotype	Proximity
Attribution theory	Exchange

Tendency of people to overemphasize personal causes for other people's behavior and to underemphasize personal causes for their own behavior.

Scientific study of the ways in which the thoughts, feelings, and behaviors of one individual are influenced by the real, imagined, or inferred behavior or characteristics of other people.

Tendency to attribute our successes to our own efforts or qualities and our failures to external factors.

The fact that early information about someone weighs more heavily than later information in influencing one's impression of that person.

Attribution error based on the assumption that bad things happen to bad people and good things happen to good people.

Process in which a person's expectation about another elicits behavior from the second person that confirms the expectation.

How close two people live to each other.

Set of characteristics presumed to be shared by all members of a social category.

Concept that relationships are based on trading rewards among partners.

Theory that addresses the question of how people make judgments about the causes of behavior.

Equity	Frustration-aggression theory
Attitude	Authoritarian personality
Self-monitoring	Racism
Prejudice	Cognitive dissonance
Discrimination	Social influence

Theory that under certain circumstances people who are frustrated in their goals turn their anger away from the proper powerful target and toward a less powerful target because it is safer to attack.

Fairness of exchange achieved when each partner in the relationship receives the same proportion of outcomes to investments.

A personality pattern characterized by rigid conventionality, exaggerated respect for authority, and hostility toward those who defy society's norms.

Relatively stable organization of beliefs, feelings, and behavior tendencies directed toward something or someone-the attitude object.

Prejudice and discrimination directed at a particular racial group.

Tendency for an individual to observe the situation for cues about how to react.

Perceived inconsistency between two cognitions.

An unfair, intolerant, or unfavorable attitude toward a group of people.

Process by which others individually or collectively affect one's perceptions, attitudes, and actions.

An unfair act or series of acts taken toward an entire group of people or individual members of that group.

Norm	Altruistic behavior
Conformity	Bystander effect
Compliance	Risky shift
Obedience	Polarization
Deindividuation	Great person theory

Helping behavior that is not linked to personal gain.	A shared idea or expectation about how to behave.
Greater willingness of a group than an individual to take substantial risks.	Voluntarily yielding to social norms, even at the expense of one's preferences.
Greater willingness to take risks in decision making in a group than as independent individuals.	Change of behavior in response to an explicit request from another person or group.
Shift in attitudes by members of a group toward more extreme positions than the ones held before group discussion.	Change of behavior in response to a command from another person, typically an authority figure.
Theory that leadership is a result of personal qualities and traits that qualify one to lead others.	Loss of personal sense of responsibility in a group.

Industrial/ organization psychology	
Hawthorne effect	
Social cognition	
Schema	
Cultural truism	

	Area of psychology concerned with the application of psychological principles to the problems of human organizations, especially work organizations.
	Principle that subjects will alter their behavior because of researcher's attention and not necessarily because of any specific treatment condition.
	Knowledge and understanding concerning the social world and the people in it (including oneself).
	A set of beliefs or expectations about something that is based on past experiences.
	The belief that most members of a society accept as self-evidently true.